Kendal

Windermere

Ambleside

Langdale

Coniston

DOW CRAG

SCAFELL

Eskdale

Wasdale

CUMBRIAN ROCK

100 Years of Climbing in the Lake District

Trevor Jones

&

Geoff Milburn

Pic Publications

Previous page: Above: Scafell Pike with Pike's Crag and Mickeldore.
Below: Dow Crag in Winter.   Photos: Rob Matheson.
Opposite: Pete Kirton on Fine Time (1972) Livesey's line up the front of Raven Crag, Langdale.   Photo: Al Phizacklea.

First published in 1988
© 1988 Trevor Jones & Geoff Milburn

Pic Publications
 25 Cliffe Road
  GLOSSOP
   Derbyshire
    SK13 8NY

Jones, Trevor, *1930-*
    Cumbrian rock : 100 years of climbing
    in the Lake District.
    1. Cumbria. Lake District. Mountaineering,
    1886-1987
    I. Title II. Milburn, Geoff
    796.5'22'094278

    ISBN 0-9511114-2-6

Distributed by Cordee
 3a De Montfort Street,
  LEICESTER
   LE1 7HD

Type origination by Bureau-Graphics Ltd. Glasgow.
Colour origination by Arneg, Glasgow.
Produced in Great Britain by the Ernest Press.
Bound by Hunter & Foulis, Edinburgh.

Front cover: Ed Cleasby pumping out on the first ascent of Astrakhan, Dow Crag.   Photo: Al Phizacklea.
Rear Cover: Nigel Bonnet on G.T.X., Raven Crag, Threshthwaite.   Photo: Al Phizacklea.

Contents

Introduction

The Lake District is the cradle of British rock-climbing which began in 1886 with the ascent of The Needle on Great Gable. The climbers who followed this event are responsible for the content of Cumbrian Rock and the book sets out to present the aura of each generation — as opposed to being a straight factual history. People are interested in other people and that is the reason for the inclusion of so much anecdotal material; it is hoped that no-one will be offended by this. Some of the material was reluctantly omitted as the laws of libel are stringent. People have climbed in the Lake District ever since the poet Coleridge descended Broad Stand on Scafell at the start of the nineteenth century. The history of Cumbrian rock climbing since then has been full of notable cragsmen in search of adventure. With some trepidation the limestone crag of Chapel Head Scar has been included in the last chapter, but only after the young Lakes climbers pointed out its merits for climbing when the high crags are storm-bound. The coastal limestone in North Wales is now accepted by Welsh climbers, whereas Chapel Head Scar seems to be taking a little longer. It was not thought necessary to be exhaustive about other fine limestone cliffs in the vicinity, but rather to give a feel for climbing on the white rock. The presentation tries to steer clear of rigid doctrines and it is hoped that it may give an insight into, or an urge to climb on, the high Lakeland crags.

Acknowledgements

This book would have been impossible without the kindness, help and guidance of dozens of Lakeland climbers, young and old, whose ages ranged from eighteen to ninety-five. Many of them have lent photographs and slides; some are breath-taking, others of extreme historical importance, such as Charlie Wilson's comprehensive set of hundreds of climbing photographs of the Thirties. In a later era Ian Roper deserves special mention for his superb black and white photographs, while the state of the art in colour is undoubtedly expressed in the 1980s by Al Phizacklea. Photographers who lent me their material as well as providing important information included:

Johnny Adams, Bob Allen, Nat Allen, Austin Barton, Bill Birkett, Marie Blake, Chris Bonington, Pete Botterill, Les Brown, Jessie Byrom, Ed Cleasby, Sid Cross, Paul Cornforth, Colin Downer, Ian Dunn, Brian Evans, Fell and Rock Climbing Club, Pete Gomersall, Rick Graham, Tony Greenbank, Peter Greenwood, Ed Grindley, Jim Haggas, Dougie Hall, John Hartley, Alan Hinkes, Ron Kenyon, George Kitchin, Bonny Masson, Rob Matheson, Douglas Milner, Mike Mortimer, Paul Nunn, Geoff Oliver, Mrs Peascod, Al Phizacklea, Colin Read, Norman Rimmer, Ian Roper, Joe Roper (95 years of age), Paul Ross, John Sheard, Colin Shone, Jack Soper, Ivan Waller, Charlie Wilson and Ken Wilson.

Others who gave valuable source material include: Nat Allen, Allan Austin, Dave Armstrong, Martin Berzins, Jim Birkett, Joe Brown, Harold Drasdo, Dennis Gray, A.B. Hargreaves, John Lockley (Golden Rule-Ambleside) and Pete Whillance. Thanks are particularly due to the Fell and Rock Club for allowing many quotes to be used from its journals which have come out regularly since 1907. At a late stage of the manuscript several people made an important contribution to help iron out factual discrepancies — in particular: Dave Armstrong, Rick Graham, Ed Grindley and Ian Roper. Ken Milburn (who first climbed Scafell Pinnacle at the age of 14 in 1928 with Bentley Beetham) worked extensively on the proofs. I particularly want to thank David Craig for assistance with the text and also his patience, whilst I struggled with the last pitch of Deer Bield Crack.

Al Phizacklea has also helped with his superb diagrams two of which were drawn to illustrate the Fell and Rock Club's guides to Pillar and Scafell.

Trevor Jones

climber silhouetted at the top of Walker's Gully, Pillar Rock.   Photo: Bob Allen.

A Pillar of Society

Radiating out like a giant wheel a series of distinctive deep valleys lies beneath Cumbria's highest peaks. Often wreathed in mist the summits remain isolated and mysterious and yet hidden amongst these mountainous folds are the great crags where the outstanding climbers of each generation have woven the threads of climbing history. The Lake District is filled with earthly beauty, despite being only thirty miles from East to West; a magical thousand square miles of lakes, cliffs, and mountains. It has several of England's treasures: its highest mountain — Scafell Pike; its deepest lake — Wastwater; and, close by at the head of Wasdale, the smallest church. Wasdale in the nineteenth century produced the greatest liar — Will Ritson, the host of the Wasdale Head hotel which was the cradle of English climbing. Proud Cumbrian Celtic farmers initially played no part in mountain exploration. They were too busy making a rugged living in a rugged region. In the central part of Lakeland only 2% is cultivated. The rest is a mass of rocky uplands fit only for ravens and peregrines, sheep and climbers. As we climb we grapple, literally with the stuff of our planet and as we perch on a belay ledge we can see, a few feet from our eyes, how the crust has been gouged and split by the volcanic and other forces which created the Cumbrian crags. Beds of lava and ash built up — the raw material of the Borrowdale volcanic series. During the colossal upheaval which also formed the Alps, the whole layered mass domed upwards, peaking roughly around the Scafell-Helvellyn axis. Waters drained outwards, and cut through to the old core forming the river-valleys which are the spokes of Lakeland — Windermere running south, the Duddon and Esk valleys south-west, Wasdale and Ennerdale westwards, Buttermere-Crummock and the Derwent valley running North, and Ullswater north east. Finally during the last Ice Age, glaciers radiating from Scafell bulldozed along the valleys, hollowing out the U-shapes of Langdale and Buttermere amongst others and left torn rock faces seamed with cracks and gullies which make our climbing possible.

Many invaders left their mark on Lakeland valleys, firstly the Romans, followed by marauding Norsemen; then the whole area was contested by Scots and English for centuries. Even as early as 1582 the natural beauty of the Lake District was appreciated by the Elizabethan historian Camden, whose description can hardly be bettered today:

'The country although it be somewhat with the coldest as lying farre North, and seemeth as rough by reason of hilles, yet for the variety thereof it smileth upon the beholders and giveth contentment to as many as travaile it. For after the rockes bunching out, the mountains standing thicke together, rich of metall mines, and betweene them great meeres stored with all kinds of wildfoule, you come to pretty hills good for pasturage, and well replenished with flocks of sheepe, beneath which againe you meet with goodly plaines, spreading out a great way, yielding corn sufficiently.'

Wordsworth, the future Poet Laureate, was Cumbrian-born, in Cockermouth, but spent most of his creative years in Grasmere, in the shadow of the high Lakeland fells.

Opposite: Top left: Rev. James Jackson.
Top right: Auld Will Ritson.
Bottom left: John W. Robinson.
Bottom right: G.A. Solly
Photos: by courtesy of the Fell and Rock Climbing Club.

He walked long distances, sometimes up to forty miles in a day, often talking to himself on his solitary poetic rambles; and not surprisingly was noticed by the common folk:

'Would walk by you times enough wi'out sayin' owt, specially when he was i'study'

Mountain-born, he was lured to Snowdon which he climbed in thick mist, then to Chamonix and the Mer de Glace, which he described as 'A motionless array of mighty waves'. Before his birth in 1770 mountains were written of as horrendous steep places to be avoided. He helped to popularise the Lakeland fell-tops and in his Guide to The Lakes (1810) described the view on an October day on Scafell:

'But how shall I speak of the deliciousness of the third prospect! At this time, that was most favoured by sunshine and shade. The green Vale of Esk — deep and green, with its glittering serpent stream, lay below us: and on we looked to the Mountains near the Sea, — Black Comb pre-eminent, — and, still beyond, to the Sea itself, in dazzling brightness.

Whilst Wordsworth was a young man restless travellers appeared in Lakeland. In 1793 Captain Joseph Budworth, a one-armed hero of the siege of Gibraltar, came for a fortnight's holiday. He walked 250 miles, trundled boulders down Helvellyn and probably made the first tourist ascent of Coniston Old Man. The gallant captain climbed Helm Crag and described his food intake in his book 'A Fortnight's Ramble in The Lakes':

'Stuffed roast pike, a boiled fowl, vealed cutlets and ham, beans and bacon, cabbage, peas and potatoes, anchovy sauce, parsley and butter, bread and cheese, wheatbread and oatcake, three cups of preserved gooseberries with a bowl of rich cream in the centre and all for ten old pence, a head.'

Not long after Budworth, another poet came to the Lake District, Samuel Taylor Coleridge, who left behind his personal millstones of illness, a failed marriage and opium, and moved in 1800 to Greta Hall near Keswick, close to Wordsworth. Soon afterwards Coleridge decided to set out on a solitary holiday round the Lake District and expressed his feelings about the area when he wrote;

'I must be alone, if either my Imagination or Heart are to be enriched.'

In August 1802 he started his 'circumcursion' or walk, described in a letter to the woman he loved, Sara Hutchinson, sister of Wordsworth's wife. He climbed Scafell late in the afternoon of 4th August, then made a historic descent across the boulder-strewn slabs leading down to Mickledore. Soon he came to the top of what is now Broad Stand and made its first descent, probably the hardest rock climb for some years:

'I came (it was mid-way down) to a smooth perpendicular Rock about 7 feet high — this was nothing — I put my hands on the ledge and dropped down — in a few yards came just such another, I dropped that too — and yet another, seemed not higher — I would not stand for a trifle so I dropped that too, but the stretching of the muscles of my hands and arms, and the jolt of the Fall on my Feet, put my whole limbs in a Tremble, and I paused, and looking down, saw that I had little else to encounter but a succession of these little Precipices — So I began to suspect that I ought not to go on but then unfortunately though I could with ease drop down a smooth Rock 7 feet high, I could not climb it, so go on I must...every Drop increased the Palsy of my Limbs — and now I had only two more to drop down — to return was impossible — but of these two the first was tremendous, it was twice my own height and the Ledge at the bottom was so exceedingly narrow, that if I dropt down upon it I must of necessity have fallen backwards and of course killed myself. My Limbs were all in a tremble — I lay upon my Back to rest myself...I arose...at the bottom of the third Rock that I dropt from, I met a dead Sheep quite rotten.....I glanced my eye to the left and observed that the Rock was rent from top to bottom — I measured the breadth of the Rent and found there was no danger of my being wedged in, so I put my Knap-sack round to my side and slipped down as between two walls, without any danger or difficulty.'

It is not fanciful to say that he had written the first climbing story. The place is easily recognisable as Broad Stand with its initial tight cleft, but more important, it is the first recorded case of involuntary leg-shakes, from which all frightened climbers have suffered. Wordsworth too clambered up cliff faces in his youth and in probably his finest poem, The Prelude, described his early pleasure in rock-climbing:

'Oh! when I have hung
Above the raven's nest, by knots of grass
And half-inch fissures in the slippery rock
But ill-sustained, and almost (so it seemed)
Suspended by the blast that blew amain,
Shouldering the naked crag, oh, at that time,
While on the perilous ridge I hung alone.'

He was also deeply interested in Pillar Rock, then unclimbed. However, on a July morning in 1826 an Ennerdale shepherd, John Atkinson, inched his way along what is now believed to be The Old West route. It was colourfully reported in the local newspaper which had one of the longest possible titles — 'The Cumberland Paquet and Wares Whitehaven Advertiser'.

'The undertaking has been attempted by thousands before him, it was always relinquished as hopeless; John is therefore most probably the first human being whose foot has pressed the tender grass upon this huge pile. His dog, the faithful attendant of the shepherd, lay by his staff at the bottom, and as if conscious of the danger his master was incurring by the attempt, uttered the most piteous cries during his absence.'

Three more shepherds repeated the ascent the same year, but it was twenty-two years before it was conquered again — not until the railway enveloped Lakeland with its tracks. Before then the normal way to get to the Lakes was to travel by ship from Liverpool to Whitehaven, then onwards by horse-drawn carriage. The next ascent of Pillar Rock was by a man of different social class, Lieutenant Wilson R.N., who made his ascent into Pillar history in 1848, followed by C.A.O. Baumgartner who was born in 1825 and had the then normal upper-class public school upbringing — Rugby followed by Oriel College, Oxford. When he was twenty-two he stayed at the Pen y Gwryd Hotel on the flanks of Snowdon and did the first traverse of the Snowdon Horseshoe, including its sensational Crib Goch Pinnacles. In 1850 he went to

Wasdale and made the acquaintance of a local expert, Will Ritson, who later was to play an important part in the social development of the dale. Baumgartner wrote of his ascent:

> 'I made known my intention to try the Pillar Stone; and was accompanied by William Ritson and another man to the Pillar Mountain. They were sceptical as to my chance of success; and, to test my powers, they diverged a little on the route, to a small but rather perpendicular rock, not more than 10 or 15 feet high I think, and requested me to climb that. It was not very easy — I forget the precise nature of the difficulty — but I succeeded in surmounting it. They then said it was all right; I could climb the 'Pillar Stone'. Ritson then took me to the top of the 'Pillar' (mountain), and to the cleft or gap that separates it from the 'Pillar Stone' or 'Rock' (it was called the Pillar Stone in those days). There we descended to the bottom of the cleft — only a short descent — beyond which Ritson would not go. Here he pointed out to me a narrow track on a level ledge of rock winding round the side of the Pillar Stone. When I reached the back of the rock, or rather the front of it, looking towards Ennerdale and Buttermere, it was simply a matter of climbing up by the hands more than by the feet, wherever the perpendicular faces of the stones and rocks appeared most practicable and presenting the best chance of access to the next stage above. On the way up, if I remember right, I occasionally piled a few stones here and there on prominent points, to serve as landmarks for the descent on the return journey — since, in some places, the only mode of getting down (except tumbling down bodily) would be by hanging by one's hands to the edge of the rock, and letting one's feet dangle down in search of a foothold on a finger's-breadth ledge, or in a crevice or cranny in the rock. I found no serious difficulty in reaching the top, where I gladly responded to Ritson's shouts of congratulation, as I reappeared to his view. No less than eight ravens, unused to visitors, flew off, protesting hoarsely against my invasion of their sanctuary.'

Baumgartner was one of the first rock-climber/mountaineers and lived to eighty-five and died in 1910. One interesting aspect of his Pillar ascent was his association with Will Ritson, who was born in 1808 at Rowfoot farm — Wasdale Head and lived there all his life. After his marriage his wife decided to provide ham and eggs for the increasing number of intellectual scrambling tourists; then he added an extension to the farm to provide accommodation for them. It was difficult for Ritson as a Wasdale local to understand the insatiable urge of the intelligentsia to climb the rocky fells. When George Seatree and John Wilson Robinson told him they had done the North Climb on Scafell he was astounded:

> "Nowt but a fleein' thing cud git up theer." Then he blurted out, "What's makkin' ye fellas fash yer'sels seea mich aboot climmin' t'crags? Isn't fells big eneugh for ye?"

One of his hotel guests was a bishop who hired Will as a guide for the ascent of Scafell. The cleric complained at their slow progress and when they reached the summit the droll Cumbrian said to his saintly client:
"Well, here ye are, Mister Bishop, ... as near Heaven as ye ever will be."
He entertained his guests with local tales, particularly of a farmer in Nether Wasdale who had finished a haystack, with his servant lad still on top who shouted: "Ah say, maister, hoo is Aa to git doon?" The farmer looked up at him and shouted in reply: "Shut thee 'ees and walk aboot a bit." More and more of the learned community came to Lakeland and Ritson's hotel. In 1859 Professor Tyndall, the conqueror of the

Weisshorn, described a stormy day in the Eighteen-Fifties in an article in the Saturday Review entitled 'A Stormy Day on Helvellyn.'

'The cold was intense, and seemed to split and scarify the skin of the face. The storm for a time seemed divided by the mountain, advancing right and left, and pouring its frozen contents into the flanking valleys; but minute crystals of snow, flying through the air with arrowy velocity, at length began to hit us. These quickly thickened to large flakes and we were soon amid the densest gloom, battered by the blinding meteor. Here was surely an antithesis to the heavy air of a London laboratory. The wind entered our clothes, and seemed to search our fibres through and through. The gloom gradually diminished as we advanced, the descending snow dwindled to a feeble hail, the wind lowered and finally we emerged north of the storm, with an unclouded heaven above us, and the most perfect calm around. It was a day of wondrous atmospheric effects — indeed, we had scarcely seen anything grander among the Alps themselves.'

The flow of tourists continued unabated. Easter 1869 saw the first recognised glissading accident which happened when descending towards Wasdale from between Great End and Scafell Pike. The leader of the party was J Stogdon who read a paper on the epic before the Alpine Club in March 1870:

'The moment we appeared there we heard a startled shout from X, saw him flung upon his back, utterly fail to stop his motion, then gliding swiftly down-wards. The slope we saw had changed from snow to hard ice, and the gradient must have been at least 45 degrees. Some big rocks cropping out of the snow came next, down which he fell head-over-heels, and then head first down another slope towards an ominous break in the continuity of the mountain side, which might mean a precipice of 100 feet. We watched in horror for the time when we should see him disappear. A little before the brink the gradient slackened; he never lost his head for a moment, grasped at a fragment of rock which struck him from his course, then at another which lay most providentially just at the right place, and his motion was brought to a stand. He lay quite still where he was on the snow quite 100 feet below us...In about three-quarters of an hour we came to him terribly shaken and almost frozen, with his clothes very much torn and his right leg almost unable to move. The next three hours were not pleasant; every step had to be cut for a considerable time and X's feet had to be put into them.'

Late in the evening they reached Ritson's hotel, where X recovered from his ordeal. Later that year there was a quickening in the pace of exploration and two proper rock climbs were done on Scafell. The first was a 250-foot climb, Mickledore Chimney, quite close to Coleridge's Broad Stand. C.W. Dymond who climbed it commented:

...'there is no special difficulty until you are near the top...the chimney is effectively blocked...and can only be scaled a la chimney sweep.'

The North or Penrith climb, also on Scafell, was scaled almost at the same time by the impeccably-named Major Ponsonby. However, Pillar Rock remained the Mecca for adventurous scramblers; and Ritson regularly provided the information regarding its ascent. By 1866 it had already had 28 ascents and that year C.W. Dymond wrote a description of the necessary details for an ascent, but added a sombre footnote:

'A guide desirable. Will Ritson never did it. Two Alpines spent two hours in vain attempts to find the way up. One in four pedestrians might do it, but no object is gained by doing it, except the reputation of having accomplished it.'

It is thought that the 'Two Alpines' referred to a party which included Leslie Stephen, one of the leading early alpinists, who made the first ascent of the Schreckhorn and the first ascent of Mont Blanc from St Gervais. By 1870 a lady, Miss Barker, climbed Pillar Rock followed in 1873 by Miss Mary Westmorland who did it with her brothers. The old stone became so popular that C.N. Williamson in an article 'The Climbs of the English Lake District' offered an important piece of advice: 'Ladies attempting the ascent will find an Alpine dress a great advantage'. Sadly the details of this intriguing garment are not available. Heavy Victorian clothing did not stop them having a party on top, which Williamson described:

'This ascent of the Pillar Rock has been an extremely enjoyable one, and has been marked by certain novel features. Mr Petty, a clever and active climber, has brought up with him his favourite guitar, to the accompaniment of which he has sung several charming melodies. Games of 'nap' and 'old maid' formed agreeable interludes between each song. It is believed that this is the first time in history that a musical instrument has been played on the top of the Pillar Rock.'

The next person to appear on the Pillar Rock scene was the Reverend James Jackson, the vicar of Rivington in Lancashire, close to the popular sandstone crags of Anglezarke Quarry. His church had a weathercock which fell into disrepair. The village stone-mason refused to repair it because of the danger; and to the consternation of his congregation, Jackson mounted the steeple and afterwards composed a short poem:

'Who has not heard of Steeple Jack, That lion-hearted Saxon? Though I'm not he, he was my sire, For I am Steeple Jackson!'

He went to live in the Lake District, where he scrambled over the fells. As he got older he became fitter and at sixty-nine walked sixty miles in under twenty hours. At the end of his life he developed a fixation about Pillar Rock and decided to subdue it if at all possible. He made preparations for his attempt and prudently took along the driver of his horse and trap — the ascent being unique, as artificial aids were used in the ascent:

'...the intrepid Hodgson had no qualms of any sort and was equal to the occasion; and the wiry old man followed in his track. The spikes, driven previously into the face of the sloping rock, were fortunately in the right place, and when by the aid of a rope we had mounted about the space of six yards, the chief obstacle was overcome, and the victory all but gained. Nothing was now wanted but a good head and a good heart, and I and my avant courier were possessed of both. After proceeding a few yards on a narrow heath- covered ledge, Hodgson disappeared from my sight, and I awaited, in hopeful mood, the result. At last a cry significant of success struck mine ear...'

illar Rock from the West.   Photo: Abraham collection.

Napes Needle from Eagle's Nest with W.P. Haskett Smith in 1936

Photo: C.Douglas Milne

However, he had not lost a sense of humour:

'If this in mind you will fix, When I make the Pillar my toy, I was born in 1,7,9,6, And you'll think me a nimble old boy.'

He had a house built at Sandwith near St Bees Head with a view of the Lakeland Fells in the distance. He thought continually about Pillar Rock during the winter months of early 1876. On his eightieth birthday he surged out again, but was defeated by mist. On May 3rd he walked nearly fifteen miles to Ritson's, getting there at teatime. Up just after 4 a.m., a quick cold breakfast, and away by 4.20 a.m. he was on the summit of Pillar Rock by 7.30 a.m.:

'After duly surveying the route I had to pursue, I was soon at the rock with the transverse nick which has to be traversed; then I scrambled to the sloping rock, which is about six yards in extent, and may be called the pons asinorum of the climb. Into this rock I drove a spike, on which, by the means of my staff, I raised the loop of a rope ladder with four rungs, hanging it on the spike; as an additional security a hand-rope was also attached to the same point; and with these appliances I gained, without slip or injury, the narrow heath-covered ledge. About six yards is the horizontal extent of this ledge, when you have again to mount upwards for 20 yards ...With ungloved hands I grasped the rugged rock, and in five or six minutes I stood proudly on the summit, and a second time asserted my claim to be Patriarch of the Pillarites.'

He was back at Ritson's by 12 p.m. after an eventful eight hours. Two years later he set out again but sadly never returned. Ritson's search party found his body lying at the foot of the Great Doup, only 400 yards from Pillar Rock. Steeple Jackson had shown astonishing determination for someone of such advanced years, and it was not surprising that his example sparked off the younger generation. The golden age of Alpine climbing, which had been dominated by the British, was drawing to a close and nearly all the Alpine peaks had been climbed. The sport of rock-climbing was in its infancy on the continent, but was now given a decisive boost by its first major English pioneer, Walter Parry Haskett Smith, who went to Eton and was the first pupil to climb its famous wall. At Trinity College, Oxford, he became a long-jump champion and cleared nearly twenty-five feet, unfortunately achieved in practice and not officially accepted. A strain of eccentricity remained throughout his life. He was called to the Bar, but never practised, and one of his few quarrels occurred when a friend sent him a brief. His coming of age in 1880 coincided with a visit to the mountains of North Wales with a group of fellow undergraduates 'when we spent a month in Snowdonia, reading and walking hard.' That winter he decided to go to the Lake District the following summer and during his preparations 'procured the Ordnance map of Cumberland, found that there was on it a sombre region thronged with portentous shadows'. He knew nothing of Wasdale traditions when he first stayed at Ritson's hotel with a group of under- graduates. He enjoyed it so much that he returned again in 1882 with his brother and had a remarkable escape on Pillar Rock when he was trying a new route. While he was levering himself over a huge block it started to fall:

'The rock came slowly over, checked every now and then by the friction of some excrescence, the pressure increasing frightfully with every minute of inclination. Meanwhile, the jagged top was buried in my waistcoat and the weight of my legs and body made it hopeless to disentangle myself. My fingers were numb with the long strain, my arms seemed to be slowly drawn out of the shoulders. It was a matter of only two or three seconds more, and I called out to my brother to go down as we had come up, and to go slowly as he would have to go alone. But at that instant an idea struck me. Letting go with my right hand I rolled over on my left side, wrenched my waistcoat free of the stone and hung over the precipice by my left hand only. If the stone did not fall quickly I was lost. It seemed to hesitate, but then came slowly over. My right hand seizing the tottering mass and weighing heavily upon it eased for a moment the strain upon my left; then as the great stone dipped for its first plunge my right foot swinging up on to it and kicking viciously downwards gave sufficient upward impetus to enable my right hand once more to clutch the hold above. It was a near thing; but a moment later I swung into the cleft just vacated by the stone.'

He was not put off, and 1882 had seen the start of his climbing career. He did seven new routes, mainly gullies all over Lakeland. The best was Great Gully on Pavey Ark, the real start of rock-climbing in Langdale and 'one of the few good gully climbs in the district'. It was of Difficult standard, hardly earth-shattering today, but in 1882 there were no rock-climbing standards, no clubs, no magazines. Haskett Smith had set the basis for the whole sport. Nearly all these early climbs were covered in vegetation, loose stones and other detritus which had to be cleared away. Many years later Haskett Smith wrote of these problems; and also the reason why he did a lot of them solo:

'Men who climb under modern conditions seldom realise how much we were hampered fifty years ago not only by moss and loose stones, but also by the paucity of climbers and the consequent difficulty of finding a companion for a climb.'

Haskett Smith was back in Wasdale in 1884 but his two new routes that year were meagre compared with his harvest in 1882. However, he met a local man who became a pillar of the Wasdale climbing community for the rest of the century — John Wilson Robinson, who was described by Haskett Smith fifty years later:

'The essence of Lake Country climbing was John Robinson! The intense pleasure he took in it, the generosity with which he gave his time and trouble to the service of anyone who wanted a climb, combined to endear him to the whole fraternity. Never was there a man more utterly unselfish, never one who so cleverly continued to give the impression that he and not you was the person benefited.'

Robinson regularly walked from his farm at Lorton to Wasdale, a distance of twelve miles. He would set off at 3 a.m. and locals often saw his lantern rising up the slopes of Scarth Gap on his way to Wasdale. He made one hundred and one ascents of Pillar Rock between 1882 and 1906 and twenty winter ascents of Deep Ghyll. On the day that he met Haskett Smith for the first time they traversed across the Napes Face of Great Gable and saw a beautiful unclimbed pinnacle — Napes Needle. Robinson said in awe-struck tones: "Would a Swiss guide attempt anything like that?" It was two years before Haskett Smith returned to Wasdale to make the epic ascent which had such far-reaching effects:

'In the year 1886 between two visits to Scotland there was just time to squeeze in a few days at Wasdale and where the party broke up my way lay by Penrith to the North and the others were to walk to the South-going train at Seascale. They were eager to do a farewell climb on

Opposite: Above: View from Mickledore, Scafell.
           Below: Moss Ghyll Grooves, Scafell Crag.   Photos: Ron Kenyon.

the way and as Buckbarrow was new to them it was agreed that we should all get up at 5 a.m. with me to act as guide for the climb and porter to the foot of Wastwater. We had had our climb and parted; but the early start and fast walk had left me with a headache, and to walk it off I went up to Beckhead and down into Ennerdale where the then unclimbed face of Great Gable merited investigation. After a pleasant climb up the Great Chimney the idea occurred to me of trying to find the ridge leading down to the Needle. This descent was readily found and the ridge followed to the gap immediately above the Needle. The drop into the gap is abrupt and the lower part of it was then very mossy. By this time my headache was gone and the Needle itself had a more attractive look about it. The main trouble lay in the cracks and crevices which were tightly packed with small stones flush with the surface of the slabs and thatched with slippery grass. The prospect from the shoulder was not encouraging. The Lingmell face of the top block was covered with a brown and brittle lichen which concealed whatever holds there might be and if the top of the block were rounded, things looked hopeless. The only test of this was to throw up a stone and, if it stayed there, it would be a proof that the top was fairly flat. Diligent search revealed only two stones on the shoulder, one the size of a snuffbox the other nearly as big as a brick. The little one bounded off and was lost; but the big one behaved better and encouraged me to follow it. There was no means of recording my visit except a small boss near the North edge of the stone round which my handerchief was tied with my brick on the top of it to keep it from being blown away. The descent was somewhat unnerving, as the lichen dust concealed all the little footholds but all went well.'

In technical terms Haskett Smith had raised the standard of rock-climbing from the scrambling level to Hard Very Difficult. He climbed it solo, but had definite views on ropes which he outlined when he did another climb:

'We were rather heretical in our attitude to the use of the rope...not having one ourselves. In the gall of bitterness, we classed ropes with spikes and ladders, as a means by which bad climbers could go where none but the best climbers ought to be.'

He was also one of the first people to write about the unspoken competition between climbers, a feature of the sport right from its start:

'...when A makes a climb, he wants B, C and D to have the benefit of every obstacle with which he himself met, while B, C and D are equally anxious to say that they followed the exact line that Mr A found so difficult and thought it perfectly easy.'

One of his great contributions to rock-climbing lay in his two volumes covering the crags in England, Wales and Ireland; for the latter country he was helped by H.C. Hart. The first red-backed volume was published in 1894 and contained a wealth of detail concerning the crags of England. The second volume published the following year covered Wales and Ireland (The companion volume on Scotland for some obscure reason did not appear). A useful innovation was that climbers could pack the books in their rucksacks or read them at home during winter evenings, instead of relying on hotel log books. He never worked and in later years travelled widely, apart from in Europe, and went to North Africa, The Rockies and even the Andes. As the years went by his attire too became somewhat cosmopolitan:

Opposite: Paul Ross on H.M. Kelly's 1928 route Kern Knotts Chain   Photo: Paul Ross.

'Another instance of this bizarre taste in dress was the outfit in which he appeared at the wedding reception of a club member. It was not an occasion for formal garments. Haskett Smith appeared in a lounge suit which was certainly very far from new, but which would have passed unnoticed had he not thought well to show it up by a pair of brand-new white wedding spats.'

Fifty years after the first ascent of the Needle the 'prince of pioneers' took part in a jubilee ascent of his pinnacle. He was driven from London in an open car, his eyes streaming from the wind. Then in preparation for the big event he did a training climb on Pillar Rock, the Slab and Notch, on a day laced with snow showers. Three hundred people gathered in the Dress Circle close to the Needle to watch the old master at work. The leader was Professor (later Lord) Chorley who in his speech on top described Haskett Smith as 'The Father of British Climbing'. The old man had been on the middle of the rope and was wearing rubbers as if to show he was in touch with the modern trend. Everyone present sang 'For he's a jolly good fellow' to the man who had set top standards when there were no standards. Someone shouted "Tell us a story". In typical fashion he replied "There is no other story, this is the top storey." H.M. Kelly, the leader of the Twenties generation, summed up his effect on future climbers:

'No other man has wielded anything like the same influence. It is no exaggeration to call him the father of British rock-climbing. The impossible became at once a target for his skill and natural ability, and his successes were many and varied. At one end of the scale is the Napes Needle, while at the other end is the long and successful siege of the North Climb on Pillar Rock. He made the Needle his very own...'

Even whilst Haskett Smith was still active all over the British Isles, a family of climbers was taking over his mantle as the leading innovator. These were the five Hopkinson brothers from Manchester, where their father had made his fortune in a classical Victorian manner. He started life as a mill mechanic, then set up in business, went into politics and then became the Lord Mayor of Manchester. The family was devotedly keen on the outdoors, and the brothers had the opportunity to explore such diverse places as Gordale Scar, Malham Cove, the Lake District, and even North Wales. In the early days of climbing the emphasis had been on the investigation of gullies and chimneys. The Hopkinson brothers however started the move from enclosed places into the open air by exploring slabs, ridges and aretes. John and Edward descended the East Face of Tryfan several years before the first recorded routes by Roderick Williams. In 1892 some of the brothers made the first climbs on the pristine North Face of Ben Nevis. They descended Tower Ridge, and ascended the North-East Buttress. When the routes were later claimed by Scottish mountaineers the Hopkinsons, via the lofty Alpine Journal, informed the Scots that they had been done before. Alfred eventually became Sir Alfred Hopkinson, King's Counsel and Member of Parliament. In 1925 he reminisced about his Lakeland adventures which spanned the years from 1857 on Fairfield to one of his last ascents on High Street in 1925.

'To the best of my belief I have never written a word, not even in the old Visitors' Book at Wasdale, on any climb in the Lake District. I do not know or care whether any of them is classed as easy or severe. I expect they have now all become easy, but I do not know their

Opposite: The steep open face of Scafell Pinnacle with a sombre feeling   Photo: Austin Barton.

names. The labels — Cust's Gully, Westmorland's Climb, Botterill's Slab, to take a few examples — convey nothing to my mind. These proprietary brands, though useful, no doubt, for purposes of identification, are sometimes a little trying to those who like to find out things for themselves. Indeed, so-called failures may have most interest.'

His attitude was extremely laid-back and suggests the Victorian pukka sahib who considered competition beneath him. Possibly they did the first ascent of Savage Gully on Pillar Rock, but all Alfred recorded was this cavalier passage:

'Even on so fine an objective as the Pillar Rock, I only remember trying five ways. One on the North Face with that charming companion and excellent mountaineer, J.W. Robinson; it had an amusing traverse, one leg being placed in a crack, and the other hanging over the edge. Another with my brother Charles as leader, rather more to the left; he seemed to be unduly long at some places, but on reaching them it appeared to those who followed that he had done well to get up at all. I suppose that now this climb which seemed to us really difficult, is as well known as Oxford Street.'

One of their greatest exploits was on 30th December 1887 on Scafell. In September Charles, Edward, and Albert had descended from the Scafell Pinnacle to a narrow ledge 250 feet above the screes where Edward built a cairn which is still known as Hopkinson's cairn. It seemed logical to them to try to reach it from the foot of the cliff and three months later, in winter conditions, Charles climbed a hundred feet up slippery rock until stopped by an icy slab and retreated. Herman Woolley, who was with him, wrote that it was 'one of the finest climbs the party had ever accomplished.' The route was not climbed until June 1912, when Siegfried Herford named it Hopkinson's Gully. It is now graded Mild Very Severe and the crux is on the first pitch, which Charles had climbed that cold winter day. Dow Crag was another of their favourite cliffs. On April 14th 1895 Charles went there with Edward and John to explore Easter Gully where he produced Hopkinson's Crack, a sustained steep cleft, which is now graded Hard Severe and is given three stars. Not far away his brothers Edward and John climbed Intermediate Gully, a two-star Hard Severe now described as 'one of Lakeland's classic struggles'. Sadly when the brothers were at the pinnacle of their achievements, an accident on the Petit Dent de Veisivi killed not only John, but also his son and his two daughters. The wives stamped down their buttoned boots, and their husbands were made to take up less dangerous sports. Exploration then centred for a while on Pillar Rock and an unclimbed problem on its North Face. In 1882 Haskett Smith had nearly been killed when his waistcoat became entangled with a falling block, as he was attempting a new route. He returned to the North Face nine years later and did nearly three hundred feet of new climbing before he reached an impasse just below the final nose, but he failed on the direct line of the future finish of the North Climb and by-passed it by descending into Savage Gully. The pace of exploration had increased dramatically by 1892 and soon another great climber solved the problem. Godfrey Solly was a pious lawyer who combined religion with an obsession for mountains and fitted in more than forty Alpine seasons amongst his legal duties and political work which resulted in his becoming both Mayor and a Freeman of Birkenhead. In the early winter months of 1892 Solly solved the problem at the top of the North Face of Pillar Rock which had defeated Haskett Smith, and produced The Hand Traverse. It was only twenty-five feet long but it was Hard Severe

Opposite: Above: Scafell Main Crag with Central Buttress.
           Below: Scafell East Buttress.   John Hartley.

and became the scene of many epics. John Wilson Robinson tried it one cold day with Dr Norman Collie, who later wrote:

> 'The day was bitterly cold, and Robinson was a short distance along the traverse. His hands, however, were so frozen that he could not hold on or get back. He called out, "I can't hold on any longer," and then fell straight on to the ledge below, bounded out into the air, turning a somersault backwards, and pitching on to a grass projection some thirty feet lower down, hitting it with his shoulder. At the exact moment that he hit the grass the strain came on the rope. If this had not happened nothing could have stopped him, and the whole party would have been dragged after him. Sheer luck had saved us.'

In the spring of 1892 Solly scaled a steep and unclimbed arete close to the Dress Circle on Great Gable, only a few feet away from Napes Needle. This highly intimidating route, Eagle's Nest Ridge Direct, was the first Very Severe in the British Isles but Solly wrote quite modestly about it:

> 'I found that the first steps of the next pitch were very difficult, and that the rock rather pushed one out. The others got out of the rope, and Slingsby, climbing up as far as possible, stood on a little step just below, with his hands on the platform. I put one foot on his shoulder and as I climbed up, making room for him, he raised himself and finally stood on the platform, helping me as far as possible. I went on and climbed the second step. Then when I came to the third I did not like it. Retreat was even less inviting, and consultation with the others impracticable. After looking round, something of a hold for each hand and foot was discovered, and I went on, with the knowledge that even if one hand or foot slipped, all would be over. Just above this the difficult part ended.'

Solly's climb was to tax the best climbers for decades. Even O.G. Jones top-roped it before he led it and afterwards wrote:

> '...the first ten feet above the nest are remarkable for steepness and smallness of the holds. If the rocks are cold and the fingers benumbed the holds cannot be appreciated at all and the place becomes horribly dangerous...No man should lead up it who has not already explored the ground from above.'

It had taken over eighty years to progress from Coleridge's hesitant steps on Broad Stand to Haskett Smith's handkerchief fluttering on the top of Napes Needle. Less than six years later technical standards had jumped by two full grades on Eagle's Nest Ridge Direct. There were still unclimbed clefts, and one of the greatest was Moss Ghyll on Scafell. Ghyll after ghyll had yielded to Victorian human pyramids, nailed boots and threaded ropes; but Moss Ghyll which split the main face of Scafell had remained inviolate. An Anglo-Scot, Dr Norman Collie, solved its difficulties in a novel manner by hacking a foothold with an ice-axe on the crux sequence. It is surprising that he was not condemned for it since its grade is only Very Difficult. Solly or the Hopkinson brothers could easily have led it. Even today it is still possible to see the light-grey chipped hold. Collie described his struggle with due self-criticism:

> 'I stretched out my foot and placed the edge of my toe on the ledge. Just as I was going to put my weight onto it, off slipped my toe, and if Hastings had not quickly jerked me back, I should instantly have been dangling on the end of the rope. But we were determined not to be

Opposite: Top Left: George Abraham on The Stable Door at Wasdale Head.
            Top right: The Collie Step in Moss Ghyll.
            Bottom Left: H.C. Bowman, C.H. Patchell and E.V. Mather on Collier's Direct Finish to Moss Ghyll.   Photo: Abraham collection.
            Bottom right: Blizzard Chimney, Dow Crag.   Photo: Eric Byrom collection.

beaten. Hastings' ice-axe was next brought into requisition, and what followed I have no doubt will be severely criticised by more orthodox mountaineers than ourselves. As it was my suggestion I must take the blame. Peccavi! I hacked a step in the rock — and it was very hard work. But I should not advise anyone to try and do the same thing with an ordinary axe. Hastings' axe is an extraordinary one, and was none the worse for the experiment. I then stepped across the mauvais pas, clambered up the rock till I reached a spot where a capital hitch could be got over a jutting piece of rock.'

A remarkable young man was now learning his climbing craft at the same time. O.G. Jones, or the Only Genuine Jones as he liked to call himself, was of Welsh extraction and in his teens he explored the Welsh mountains. In 1888, completely untrained, he made a solo first ascent of the Cyfrwy Arete on Cader Idris wearing boots which had no nails. In a short time he made himself into a good climber by relentless training. He weight-trained, climbed on Cleopatra's Needle and even traversed round a railway engine using the rivets as both hand and footholds. His strength became legendary: one particular feat was described by George Abraham:

'One Christmas time an ice-axe was arranged as a horizontal bar. Some marvellous feats were shown by experts, but Jones who had been watching retiring from the end of the room came forward and astonished everybody. He grasped the bar with three fingers of his left hand, lifted me with his right arm, and by sheer force of muscular strength raised his chin to the level of the bar three times.

He had poor sight and needed thick spectacles which caused Haskett Smith to remark:

'In a perverse way, his myopia was an advantage; it shielded him from realising the true extent of his exposure and it led him into places which called forth the utmost exertion of his phenomenal strength and gymnastic genius. His capacity for getting into difficulties on the crags was more than equalled by his ability to find his way out of them.'

One afternoon in 1891 he looked in the window of Spooner's photographic establishment in The Strand and saw a picture of Napes Needle. He bought a print, hung it on the wall of his room for inspiration, and a fortnight later reached the top of the crag. He wrote that he had descended without serious difficulty, but this is not in accordance with Collie's account:

'We had just climbed the Napes Needle and come down again. Two men who had been watching us then started up it. They got to the ledge underneath the top, but could get no further, so I climbed up to help them. One of them got into the crack but could not find sufficient hand-hold around the corner, and wanted to know if there was no other way. Finally he got on my shoulders, and I pushed him up till he got a hand-hold on the top; he then scrambled up. I went down and began climbing the ridge behind the Needle but I had to come down again, and once more climb up the Needle for the last man could not get off the top; I got him off safely, and the man was Jones. It was, I believe, his introduction to climbing at Wastdale.'

Opposite: Kern Knotts Crack (1897) and its celebrated neighbour the Innominate Crack (1921) Great Gable.   Photo: C. Douglas Milner.

Although Jones was immensely strong and determined, he did not advance the standards already set by Solly, but the sheer number of his new routes in widely different surroundings impressed everyone who climbed with him. One of his friends W.M. Crook praised him:

'His wonderful grip of rocks, his steady head, his extraordinary power of balancing himself on one foot in what seemed to me then almost impossible positions.'

A typical struggle was on the North Climb on Pillar Rock in 1893 on which occasion his companions were John Wilson Robinson and F.W. Hill. The latter saw Jones fall to his death in the Alps several years later. Complicated combined tactics were used:

'The operations commenced by Hill fixing a foot in the stirrup and lifting it a couple of feet as Robinson hauled up his rope. Then, with Robinson simply holding on firmly, Hill straightened himself in the stirrup using it as a foothold, while I pulled up the couple of feet of slack in the waist rope. Next it was my turn to hold hard as Hill raised his stirrup foot, and then Robinson's to keep the foot firm while Hill lifted himself on to it. These two moves were repeated again and again alternately. It will be perceived that all the actual lifting of Hill's weight he managed himself during the straightening out on the stirrup, and that we others were at the most called upon only to hold his weight.'

Many of his finest climbs were done with the Abraham brothers who lived in Keswick. They started climbing some years before they met Jones and saw him for the first time on a fine April morning in 1896 at their photographer's shop in Borrowdale Road. In their early teens they had scrambled on the fell sides above Keswick for better photographic vantage points. Ashley, the younger brother, was only fourteen when they did the first ascent of a gully called Sandbed Ghyll in St Johns in the Vale. One of George's first climbs was made while hunting for kestrel's eggs on Falcon Crag in Borrowdale. At the nest he found that he hadn't anything to carry them in, so he put the eggs in his mouth. Suddenly an irate gamekeeper shouted at them causing George to slip and bite the embryo-filled eggs, but his violent retching turned the gamekeeper's wrath to laughter. Easter 1896 started off one of the most productive partnerships in Victorian climbing. Jones and the two brothers went to Scafell, where he led them up a route from Deep Ghyll on the face of Scafell Pinnacle. The brothers were not outclassed however by their flamboyant friend.

Mouse Ghyll was climbed in September 1897 by Cecil Slingsby and less than a week later, George did a harder finish which is still graded Very Severe — the first of its standard in Borrowdale.

1897 was a golden year for Jones. At Easter he and the Abrahams were in Wales, where they grappled with Lliwedd. Jones then left his companions and went to Coniston, where he met Godfrey Ellis. Jones was interested in an unclimbed fissure between 'B' and 'C' Buttresses on Dow. At the start a sharp-edged crack sliced into his fingers and made them bleed badly. Another crack over-stretched his strong arms and he had to bring up Ellis to fling the rope over a small spike and protect subsequent difficulties. Central Chimney acquired a fearsome reputation and was thought to be the most dangerous climb in the district, although it has now mellowed to a one-star Severe labelled 'an old classic climb which remains popular.'

Four days later Jones did the first ascent of Kern Knotts Chimney and next morning went to the foot of the then-unclimbed Kern Knotts Crack. He had already worked out

Opposite: Top left: Brown Slabs Arête, Shepherds Crag.
            Top right: Peter Martin on Harrow Wall, Grey Crag, Birkness Combe.
            Bottom left: Dave Harber at the Crevasse leading to Slingsby's Chimney.
            Bottom right: Peter Martin in Kern Knotts Chimney.   Photos: G. Milburn.

that the wall was not vertical, merely at an angle of 75 degrees. However John Wilson Robinson thought that it was unjustifiable and with tongue in cheek told Jones that if he climbed it he would never speak to him again. Jones top-roped the route on a cold winter's day in December 1895 and on the next occasion tried to lead it with the aid of an ice-axe, but a projecting block jammed into his neck and he retreated. Finally he emptied his pockets and top-roped it again. However at Easter 1897 he finally climbed it and descended Kern Knotts Chimney in a total time of seven minutes. Although only seventy feet long and Mild Very Severe, it became a classic and has remained so ever since. In 1897 Jones recorded his intensive few years of Cumbrian experiences in 'Rock Climbing in the English Lake District'. It was the first rock-climbing book in what we can now recognise as the modern idiom, and it was important for an emerging generation of climbers. The book had clear detailed route descriptions and strikingly clear photographs by the Abraham brothers, and it incorporated Jones's own climbing philosophy:

> 'It satisfies many needs; the love of the beautiful in nature; the desire to exert oneself physically, which with strong men is a passionate craving that must find satisfaction somehow or other; the joy of conquest without any woe to the conquered; the prospect of continual increase in one's skill, and the hope that this skill may partially neutralize the failing in strength that comes in advancing age or ill health.'

Probably the most important innovation was his invention of the grading system, which in a modified form is with us today. He split climbs into four categories: Easy, Moderate, Difficult and Exceptionally Severe. This system was based on four components: the angle of the climb, the type and size of the hand and footholds, and the pitch lengths; and it is interesting to compare the grading of his hard climbs with today's grades:

EXCEPTIONALLY SEVERE COURSES	MODERN STANDARD
Doe Crag Intermediate Gully	Hard Severe
Screes Great Gully	Severe
Shamrock Gully (new route)	Severe
Doe Crag Central Chimney	Severe
Scawfell Pinnacle by Deep Ghyll	Not now climbed as a summer route
Scawfell Pinnacle by Professor's Chimney	Difficult
Kern Knotts Crack	Mild Very Severe
Doe Crag Easter Gully	Severe
North Face of Pillar (by hand-traverse)	Hard Severe
Sergeant Crag Gully (direct route)	Severe
Walker's Gully	Hard Severe (Very Severe for a short man)
C Gully of the Screes	Mild Very Severe
Eagle's Nest Ridge	Mild Very Severe
Scawfell Pinnacle Direct from Lord's Rake	Hard Severe

In the introduction Charles Pilkington warned of the dangers of attempting the very hard routes:

> 'The novice must on no account attempt them. He may console himself with the reflection that most of these fancy bits of rock-work are not mountaineering proper, and by remembering that those who first explored these routes, or rather created them, were not only brilliant rock gymnasts but experienced and capable cragsmen.'

Climbing and physical fitness dominated his life. On one occasion he bicycled from London to Brighton and back in a day on dusty untarred roads. The Alps too were treated as if they were an endurance test, and in 1898 he climbed 24 mountains, several of them 4000 metre peaks. When he suffered frostbite on the Dom in Switzerland, he tried a cure by sticking his fingers in boiling glue which caused them to be permanently mis-shapen. His sequence of brilliant successes was marred by several incidents where he was lucky not to be killed. L.S. Amery was polite when he wrote that 'he was a fine, if over-bold climber'. During an ascent of Iron Crag Chimney he had an epic ascent which George Abraham described:

> 'After a few seconds he gave a cheer and called to my brother to follow him. This he had just begun to do and had left the ledge about five feet, when I heard a dull ominous crack, and, on looking up, saw the whole thing coming down. There was no time to do anything but squeeze into the chimney and warn my father. I succeeded in getting far enough inside to escape serious damage, but the heel of my left boot, which projected a little, was torn entirely away. My father's escape was more marvellous, for it seemed that nothing could save him; but on looking down I saw the great rock strike a projecting piece of the chimney only a few inches above his head, and spread out like a fan into a thousand splinters which shot far out into the air, falling again near the foot of the chimney; and thus we escaped with only a few slight bruises. One shudders to think what would have happened if the ledge had fallen when Jones and my brother were on it.'

Perhaps it is not surprising that the elder Abraham commented; 'Is he subject to fits?' On another occasion he fell off while soloing Moss Ghyll but a back-rope stopped him and he escaped with two broken ribs. On Shamrock Gully on Pillar Rock he had an even more blood-curdling experience:

> '...the oppressive silence was broken by the words: "I cannot get up or down safely!" The position was alarming for the jaws of the gully dipped deeply below, and, though the rope was secured to us and the great boulders, a fall would have been serious. A few moments later Jones, with remarkable foresight and judgement, espied a small piece of jutting rock no bigger than the top of an egg-cup. This was just above him on the right, but it was possible to swing the rope up to and over it; and he began the ascent thus secured. We paid the rope out from the cave and all went well for a time. Then suddenly there was a cry of warning, and something of a more solid nature appeared. "Hold tight!" was the startled shout, and Jones came swinging in pendulum fashion across the wall with astonishing impetus. The rope held over the belay, and he crashed pell-mell amongst us in the bed of the cave. We collapsed like ninepins, sprawling in all directions. In the melee the rope flew out of my hand, and I well remember how Jones sat up presently on the snow, rubbing his bruises and accusing me of losing my head and the rope simultaneously.'

In 1898 he rose above everything he had done before in a brilliant display of courage and route-finding when he climbed from Lord's Rake direct to the Waiting Room, then in stockinged feet negotiated the precarious Mantelshelf. It was one of his best climbs, and it was carried out in gathering gloom:

'Darkness was coming on apace, and we had yet a most awkward corner to negotiate before finishing our appointed business. Standing on Walker's shoulders I screwed myself out at the right-hand top corner of our waiting-room, and started along a traverse across the right face of the nose. The toes of the feet were in a horizontal crack, the heels had no support, and the hands no grip. It was only by pressing the body close to the wall which was fortunately a few degrees away from the perpendicular, and by sliding the feet along almost inch by inch, that the operation could be affected. It was with no small sense of relief that the end was reached in a few yards, and a narrow vertical fissure entered that gave easy access to the top of the nose.'

Jones was now thirty-one and at the height of his powers. In the first days of 1899 he made another great effort; the weather had been bad in Wasdale, and almost everyone had gone home. Jones's ambitious target was one of the last great unclimbed gullies in the Lake District — Walker's Gully on Pillar Rock. The cleft had been named after an unfortunate of that name who had fallen down it in the Eighteen-Eighties. Jones and George Abraham waited for the weather to improve and by January 7th were getting desperate. Jones decided despite the sleet and icy rain to make his attempt. The gully was dripping with icy water but they persisted until the final obstacle. Three enormous jammed boulders had defeated previous explorers. Jones flung off his Norfolk jacket and boots, and in stockinged feet and sub-arctic conditions provided a final solution to the great cleft. Even now it is Hard Severe in the summer and the guidebook advises that t 'he top pitch may be found Very Severe if the climber is short'. Jones described his epic struggle:

'Next the right wall was tried and I blessed the previous three months' monotonous training with heavy dumb-bells. The strain of the arms was excessive. Fortunately, there was no running water there, or the cold would have been unendurable. At the worst corner, by hanging on with the right hand and with the left looping part of my rope through the recess at the side of the boulder, a good grip was improvised. Of natural holds there was none on that smooth icy wall and the loop was a perfect boon. Even a perfect boon is hard to utilise when hands and toes are benumbed and all one's muscles are racked with prolonged tension. But the loop served its purpose, and after a few more struggles in the crack a ledge was reached from which it was evidently an easy scramble to the head of the gully.'

The others followed and they all rejoiced at the top:

'I put my frozen feet into others' pockets, my dignity into my own, while we ate the crushed remnants of our lunch and discussed the day's excitements. When the grateful diffusion of animal heat had brought sensation to my extremities, and the spare energy of the whole party had spent itself in dragging on my boots, we started off again and made our way over the snow-covered fells down to Wasdale.'

It was his last great new route in the Lake District and his success was typical of brilliance and impetuousness. He had transformed Lakeland climbing with the scope and quality of his new routes, but his training habits had more in common with modern rock gymnasts than with his Victorian contemporaries. A few weeks after Walker's Gully he and George Abraham sat at the top of the Devil's Kitchen in the Ogwen valley in Snowdonia and discussed the possibility of a joint trip to the Himalayas. He went to the Alps as usual in the summer and did fourteen peaks before attempting the West Arete of the Dent Blanche on August 27th with F.W. Hill and three guides. The leading guide fell and all were killed except Hill. In the past Jones had often got into places which were almost beyond strength and will but he always rose magnificently to the occasion. He was the first rock athlete; but that last climb merely proved that he was after all human. Only a memory remains — thick spectacles, buttoned cap, knickerbockers and all.

ENNERDALE

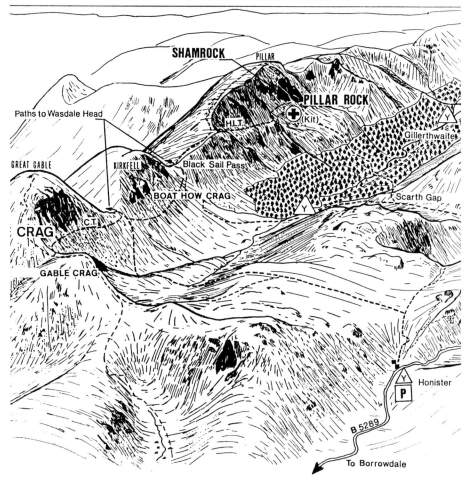

Opposite: Left: Eagle's Nest Ridge (1892).
           Right: Bracket and Slab Route (1923) Gimmer Crag.

Photos: C. Douglas Milner.

Botterill's Slab (1903), Scafell Crag — now a classic VS.

Photo: Ian Rop

Breathing nearer Heaven

A new century dawned, and the remaining Victorians, like old soldiers, began slowly to fade away. At the same time other climbers appeared to rejuvenate the closely-knit Wasdale community and it was the Abrahams in particular who helped to inspire these new climbers.

There was however some lingering tradition in that nailed boots still lined the entrance hall of the hotel and soaking Norfolk jackets still cluttered the drying room. During one incessant wet period a visitor asked an old Cumbrian if it ever stopped raining:

"Yaas" answered the dalesman, "it sometimes snaws."

However, the restless climbers would not be cooped up, and spreading out in search of adventure they climbed on the hotel's stone walls. The Barn-Door Traverse was a favourite test-piece and a contemporary photograph shows one of the Victorian rock stars, Dr Joseph Collier — his left arm locked off, tension in a strained hand, left leg splayed out horizontally — as he tried to curl his boot round the upper edge of the barn door which had POST HORSES painted boldly on the lintel.

If the weather was too frightful, they even climbed indoors. One day, on a traverse of the billiard room, O.G. Jones slipped and burst through a thin partition into a group of ladies who were taking tea on the other side.

Owing to its popularity the hotel often became full to overflowing at Christmas and on one occasion a guest slept in the bath, his repose disturbed in the middle of the night when someone turned on the cold tap.

The photographs of the Abraham brothers had dramatically illustrated Jones's book and they themselves were involved in many spectacular explorations. Curiously, in 1901, George stated: "experts and novices alike have declared Wasdale to be an exhausted centre". The total number of climbs in the Lake District had reached about a hundred; today there are many thousands, and perhaps he had second thoughts when he devised New West on Pillar Rock. The 1977 guidebook states; 'the situations are superb and the climb is one of the best routes of its standard in the Lake District'.

George and Ashley carried on at a high standard all over the British Isles. Their critics felt it was wrong to make money out of the mountain environment and labelled them professional exploiters — a snobbish verdict on one of the first artistic rock- climbing teams. They carried bulky wooden cameras and clumsy tripods on the high cliffs. Once Ashley emerged from under a black cloth after exposing a plate and stepped off a ledge; fortunately a short rope was attached to his brother and he was saved. The Abrahams became respected elder statesmen of British climbing. Their book 'Rock Climbing in North Wales' (1906), was started by O.G. Jones but the Abrahams finished it after his death. The most important of their books was written by George — 'British Mountain Climbs' (1909) — and standing the test of time it reached its sixth edition in 1948, though it did not have the dynamic spark of Jones's book. The Abrahams carried on climbing as their hair whitened, and their last new climb together was the New West on Pillar Rock. George survived until the early Nineteen-Sixties when he died at the age of ninety-three.

The number of climbers continued to multiply and soon another leading pioneer emerged, a Yorkshireman, Fred Botterill, who lifted climbing delicately upwards to new concepts of technical difficulty. He was the first of a long line of gritstone experts from England's largest county, who have enriched Lakeland climbing. Fred's natural abilities were honed on the sharp cracks of Ilkley Quarry and the moulded joints of Almscliffe, where he initiated many of the boulder problems, and pioneered classics such as Stomach Traverse and the puzzling Bird's Nest Crack. Botterill was to surge upwards into the unknown with his unique inclined slab on Scafell.

Five years before, O.G. Jones had inched his way in stockinged feet on the 'Direct from Lord's Rake', a Hard Severe. In 1903 Botterill climbed his eponymous Slab in boots thickly encrusted in nails, on a route far harder than its contemporaries and with a pitch length of over a hundred feet. A narrow light-coloured ramp slopes intriguingly upwards near the left edge of Scafell Pinnacle Face:

'Clearing away the moss from little cracks here and there I managed to climb slowly upwards for about 60 feet. The holds then dwindled down to little more than finger-end cracks. I looked about me and saw, some twelve feet higher, a little nest about a foot square covered with dried grass. Eight feet higher still was still another nest and a traverse leading back to where the crack opened into a respectable chimney. If I could only reach hold of that first nest what remained would be comparatively easy. It seemed to be a more difficult thing than I had ever done but I was anxious to tackle it. Not wishing to part with the axe I seized it between my teeth and with my fingers in the best available cracks I advanced. I cannot tell with certainty how many holds there were; but I distinctly remember that when within two feet of the nest I had a good hold with my right hand on the face, and so ventured with my left to tear away the dried grass on the nest. However, the grass removed from the ledge, a nice little resting place was exposed,— painfully small, but level and quite safe. I scrambled onto it, but on account of the weight of rope behind me, it was only with great care and some difficulty that I was able to turn round. At last I could sit down on the nest and look around me. The view was glorious. I could see Scafell Pike and a party round the cairn. Far below was another group intent on watching our movements, a lady being amongst the party. I once read in a book on etiquette that a gentleman in whatever situation of life should never forget his manners towards the other sex, so I raised my hat, though I wonder if the author had ever dreamed of a situation like mine. I now discovered that our 80 feet of rope had quite run out, and that my companions had already attached an additional 60 feet. Further, I began to wonder what had become of my axe and concluded I must unthinkingly have placed it somewhere lower down. There it was, stuck in a little crack about five feet below me. Not knowing what was yet to come I felt I must recover it, so I lowered myself until I could reach it with my foot. I succeeded in balancing it on my boot, but in bringing it up it slipped and clattering on the rocks for a few feet took a final leap and stuck point downwards in the Rake's Progress. Standing up again I recommenced the ascent and climbed on to the second nest, a cheval, from where, after a brief rest, I began to traverse back to the crack. This was sensational but perfectly safe. As usual I started with the wrong foot, and after taking two steps was obliged to go back. The next time I started with the left foot, then came the right, again the left, and lastly a long stride with the right, brought me into the chimney. The performance was what might have been called a pas de quatre. Complimentary sounds came from my companions below, but without stopping to acknowledge these I pulled myself up ten feet higher onto a good grass covered-ledge to the right of the crack, smaller

The New West Climb on Pillar Rock. (1901).

Photo: G.D. Abraham.

but very similar to the Tennis Court Ledge of Moss Ghyll.'

Three stars in the 1984 guide book, which describes it as; 'compelling...an outstanding pitch...an amazing lead.' The first Very Severe slab of over one hundred feet high and similar to the hard slabs climbed twenty-five years later in both Wales and the Lake District. Mickledore Grooves, very close on the East Buttress of Scafell, put up nearly thirty years later by the master slab-climber Colin Kirkus, was of the same grade, 4c, and was climbed in rubbers, not nailed boots. Botterill found the first modern slab climb, and had thoughts similar to those of a modern climber:

'Be his bed the soft one of home or the hard one of camp;
Be it in the jolting train or on the restless sea;
Be it in the desert heat or on the cold glacier;
what climber as he lays him down, has not recalled
his past failures, his future triumphs.'

1903 could have been the start of another great surge but it was not to be. Monday 21st September 1903 was not a good day for climbing. The wind was strong in Wasdale, and even stronger two and a half thousand feet higher on the summit of Scafell, as three parties made their way towards England's highest altitude crag. One party consisted of R.W. Broadrick, A.E.W. Garrett, Henry Jupp and Stanley Ridsdale. Marples and Lucas made up the second party, while the third consisted of Webb, Slade and Williamson. The latter climbers lunched with the first party, then went exploring. Broadrick was the leader of the first group. His climbing credentials were excellent. With his brother he had helped to pioneer two new routes on Dow Crag, one of them Broadrick's Crack, which is still graded Hard Severe. The latter was much more difficult than the climb he was aiming at. The previous year he had walked seventy miles over the Lakeland fells in twenty-four hours, and covered 18,500 feet of ascent which put him in the front rank of British mountaineers.

   Years before one of the Hopkinson brothers had built a cairn on a ledge just over one hundred feet above Lord's Rake. There had been several attempts to reach it from the ground, yet all had failed. Broadrick, on that September afternoon in 1903, felt tired and passed the lead to the less-experienced Garrett. Suddenly he slipped. With a scraping of boot nails the rope came taut, then all four plumeted to the foot of the face. Slade heard a shout and moved along foot of the cliff where he saw the four men scattered on the rocks. Ridsdale was still just alive and managed to gasp out:

   "I've been shouting for hours, I'm afraid the others are all gone, but look after them and don't mind me.'

Another account of what Ridsdale said was:

   "Broadrick was first, Garrett second, myself third, and Jupp last. Then Broadrick and Garrett changed places. Broadrick said he was tired. Garrett slipped."

Harold Spender, a member of the Alpine Club which frowned on rock-climbing, unleashed a thunderbolt in the Manchester City News:

   'How long is this to go on and how many more lives are to be lost? ...the peculiar danger

Opposite: Top left: Gilbert Peaker on Pillar Rock.
         Top right: Mrs. Kelly (?) on the front face of Scafell Pinnacle.
         Bottom left: Gilbert Peaker descending from Scafell Pinnacle.
         Bottom right: Knife Edge Arête to Scafell Pinnacle.   Photos: C. Douglas Milner.

of the Lakes climbing lies in the natural rivalry that springs up amongst the climbing parties at Wasdale Head. No party likes to be beaten by another.'

He overstated his case: the losses amongst climbers were minimal when one considers the high general mortality at the turn of the century; and certainly compared favourably with the death rate in the Alps. Gloom again descended on the climbing community at Wasdale Head.

After a respectful interval of inactivity, 1906 was the next important year; and again it was the fleet-footed Botterill who went to investigate the North Face of Pillar Rock. The result was another hard slab, North West Climb, which was over four hundred feet and Very Severe. George Abraham gave it the full treatment:

'...the start is well marked by the boot nail scratches, most of which have doubtless been made by returning parties...A slip on the part of the leader on the upper section would almost certainly mean that none of the party would take any further interest in old age pensions.'

In his book British Mountain Climbs he further described it:

'The North-west Climb. — This is an extremely difficult course, and dangerous withal on account of the absence of really good anchorage. None but seasoned experts should attempt it, and then preferably at the end of a climbing holiday when the physical powers are at their best. It speaks ill for the judgment of the newer generation of climbers to say that until the end of 1908 most of the parties that had tackled this course had to be rescued by means of a rope from above, or had to descend at considerable risk. The latter alternative, beyond a certain point, is almost impossible.'

Botterill was the first Lakeland climber to pioneer two routes that are still graded Very Severe in the Nineteen-Eighties.

Most of the early pioneers had been members of the Alpine Club, which had been founded in 1857. By the turn of the century it was generally felt that its attitudes were out of touch with rock-climbing. A Lakeland group decided in November 1906 to form a Lakeland climbing club. It was called the Fell and Rock Club of the English Lake District; and its ideals were contained in its first membership ticket:

'This Club was founded in November 1906, with the sole object of fostering a love of mountaineering and the pastime of rock-climbing in the English Lake District; and to provide such facilities for its members as to enable them to meet together in order to participate in this sport in one another's company; also to enable lovers of this branch of athletics to become acquainted with one another; and further, to provide information and advice on matters pertaining to local mountaineering and rock-climbing.'

Being forward-looking they admitted women; whereas the Alpine Club, the Climbers' Club and the Scottish Mountaineering Club remained male preserves for many decades. The main bulk of the members were local business men, professional people and others engaged in Northern business life. It was the first break in the ascendancy of the Oxbridge climbers who had dominated early climbing society.

The first President was Ashley Abraham; and J.W. Robinson, the most experienced climber in Cumberland, was made Vice-President. He had climbed Pillar Rock 101

Photo: C. Douglas Milner.

times, Scafell more than 50 times, and Great Gable more than 30 times. He died soon after the founding of the club, but his enormous circle of friends built a large cairn close to Pillar Rock and it was unveiled on one of the stormiest days that most who attended could remember.

The first journal produced by the new club was remarkable for an article by Ashley Abraham who enquired;

'Have any of you ever noticed a bayonet-shaped crack descending from the skyline about midway between Moss Ghyll and Botterill's Crack on Scawfell? Has it never occurred to you that between these two climbs there is a stretch of nearly two hundred feet of unscaled rock?'

One might think that the Abraham brothers could only see gullies and chimneys, yet Ashley had spotted one of the great untouched features, which remained unscaled for another quarter of a century.

Another article in the same journal by Andrew Thomson, described the lay-back technique which was used to overcome Amen Corner, part of 'B' route on Gimmer Crag:

'It was ultimately climbed by gripping the edge of the crack with both hands and walking up the left wall, the body being almost in a horizontal position. The strain on the arms is terrific, and one gets into a position with a hand actually on the double hand-hold by which the final pull-up is effected, yet one is too exhausted to do so.'

C.H. Oliverson also wrote 'The Rope as used in Rock-Climbing', describing the techniques then in use. The rope was passed through the hands of the second man, who just gripped it if the leader fell. Climbers still did not tie on to spikes or pinnacles, but merely passed the rope around them. Oliverson suggested that the best number of people was three:

'One of the best methods of attacking a climb is for the third man to belay the second, the second man then has his hands at liberty in order to guide the rope for the leader. If the leader should slip the second man can pull in the rope quickly and at the proper moment, which he could not do if he passed the rope over an ordinary belay upon the way to the leader.'

It was still thought that the ice-axe had a part to play:

'Artificial Belays — Ice Axe Belay — In some instances there are no natural belays upon the rocks, and then it may be necessary to form one in some way. Each end of the axe is jammed in some rough part of the rock, with the head of the axe rather higher than the other end. The rope is then tied round the head of the axe in such a way as to prevent its slipping down the shaft of the axe, and also so as not to pull the axe away from the rock; when any strain is put upon the axe it will be more firmly fixed in its place.'

His comments on rope lengths were just as primitive and he recommended that four climbers needed no more than one hundred feet of rope and therefore only twenty-five feet of rope between any two climbers. It is surprising that there were not more fatal accidents. Perhaps the best judgement on his recommendations is to quote another of his comments:

Opposite: Above: Mal Richardson on Troutdale Pinnacle (1914) in the early Seventies.   Photo: Alan Hinkes.
Below left: Rope and rubbers.   Photo: Norman Rimmer.
Below right: The Gangway, Gimmer Crag.   Photo: C.D. Milner.

'Play the rope as though you were trying to tire out a whale with a piece of string.'

An example of the dangers of these techniques was described by George Abraham concerning a party on the New West on Pillar Rock:

'They arrived in darkness at the foot of the slabs and found them glazed with ice. The leader attempted in vain to make progress further than a ledge 15 feet above the shattered rocks. Prolonged effort led to a sudden and unexpected descent. The second climber apparently possessed no belay, but when the fall occurred he instantly hitched the rope around a slight excrescence and braced himself for the strain. The leader went flying away out over the ledge; the rope held and he hung suspended in darkness over the abyss. The last man on the rope, anchored by his companion in front, was just traversing around the sensational corner from the chimney at the time. The sight of the flying leader so startled him that he also lost his balance and swung pendulum-like into a crack in the cliff, where, fortunately, he became wedged, in a more or less dazed condition. In due course the leader realised his position, and after many terribly exciting efforts, which were for some time futile, he was eventually hauled up to the ledge. The last man was rescued, and then, remarkable to relate, it was ascertained that no bones were broken nor had any serious damage resulted.'

George Abraham brought out his book 'The Complete Mountaineer' in 1907. The brothers were prototypes of the climbing photographic journalist and outstanding pioneers, but George's advice on rope techniques was no better than that given by Oliverson:

'On even the most difficult routes yet made there are ledges at intervals where the leader can safely stand, or sit and hold the rope, while the second climber ascends to his level. If there is any danger of a slip the rope should be held firmly even to the extent of hauling slightly, but if it is possible to work the rope around a projecting piece of rock that may not be necessary. It is astonishingly easy to support the weight of a dangling companion if the rope is thus secured. If any knobs of rock are available — and the efficient second will generally discover something of the kind — the rope should be paid out, or belayed round this. This process is called belaying and the word belaying-pin is often used to signify the rock used for this purpose.'

Even in one of his later books, 'First Steps To Climbing', George's advice was still fundamentally wrong:

'Before the age of twenty-one serious work such as leading should not be undertaken.'

He and his brother were in their teens when they started doing new routes and the two leaders of the next generation were under this age. Naturally he had decided views on footwear and favoured nailed boots:

'Rubber-soled boots are favoured by many experts. Their drawbacks are very similar to those of scarpetti, but if the thick red-soled variety is chosen they have advantages, one of which is that they withstand general service; they can also be worn for the walk up and down to the rocks.'

Another fatality then occurred which involved Fred Botterill. He was climbing on

Opposite: Rusty Westmorland leading Gillercombe Buttress, first done in 1912 by H.B. Lyon and A.S. Walker.   Photo: C. Douglas Milner.

Central Buttress, Scafell Crag, with a climber on the Great Flake.

Photo: R.F. Alle

Great Gable with Thomas Rennison, who was keen to try Eagle's Nest Ridge Direct, Solly's tour de force of 1892. They rose at 5.30 a.m.:

> 'At 9.40 by R.'s watch B. advanced to the belay pin which is some sixty-five feet above the Dress Circle. R. joined him there, and after a moment's rest advanced. It is necessary at first to climb slightly, perhaps three feet, to the left before going upwards. R. had gone to the left and advanced upwards about ten feet. His arms were both outstretched, his knees and toes occupying two parallel cracks. His feet would be within eight feet of B.'s head. He had not spoken since commencing, perhaps three minutes. He had not moved a limb for twenty seconds when ... he slipped ... all points of contact coming away simultaneously. He made no effort to save himself — uttered no cry — never turned his head — exactly like a man with palpitation. At that moment the knot at his waist was within thirteen feet of the belay in an oblique line, the belay being level with B.'s waist. There were from fourteen to eighteen inches of slack paid out for the leader's next forward step; there were also fourteen to sixteen inches of rope round the belay. B. instinctively placed both hands on the rope, feeling sure of pulling R. up, and crouched to meet the jerk. B. was not in a good position, quite unable to lean backwards. There was no time to take in any slack. The jerk came immediately and the rope broke with a loud snap, six inches above B.'s right hand.'

Fortunately for Botterill the rope had snapped round the rudimentary running belay that he had contrived and this almost certainly saved him from being killed. The accident had a profound effect and he never climbed a hard route again.

Another man stepped briefly into the gap left by Botterill's voluntary abdication. Hugh Rose Pope, a six-footer from Eton and Oxford, had been trained in the Pen y Pass stable of young climbers then presided over by Geoffrey Winthrop Young, 'the eminence grise' of Welsh climbing in the Edwardian age.

The fine old ramparts of Pillar Rock had slumbered for five years since Fred Botterill had produced North West. Pope climbed South West, an elegant slab, four hundred feet long, Very Severe in standard, which undoubtedly deserves the praise later given in the 1977 guide-book: 'an exceptionally fine slab climb...'

Pope was only twenty-two, at the height of his powers. The following year he went to France to learn the language and was killed scrambling alone on the North Face of the Pic du Midi.

However, the growth in the number of Northern gritstone climbers continued to raise standards and produced another rock star, Siegfried Wedgwood Herford, born in Aberystwyth in 1891. He went to Manchester University in 1909 and immediately took a liking to gritstone climbing. He went to the Pen y Pass climbing parties and undoubtedly impressed Geoffrey Winthrop Young with his ability on rock:

> 'Siegfried Herford had something of a Norse wind-god in his fairness and sudden apparitions on high, unlikely pinnacles. He was an originator; but his first wish was admiringly to repeat all Pope's climbs. His lead up the Flake Crack on Scafell, undertaken for a climbers' guide to the Lake climbs similar to our Welsh guide, which I had arranged with the Oxford Press, is sometimes cited as the beginning of the transition to modern methods and standards...An engineer, with a deep strain of poetry and romance, his style of rock-climbing would have been at home among recent developments. From his knee to his shoulder there looked to be a single powerful spiral of muscle, which enabled him to straighten in balance upon infinitesimal stances.'

Gritstone climbing was short and compact and a great many feet of climbing were possible in a day. It was the start of an era when climbers climbed solely for enjoyment, not as a prelude to Alpine mountaineering. Winthrop Young analysed this:

'The boulder practice such as we obtained on rocks near our base, on off or wet days, was a limited exercise which could do little to improve the technique of the time. It was not until the climbing infection spread over areas without hills, where the solitary outcrop of gritstone or sandstone played the part of the local mountain, as it did in the Peak District, that bouldering, as we call it, could come into its own as practice on a large scale, and produce its experts. Herford and Laycock were original and conspicuous examples of a truth which only became recognized fifty years later, that practice and a progressive training on relatively low and technically difficult rocks of this character are the essential preparation for attempting modern severe rock problems.'

During his undergraduate period Herford started to climb with John Laycock, a keen outcrop climber who wrote 'Some Gritstone Climbs' (In Derbyshire and Elsewhere) — the first guide to outcrop climbing which was dedicated to Herford, who did the Girdle Traverse of Castle Naze; an outcrop near Buxton.
During 1912 Laycock and Herford spent a hundred days climbing together, and the relentless determination of Herford soon overtook Laycock in technical ability.
Laycock wrote later somewhat wanly:

'...he almost always led, because it was his right...To all but his intimates he was rather reserved in manner. To them he was the truest, kindest and most generous of friends, our idol and our pride.'

In 1911 Laycock led Herford up the delightful Middlefell Buttress in Langdale, which is the most pleasant way to gain height en route for Gimmer Crag. Laycock also introduced Herford to George Sansom and in 1912 they went to the Dolomites together, then they returned to Glencoe and Skye. No man had experienced such a concentrated apprenticeship and Herford lived up to Laycock's judgment that 'he was the greatest rock climber England has yet produced.'
Sansom was slightly older than Herford. Born in 1888, he went to University College London, and was as fanatical about rock-climbing as Herford. He went to Wales but didn't like it:

'I did climb in Wales for a few days but strangely enough, I can't recall a single day's climbing there that I really enjoyed.'

Sansom was enthralled by the superb Abraham photographs and George arranged for his younger brother John to take Sansom up his first Cumbrian climbs. He gravitated to Wasdale and its historic climbing community. He summed up his feelings to it by quoting George Basterfield's poem:

'There are no hills like the Wasdale hills when Spring comes up the vale.'

Sansom had the good fortune to be taken climbing by Fred Botterill and credited him with 'elegant, effortless climbing; in fact I have never seen a neater climber.' Sansom was the better planner of new routes, whilst Herford provided the technical skill. April

Opposite: A modern team on Jim Birkett's North West Arête, Gimmer Crag.   Photo: Ron Kenyon.

1912 saw the start of their new assaults on the Cumbrian crags when Sansom ascended the West Buttress of Kern Knotts. A poor stance at the foot of a groove, then a swing left to a good foothold, gave him his first new Very Severe. Five days later it was Herford's turn, but this time it was on the main face of Scafell. A sombre aura had surrounded it, ever since the four deaths nine years before, but they trod warily and produced the Direct from Lord's Rake to Hopkinson's Cairn, now a popular two-star Severe. In an article in the Fell and Rock Journal for 1912, 'The Climbs on the Scafell Pinnacle', they outlined their views on rope-lengths, footwear, and the skills needed to pioneer hard climbs:

'We see no reason, therefore, why the climbs on the Pinnacle Face should be regarded as intrinsically dangerous, but at the same time we would most emphatically urge that they be not attempted by any but the steadiest and most skilful of leaders, who, moreover, have had considerable experience of difficult slab climbing without boots. We would most strongly emphasise the point that boots should be taken off; the holds are so sloping in places (up to 40 degrees) as to render the climbing in boots excessively dangerous. These climbs are undeniably best tackled alone. We have both experienced the weight of 130-odd feet of rope, while negotiating the exposed traverse below the Waiting Room, and must say that it is more dangerous than useful... We do not think that sufficient distinction has been made between difficulty and danger in climbing. In the case of a climb lying on perfectly clean and sound rock, the apparent difficulty varies inversely as the skill of the individual, although the intrinsic or technical difficulty is of course the same for all. It is when the skill begins to be taxed to near its limit that danger is present. The danger, therefore, depends on the skill of the individual, and can be eliminated if the skill is sufficiently great.'

Their recommendations about rope lengths were as severe as their climbs. In their description of the Direct from Lord's Rake via Hopkinson's Cairn they wrote:

'Very severe. Perfect rock. A very difficult and exposed slab. Comparatively easy above the Cairn. No belays in the lower part. Best number, one, or if two, both capable of leading. 150 feet of rope needed.'

The next ghost to be exorcised was Hopkinson's Gully which had been inviolate since the Hopkinson's icy assault in 1887. It was to be another Very Severe three-star route, and the latest guide-book calls it 'The best line hereabouts.'

In stockinged feet and without proper belays, they changed the face of British climbing. Herford had developed a taste for girdle traverses on gritstone and it seemed to him that Scafell could yield a similar prize:

'On the face of it, Scafell seems scarcely a suitable place for a Traverse. The great unclimbed Central Buttress appears to block the way effectually and there are several other serious obstacles. I was all the more pleased, therefore, when Sansom wrote to me early in September, suggesting a feasible route right across the crags.'

It was over a thousand feet long and they had to abseil down some of the awkward parts. In this way they were able to examine at close quarters the great unclimbed Flake Crack in the middle of the face:

'The ledge on which we now stood is in many ways unique, and is certainly one of the most remarkable places in Cumberland. Above it the wall of the Central Buttress rises sheer for several hundred feet, almost hopelessly smooth and steep.'

Just as they reached the tantalising position where they could make an inspection, it started to get dark and so they retreated but they returned two days later:

'It was our idea to see whether we could not make a traverse across the upper part of the Central Buttress, leaving, for the time being, the route we had previously tried. We therefore followed Moss Ghyll to the belay above the Collie step, from which point Sansom led us straight up the wall ahead, as far as a good grassy ledge which was to be our starting point for this section of the Traverse. A most sensational corner was first rounded on unsatisfactory holds. Here the chief excitement was reserved for Brunskill, who came round last. He was wearing for the occasion a long female garment showing an elegant waist, which he had appropriated from the large collection of relics in Walker's Gully, and was the cause of much ribald laughter as he swung round the corner, his coat-tails flying in the air, over a drop worthy of the Dolomites.'

After the girdle traverse, Herford decided to investigate the top of the flake by traversing along a narrow step now known as Jeffcoat's Ledge. It narrowed alarmingly, until it became a wafer-thin flake, perforated in a few places, which added to his insecurity. He realised that the only feasible side of the crack for him was its right-hand side. Jeffcoat held the rope as Herford descended and started a desperate struggle upwards. The rope jammed, then freed, and Herford got back on top of the Flake exhausted, but thought it might just be climbable.

As in all good thrillers a third man then appeared, C.F. Holland, who was to help in the solution of Central Buttress. He survived the war and provided an invaluable link with pre- and post-war climbers. Holland was the son of a Church of England Minister of modest means. First he went to Westminster School with a charity award and then went on to Oxford during which time he met Herford on a train from Bangor to Bethesda:

'Opposite sat a tall young man of striking appearance, obviously alien in every way to the quarrymen and suchlike who filled the carriage, jabbering some strange language, presumably Welsh. According to the usual custom of the English under such conditions we did not exchange a single word, but when on reaching Bethesda we found we were both bound for Ogwen we agreed to share a vehicle.'

They stayed at Ogwen Cottage, where Herford found that he had to share a bed with a stranger, a common practice in the middle ages and one which survived in Wales until the twentieth century.

'Herford was sharing a bed with one who desired to have more than his fair share of bedclothes. On being expostulated with, the other man had refused to yield any portion of what he had acquired, and was promptly thrown onto the floor, albeit carrying with him the entire bedclothes, purporting, I imagine, to sleep where he lay. Thereupon Herford twisted his toes to induce him to part with the integuments (I am not quite sure of this word, but it sounds good), in which he had now wound himself after the fashion of a cocoon. In its agony the cocoon rolled about and eventually went under one of the beds. Now it so chanced that

Opposite: Top left:, top right and bottom left: Central Buttress yielding to combined tactics, in old style.   Photos: Eric Byrom collection.
           Bottom right: Charlie Wilson belaying Len Muscroft on Central Buttress.   Photo: C.R. Wilson.

it was the bed of one who had acquired the strange habit of placing his false teeth under his bed. Hence the loud shout as he sprang forth to rescue his property from their imminent danger, while the final dominating scream emanated from the cocoon, who had apparently been severely bitten.'

Holland joined Herford on a Hogmanay attempt on Walker's Gully on Pillar Rock which was in similar wintry conditions to that of the first ascent by O.G. Jones. Herford got into difficulties:

'The first attempt failed, as the scree went on strike and the leader's quiet remark, "I am coming off now", was immediately justified. The thread did its work and a second shot was successful...For the next hour or so important threading operations ensued. Finally Herford performed marvellously on the right wall, assumed a backing-up position and disappeared. Now it was Sansom's turn to do surprising things on the wall, apparently preserving his status quo by sticking his head into ante-chambers in the rock while he unthreaded. Meantime, he who tells the tale had retired into the recess of the cave and kept the octopus quiet by sitting on it. Subsequently this went aloft guarded by the ice-axe, which throughout displayed great strength of character.'

Herford was again spurred into wintry activity on the unclimbed Central Buttress, and Holland later described the exploits of a snowy day in January 1914:

'Under the prevailing conditions the expedition seemed to me a most perilous one, and the two corners we had to pass places of some severity, easy as they may be on a hot summer's day. Eventually we reached the belay near the end of the ledge, and prepared to rope down. As a matter of fact, Herford climbed down successfully, in spite of the snow, though he announced that it was pretty near the limit.'

Later, on April 19th, Herford, Sansom, Gibson and Holland went up Brown Tongue to the foot of the cliff. Gibson traversed to the top of the Great Flake and set up a top-rope, then Sansom climbed the ferocious crack, but his arms gave out on the final overhanging section. Herford followed and managed it without any assistance but felt that he was near his limit. They all then descended to the foot of the cliff where Sansom proposed rope engineering to overcome the problems; so he soaked two ends of one rope in wet moss to make them stiff and easier to thread round the chockstones at the foot of the final difficulties. Sansom set off but got into difficulties before he reached the chockstones; Herford then shot up the lower part of the crack at great speed, and jammed himself into the crack, where Sansom used his shoulder to get to the chockstones and thus was able to fix double loops.

They both had a brief rest, then each tried the final problem; but their exertions had taken their toll and they decided to retreat after seven hours of exhausting effort. Fortunately the threaded rope was in position round the chockstones and was ready for their return the following day.

Despite snow still lying in deep clefts the weather was brilliant, one of the best April days that Sansom could remember. Herford and Sansom went up again safeguarded by the threaded rope. Sansom later described an incident during a rather critical phase:

'A most remarkable incident had occurred while the crack was being led. Sansom was hanging on by indifferent sloping handholds on or near the lower end of the great chockstone, and Herford was standing on his shoulders, about to make the first step of the last tremendous solo effort. The initial difficulty confronting him was that of getting a purchase with his left foot in a groove unsuitably shaped for that purpose. Sansom's left hand began to slip under the great strain, and must inevitably have given way very soon, in which case he would have come off, though only for a foot or two, on to the loops. Herford's fall, unavoidable if this had happened, would have been a very serious affair indeed, and even if his rope had held it is impossible to see how we below could have given any assistance, beyond keeping the ropes tight, if either had been injured in any way. At this moment, however, the great goddess of luck took a hand in the game. I call it "Luck"; there are those who would name it differently. Finding himself unable to get his foot as he wanted it, Herford stepped back and accidentally put his foot on the slipping hand, thus holding it in position; and the difficult step was made so quickly at the second attempt that Sansom was able to support the double weight till that of the leader was removed.'

They were now close to a brilliant success, as Sansom described:

'He used my shoulder as footholds. Directly he vacated them I climbed three feet higher and hung by my hands from the top of the chockstone, whilst he again employed me as footholds, which are most sorely needed at this point, for the crack is practically holdless and overhangs about 20 degrees. A minute or two of severe struggling and he reached the top to the great joy of all members of the party.'

It had been at the very limit of Herford's abilities and he sank exhausted on the top of the flake, his right knee jammed into the crack. Holland described his state when he climbed the flake:

'I was left, forlorn and frightened, ready to give all my wordly wealth to avoid what lay before me. Over the ensuing struggles I will draw a veil; suffice it to say that I had two ropes on, and climbed up a third; failed miserably to cut away the thread as I was asked to do, and finished in a state of utter exhaustion, after a wild haul at a knotted loop that Herford had with characteristic thoughtfulness placed in just the right position.'

This was not the end of the difficulties as there were still two hundred feet of unclimbed rock above. However, they were well satisfied and returned two days later to finish the climb. The prospect at the top of the Great Flake was uncompromisingly steep, so they traversed off right for the final solution. This took them under the Bayonet-Shaped Crack seen and named by Ashley Abraham.

'Herford first tried the Bayonet-Shaped-Crack. But it looked repulsively difficult and he abandoned it in favour of a most exhilarating traverse across its foot, onto the vertical wall beyond, and upwards across the latter for 30 feet to a steep slab, which he followed for another 25 feet to a good belay at the top of the lower section of the crack. We soon joined him here and climbed easily up the left wall of the upper portion of the Bayonet-Shaped-Crack to the top of the crags.'

Sansom led the last pitch, a delicate 5a by modern grading which led to easy ground. It was the greatest climbing achievement in the British Isles. In 1924 Holland produced a guide-book to Scafell and rose to the task of describing the magnificence of Central Buttress in which he had played a useful part ten years previously:

> 'For some distance the bare cliffs tower overhead, and the Great Flake is conspicuous, though the ascent looks utterly hopeless. Its conquest however, was accomplished by the late S.W. Herford, and is perhaps the finest achievement associated with that great climber's name. The Central Butttess. The most arduous ascent in the Lake District; unexampled exposure; combined tactics and rope engineering essential at one point; not less than three climbers. Rubbers.'

Herford had advanced the technical standard of rock-climbing up to a modern 5b grade, and it was to be over thirty years before it was exceeded anywhere in the British Isles. Some climbs soon after the war equalled but did not exceed it. The 1984 guide-book gives the route respectful treatment. It has a three-star accolade and the crux is described as having 'a fearsome finish.'

The war started a few months later. Herford joined up and wrote jokingly to Laycock:

> 'I'll write your obituary for the Fell and Rock Journal. You can do the same for me.'

Herford applied for a commission which was refused, then on the 28th January 1916 he was killed by a rifle grenade. His magnificent climbing ability, locked in precious neurons, was blown apart in a second by a piece of Ruhr steel. However he did leave his greatest memorial on Scafell.

Samson was awarded the Military Cross in the Army, then transferred to the Royal Flying Corps in which he won the Distinguished Flying Cross. After the war he became a Doctor of Science, a Fellow of University College, London, and finally a marksman at Bisley. He was also a skilled cabinet-maker and invented a mechanical cat to scare birds away from his garden. The cat emerged from its hutch every two minutes, its eyes lit up, it turned its head and mewed.

Fortunately Sansom lost none of his agility during the war and returned to Wasdale, then soloed the Very Severe North West climb on Pillar Rock. Harry Griffin, the Lakeland author, was led up it by Sansom and remembers:

> 'He used to smoke a cherry-wood pipe and eat barley sugar — useful for making fingers stick to holds as he told me.'

Even in his eighties his heart was still in Wasdale contemplating the happy memories of his days of glory with Herford sixty years previously when he was young and his world so different before the First World War smashed his climbing life.

> 'As I am 85 this year, I fear that my climbing days are over but my love for the Wasdale fells will endure for ever.'

Perhaps Tennyson might have been thinking like a rock-climber when he wrote;

> 'The joy of life in steepness overcome
> And victories of ascent and looking down
> On all that had looked down on us
> And joy in breathing nearer heaven.'

Opposite: Top left: A.T. Hargreaves boldly leading Kern Knotts Crack.   Photo: Sid Cross.
           Top right: Reg Schofield starting up Innominate Crack, Great Gable.   Photo: C.R. Wilson.
           Bottom: A Fell and Rock group in the early 1920s:
                      (back) J.H. Doughty, B. Eden-Smith, H.M. Kelly, N.L. Eden-Smith
                      (front) G.S. Bower, R.E.W. Pritchard, R.S.T. Chorley. W. Eden-Smith, H. Coates.   Photo: H. Coates.

A Hundred per cent He-man

In the first year of peace surviving climbers streamed back across the Channel from the trenches, eager to get on the crags again. Some had been crippled, others had had limbs blown off. In Holland's case his arm was still in plaster as a result of gunshot wounds.

Before 1914 there had been occasional flashes of brilliance, but after the war high-standard new climbs became commonplace during the summer months. One of the main reasons was the transport revolution inspired by the war's need for hosts of motor vehicles. This caused a change in climbers' leisure patterns. When hostilities ceased the manufacture of military vehicles was transferred to motor cars, which made regular weekend climbing possible. More important, it eliminated the difficult problems of rail connections between different areas and valleys, and resulted in a steady stream of new routes as soon as the winter snows of early 1919 had melted.

Post-war British climbing became centred in the Lake District, partly because it was near the Vickers engineering works at Barrow in Furness, whose output of warships had proved an important factor in victory. Vickers employed many trained engineers and scientists; and some of these became bewitched by the Cumbrian fells.

Herford, Sansom and Holland were part of the climbing elite at the beginning of the war. The latter two survived and came back to the Lakes almost immediately, but Sansom felt the death of Herford keenly and he lost the essential drive for hard climbing. Holland on the other hand was made of sterner stuff, having been shot in the arm and awarded the Military Cross for bravery in fierce fighting in the Hindenburg Line.

After one heavy German bombardment he had made a solemn vow; 'If I get out of this alive the first thing I'll do when I get back to England will be to go to the top of Napes Needle and sing 'God Save The King.'

One of the more endearing anecdotes about him was told by a companion of his called Wilson:

'Holland and I were once leaving the New Hotel on our way to Gimmer when a new member arrived on his bicycle and asked if he could join us. Knowing that he was the Income Tax Inspector for Holland's own district I warned him that it would be putting too great a temptation in Holland's way, but he came and all the way up to the crag Holland gloated over having him in his power. The inevitable happened when we were coming down Gimmer Chimney. The Inspector was on a large stance about 80 feet down and I waited on my holds, owing to shortage of rope, to enable Holland to come down to a turf ledge about twenty feet below the top of the chimney. No sooner had Holland stepped on the ledge than a stone about the size of a cigar box fell from the underside of it and dropped clear on to the Inspector's head.'

The tax man spent some months in hospital. It is not known whether Holland's assessment was increased.

His heart was always in the Lake District. Once in the Dolomites beneath the great rock walls of the Langkofel, there was a sudden silence at meal-time, broken by

Opposite: 'Destry Rides Again". George Bower leading Giant's Corner, Dow Crag in 1951 — 31 years after his first ascent.
Photo: C. Douglas Milner

Holland saying, "Gentlemen, a toast — Slab and Notch." (The Easy Way up Pillar Rock).

He had been a keystone in the successful Central Buttress party in 1914 and five years later was the linchpin of a trio that revitalised Lakeland climbing. Another member of that 1919 trio was Harry Kelly, an agnostic and a socialist, who escaped the carnage of the trenches. He was already thirty-five, but at the brink of a glittering new route career, during which he put up nearly fifty new routes over the next decade. He did not advance existing standards, but he had a superb eye for a new route combined with an obsessive urge. A possible new route up uncharted rock spurred him to even greater efforts. The Welsh star climber Fred Pigott said about him:

> 'To a natural gift he added great application and had achieved a precision in smooth and delicate balance that had probably not been reached by anyone on British rocks before.'

He tried to descend all his routes and often explored potential lines on a top-rope. For footwear he wore the cheapest rubber plimsolls. As with Herford, his base was in Manchester and he became an expert on gritstone.

There was a third man, C.G. Crawford, who had a natural optimism that buttressed the abilities of the other members of the trio. Soon he became one of the more staunch Himalayan mountaineers of the Nineteen-Twenties. Their separate qualities were summed up neatly:

> 'Holland formed a direct link with pre-war climbing: he had been with Herford and Sansom on their exploration of the Central Buttress. A great climber, an even greater inspirer, he has probably exerted more influence on ambitious youth in the climbing world than any other man of our time. His knowledge of the crags was extensive, his courage boundless, his temperament ideal... Holland's eye for a route, Crawford's cheery optimism in conjunction with his remarkable aptitude for the sport, and Kelly's technical skill in leadership formed an irresistible combination when these three got together.'

In the summer of 1919 Holland, who was still recovering from his wartime wounds, felt the climbing urge and sent a telegram to Kelly, who had been expecting to spend a solitary holiday in Wasdale, 'Bring one pound of Capstan and two pairs of rubbers. Holland.' (Capstan was a strong pipe tobacco.)

It was a memorable meeting. Kelly, Holland, and Crawford who later joined them, did all the existing routes on Scafell Pinnacle during one July week and interleaved them with two new Mild Very Severes — Waiting Room from the First Pitch in Steep Ghyll and Pinnacle Face from the same point — these were Crawford's contribution with Low Man by the Right Wall of Steep Ghyll by the indefatigable Holland.

Kelly decided on a route up a set of grooves that slanted steeply upwards from Moss Ghyll. He tried the line twice during that eventful July week, but failed and had difficulty in retreating. He tried the second ascent of Herford's Central Buttress but failed, and afterwards referred to it as 'that awful Great Flake'. This was significant because succeeding generations need to climb on the shoulders of the previous 'greats' and do their routes with relative ease. Kelly however was too old to make such a leap forward. The trio spent several days on Pillar Rock and each climber shared leads on new routes. Holland started off with a Severe called Rib and Slab, still one of the best climbs of its standard on the cliff. Kelly and Crawford then added three more routes in the next few days, and finally Kelly returned with Holland to add two Very Severe routes which were gems. Holland described the hard moves on the first one:

'The traverse across the Chimney leads to a very hard swing round the corner and for some thirty feet the climbing is phenomenally steep, the holds are small and unsuitable, lichen and moss are at present abundant, and altogether the whole section seemed to me most severe, and dangerous in addition, as I could see no means of safeguarding the leader. With any moisture about the pitch would scarcely be justifiable, as the holds when dry are only just adequate.'

Five pitches on the West Face of High Man gave nearly three hundred feet of enjoyable friction-climbing. Eager to do another climb, Kelly immediately set off again up the West Face. Holland followed and was hard pressed:

'I cannot refrain from saying something about Route 2. The line we intended following soon brought us up against obstacles of a most uncompromising character and Kelly was forced into a chimney, or rather a right-angled corner of extreme severity. I found this too hard at one point, and after great exertions to preserve my status quo had the unpleasant experience of falling off backwards and dangling, as Kelly was seated on a projection. Hardly had I re-established myself when the unkindly rope removed my pipe from my mouth and not long afterwards completed my discomfiture by dislodging a stone which hit me on the head. Our exit was also in keeping with the rest of the climb, which as a whole was one of the severest and most unpleasant I have ever experienced.'

Holland had been polite in the extreme in his written account, whereas Kelly wrote more forcefully that not only had he nearly split Holland's skull, giving him a 'bloody coxcomb', but even more serious, had committed the unpardonable sin of using a split infinitive in his apology. The atmosphere was silent and frosty as they returned along the High Level route. Normally after a new route climbers tell and re-tell their hairs-breadth escapes needed to overcome the problems, and talk about possible route names. No conversation took place on the afternoon of August 9th 1919; but when they neared Burnthwaite Farm Holland at last broke the long silence, and said; "Kelly, if you don't have names for those climbs we've done today, I've got a couple — Sodom and Gomorrah."

The names were too strong for the Fell and Rock and the routes were blandly labelled Route 1 and Route 2. It was nearly fifty years before the original names were rightfully restored. Towards the end of the holiday Kelly slipped away to Kern Knotts, and in three days added three more Very Severes to the list. Their varied abilities were summed up later by Kelly:

'In some way Holland appears to have been the inspirer of the climbs, while Kelly was the leading executor. Holland was constantly praising his imperturbability, his calm assumption of responsibility, his detachment in moments of danger. "I like to think of him", he once wrote, "leading his devoted party up the North-West (on Pillar) in pouring rain, measuring all the pitches without any of the hurry usually associated with cold and wet." Yet it would be wrong to parcel out too definitely the responsibility, to assume that new climbs were always made as the result of a deeply-laid plan. It is interesting to contemplate that at least half our climbs were discovered in a casual (one might almost say accidental) fashion, whereas one might think the majority were first done by laborious studying of the rock-faces.'

Much later Holland wrote about the mystique of hard climbing and sketched a philosophy about it:

'I would urge younger climbers with practically all their climbing life yet to come, to set up an ideal, to abandon all ideas of safety first, and to climb dangerously, though it is important to add that incessant and conscientious training is necessary in order to be able to do this justifiably... Climbing should be a religion and not a recreation, that is to say a pleasant way of spending an occasional holiday. In the case of the other great sports, such as rugby and boxing, a man is approaching the sere and yellow at the age of thirty, but we can carry on at least to seventy if trouble is taken to keep the limbs supple and the mind young. ...So many men climb enthusiastically for a few years, five years is a climbing generation, and then abandon the sport except for a holiday from time to time when probably they get one of a later generation to lead them safely and gently up a few of the more moderate ascents; I notice incidentally that this is particularly common in the case of those who have been rock specialists, while the mountaineers usually carry on year after year. Sweep away all the usual considerations that make one give the sport up, the qualms as to its being justifiable now one is married, either on the score of danger or expense; and, when you climb, be a whole hogger, a hundred per cent he- man... You may be killed, but what if you are? The only sane way of viewing life is as one step of a series in an upward progression and not as an end in itself, and that what matters is not the manner or time of its end, but the spirit with which we have faced its difficulties.'

His philosophic thoughts can hardly be bettered in the Nineteen-Eighties.

Holland, Crawford and Kelly had done wondrous things, but all their deeds were eclipsed a few weeks later in the autumn by one route put up on Dow Crag by an unknown climber from Barrow in Furness — Joseph Igal Roper. He began climbing in 1918 after scrambling over the southern Lakeland Fells with a Barrow group. Roper was born in 1893, and at his home in Bakewell at the age of ninety-five remembers those heady days in 1919 when his Great Central Route equalled Herford's 5b Central Buttress. Joe had many talents. He went to Ruskin College, Oxford, and one of the reasons he reached the top in rock-climbing was his extraordinary strength, caused by working on his uncle's chicken farm. On piece-work payment, he had to wring their necks, then pluck them and had to work hard to make a living. The deaths of many thousands of chickens resulted in outstanding muscular strength which, combined with a keenness for ballroom dancing, gave him faith in the co-ordination of his hands and feet.

In September 1919 Roper went to the Easter Gully of Dow Crag, to an attractive unclimbed pillar. On the first attempt he slithered off its crux (which came to be named Bandstand Wall) and sprained his ankle. The Bandstand Wall was guarded by the South America Crack, so-called because its outline looked like that continent. Roper hand-jammed up it, while future ascensionists were forced to layback the pitch. Joe described his ascent:

'A vertical wall is the next difficulty, and a small grass ledge the immediate goal. The holds on the wall are all in miniature, and this pitch provides the greatest difficulty of the climb. On both occasions it was climbed on the left of the grassy ledge, though at first view the right side of the grassy ledge appears to be the best route... The get-away from the 'bandstand' can be facilitated by the second man holding the leader's foot on a tiny knob of rock, until

Opposite: Joe Roper's 1919 HVS, Great Central Route on Dow Crag. The leader, Bill Smith of Burnley, is on the South America Crack. Note the
            Marks and Spencer's black pumps.   Photo: John Hartley.
            Inset: Joe Roper in his 95th year.   Photo: Trevor Jones.

John Kingston leading H.M. Kelly's 1923 route Tophet Wall on Great Gable.

Photo: Ian Ro[

a very unsatisfactory finger-hold is grasped and passed quickly, as the vertical character of the rock gives the body and feet no effective purchase.'

The climbing above the ledge was still hard with little for the feet. Grudgingly the wall relented until Broadrick's Crack was reached and a good ledge on the front of the pillar. In the first Lake District rock-climbing guide, 'Doe Crags and Climbs round Coniston', George Bower gave Great Central Route full treatment:

'Exceedingly Severe; rubbers or suckers essential... The way is desperately severe, and starts to the left of the slight nose formed by the buttress. Belayed by the third man the second steadies the leader's foot, rattles the bag of acid drops, or performs any other service required of him.'

Roper had climbed the first 5b pitch without top-rope inspection. The latest guide-book (1984) grades the climb Hard Very Severe 5b and calls it 'A climb of great tradition, characterised by both delicate and strenuous climbing with exposed positions.'

Its reputation was reinforced when the great Welsh climber Colin Kirkus fell off it and not only broke his toe, but also burnt his second's hands to the bone.

The pace of exploration barely paused the next year and George Bower came into prominence in his own right. Since his move to Barrow in 1917, he had spent most of his leisure hours in the hills. His involvement with the Yewdale Vagabonds brought him many benefits. He climbed with Roper, the group's greatest star, and another prominent member, George Basterfield, whose daughter eventually married Bower. Almost as soon as Bower had settled down in Barrow he wrote a memorable treatise on rope techniques which laid the foundation for safe modern belaying. First of all he suggested using a light Alpine line to lessen the weight on a long run-out. In the short note that he published in the Fell and Rock Journal his suggestions were for safer belaying for all members of a climbing party:

'Whilst on the subject of belays, the correct method of belaying the leader may be described, since it does not appear to be universally known. It is no use the second passing the leader's rope round a rock belay, for, should the leader come off, on steep open rocks, the rope will assuredly break. The correct method, it cannot be too strongly urged, is for the second to belay himself to the rocks with his own end of the leader's rope, and to pass the latter over his shoulder, controlling it with his two hands. The shock of the leader's fall is then taken up gradually, by the friction of the rope over the body of his companion, and, only when all the slack has thus been taken up does the strain come rigidly on the rock belay.'

His suggestion for the shoulder belaying and attachment of the belayer's rope to the cliff made climbing safer for the next fifty years until his techniques were refined. Before then climbing had been like a war where even a slight mistake could be fatal, as in the tragedy of 1903. Bower was the first trained scientific mind to lift rope management into the twentieth century. It seems surprising that so many previous brilliant climbers who had been Fellows of the Royal Society had not solved the belaying problem. The Barrow in Furness climbers had a profound effect on post-war climbing out of all proportion to their numbers and in 1920 on Dow Crag, Roper distinguished himself again.

In Easter Gully to the right of Great Central Route is a gloomy black wall. It was not an inviting place, but a tenuous line up it gnawed at the thoughts of several people including George Bower, who top-roped it. When he heard that Roper was interested he stood down and made way for him. Roper went for it with George Basterfield, and later related his experience:

'The crux of the climb, as I remember it, was to pivot awkwardly with the left hand and foot and to make a grab with the right hand to reach for a handhold in the crack above the overhang. I had great confidence in my own hand which was always peculiarly strong, but George insisted on arranging a belay in the wide chimney to the East of the crack. He had the comfortable thought that if I missed the hold I would get merely a spectacular swing on the rope. I had great trust in George. But just as I was making the critical grab there was a thunderous crash of falling stones and scree. I thought George had "gone". However I straightened up on the overhang and later George explained that when I was making the critical move he pulled in the rope vigorously and disturbed the main chock which released several tons of scree.'

It is interesting to note that Bower had a hard time a week later while he was making the second ascent.

Just as suddenly as he appeared on the top level of Lakeland climbing Roper disappeared from the scene — the shortest, most dazzling career to enrich the Cumbrian cliffs. For many years his two routes were rightly regarded with awe.

The next great climber from the Yewdale Vagabonds — Bert Gross — top-roped Black Wall, struggled, but never led it. Later when Ernest Wood-Johnson was asked if he had done Black Wall he replied:

"No I climb only for pleasure."

Black Wall is still graded Hard Very Severe, the same as Great Central Route. Perhaps the last word should come from Bower's 1922 guide book:

'Exceedingly severe; rubbers essential together with perfect conditions and good form.'

Scafell was again the scene for another of Kelly's inventions. Deep Ghyll is one of the classic clefts of the mountain, separating The Pinnacle from an imposing buttress which Kelly decided would provide an imposing climb. One of its attractions may have been that it would finish higher than any other climb in England. Upper Deep Ghyll Buttress gave a starred Mild Very Severe and continued the trend so that, when the summer temperature dried out the high cliffs, a new supply of Very Severes was added to those already in existence.

One of the main events of 1920 was the discovery by George Bower of Esk Buttress, one of the most remote big cliffs in Lakeland. Unusually for a high crag, it faces south-east and dries quickly. It played a major part in climbing scenarios for the next half century. Bower's Route was over four hundred feet long, a Hard Severe, and was regarded as a classic climb for decades.

Bower's influence on Lakeland climbing in the early Twenties was profound. He made the second ascents of Roper's Great Central Route and Black Wall, and although he left the Lake District in 1921 to lecture at Loughborough College, his influence and production of new routes continued unabated. In 1921 he produced

Opposite: Gimmer Crag with teams on The Crack and Kipling Groove.   Photo: Ron Kenyon.

one of the great miniature classic climbs of the whole area, Innominate Crack on the Kern Knotts Face of Great Gable, on a wall to the right of Kern Knotts Crack. The wall was crazed by a sequence of cracks just wide enough to admit finger-ends. Bower top-roped it several times, then led it early in April 1921. He mentioned in his description that a belay could be found round a small block at thirty feet; in fact he meant a running belay, a rope-loop tied round the main climbing rope. It was only a sixty-foot Very Severe, but it became a test piece for hard climbers for several decades.

In 1922 another hard climber emerged, Bert Gross, who was also a member of the Yewdale Vagabonds and a close friend of Bower, George Basterfield and Joe Roper. He had been in the trenches in the War and this had affected his health. However, he had a good build for a climber, being tall and thin with an excellent power-to-weight ratio.

In the spring of 1922 Bower was hard at work completing investigations for his forthcoming Doe Crag guide-book. The name was Bower's choice and different from the more modern name — Dow Crag. Bower shrewdly promised Gross a new route as a reward for help, as Bower wanted to do a girdle traverse of the whole crag. This had been thought of by others who had been put off by the beetling overhangs of 'A' Buttress. The cream of the Yewdale Vagabonds assembled for the climb — Gross, Bower and George Basterfield. 'A' Buttress was solved in three pitches, although they had to take an inferior higher line on the third pitch because of threatening weather. Bower commented on the difficulties at a critical point; 'The hyacinths grow 60 feet below the traverse and great care is required to keep them at this distance.'

Two more pitches were done on 'B' Buttress before they were engulfed in damp mist. Bower produced a length of Alpine line from his rucksack, so that they could abseil off before walking back to Coniston in pouring rain. Unfortunately Bower could not be there the following weekend, so Gross's great opportunity had arrived. He missed out 'A' Buttress as its problems had already been solved, then did three more pitches before rain again stopped play, but not before Gross had inspected the next major problem, which was named 'Giant Grim'. When they returned the weather was again poor, but it slowly improved. The wet rock reluctantly dried in a thin wind but the Giant Grim proved to be awkward and off-balance, and was the hardest move that Gross had made up till then.

Immediately afterwards came the unclimbed key to the whole expedition, the central wall on the extreme edge of 'B' Buttress. Many attempts proved fruitless as Gross tried to reach a tiny corner in the middle of the wall. He retreated and decided to top-rope it but even with this aid he found it hard:

'Frenzied search found nothing but a tiny wrinkle for the fingers, and in desperation this was used for the pull up. Balance disappeared to a vanishing point...'

He returned two weeks later, led the Giant Grim, then dealt with the Central Wall in perfect control. He had arrived as a leading climber. The girdle traverse had solved some daunting problems on each separate buttress. On 'C' Buttress Gross realised that there could be an independent route straight up, if he was able to link it with satisfactory pitches from below. Seven days later he did Eliminate 'C', now given two stars. It has two 4c pitches, and despite its age, the modern guide book calls it 'a very enjoyable outing.' It was the first of Gross's new routes which transformed Dow Crag into the cliff for hard routes. However the uncompleted girdle-traverse gnawed at him

Opposite: Geoff Oliver on pitch 1 of Bentley Beetham's 1948 route, Devil's Wedge, Shepherds Crag in 1959. Photo: Geoff Oliver.

and he returned to 'A' Buttress to improve the third pitch with a tricky traverse under a huge roof, then a strenuous corner which resulted in the Hyacinth Traverse. The rope then jammed and this meant another abseil retreat. A typical English summer followed — week after week of torrential rain — then belatedly on October 8th a weak autumn sun appeared and Gross and the faithful Basterfield, after seven and a half hours of intensive effort completed the thousand-foot Girdle Traverse which had taken five months to solve. The achievement instantly made Gross's reputation. The following weekend he was back on Dow Crag at the foot of 'B' Buttress with Basterfield. Their third route together was Eliminate 'B', which was three hundred feet long and another Hard Very Severe with two 5a pitches, an action-packed route that even the resourceful Bower was pressed to describe:

'Excessively Severe; rubbers; insurance policy.'

An excellent denouement to an eventful year which had produced two eliminates and a girdle traverse, fifteen hundred feet of new climbing, and twenty-five pitches. Next summer Gross and Basterfield produced a masterpiece on 'A' Buttress — Eliminate 'A', one of Lakeland's greatest three-star Very Severes and a fine addition to their joint efforts. Although Roper and Gross between them had put up half a dozen Very Severes and Hard Very Severes on Dow Crag, this still did not topple the popularity of Scafell and Pillar Rock, although nowadays Dow is much more frequented than Pillar, partly because the Walna Scar approach allows cars much nearer than is possible on the Ennerdale road with its Forestry Commission restrictions. Curiously Gross's tenancy at the top of the climbing tree was almost as short as that of Joe Roper. In 1924 Gross decided to emigrate to New Zealand, to work as a sculptor alongside his brother who was already there. Apart from his climbs, Gross left two tangible reminders of his short and brilliant career on rock. He carved the mould for the memorial plaque to those members of the Fell and Rock Club who had been killed in the Great War.

A more useful legacy came from a fortnight's strenuous efforts in perfect summer weather, just before he emigrated, when he climbed all the routes on Great Gable, together with some variations of his own, so that he was able to work on the draft of a guide book to Great Gable while on the boat which took him far away from Lakeland.

Three years later he returned to climb again in the Lake District, but was never able to reach his previous heady heights. Misfortune overtook him several times, first a motorcycle accident, then a glider crash which resulted in unconsciousness for several weeks and left him with double vision. Late in life he married but after only two years his wife died, which broke his will to live, and a year later he killed himself.

In 1922, Bower's 'Doe Crags and Climbs around Coniston' was published. It was pocket-sized and bound in waterproof cloth. In 1918 Bower had laid the foundation for modern rope techniques. Now he had produced a reference book which could be consulted on a stance if the climber was nervous, apprehensive or forgetful about the difficulties above him. Bower advocated the use of rubber-soled footwear on the hardest climbs, suggested rope lengths for a particular climb, and used the O.G. Jones system of classifying routes, but modified it for the hardest routes.

Eliminate 'B' was Excessively Severe, Great Central Route — Exceedingly Severe. Holland too had suggested that climbs should be graded according to order of desperation. Both men came very close to our modern system of E grading climbs.

Bower infused a thread of humour into his narrative. For Intermediate Gully he suggested rigorous preparation: 'Train on raw meat and stout, use Bulldog Buttons ...' Sadly the function of Bulldog Buttons has not come down to us.

However, the use of rubbers on hard climbs alerted one of the traditionalists J.H Doughty, who waged a fierce rearguard action in defence of nailed boots:

> 'I remember', he wrote, 'listening to a well-known climber who objected to the ascent of the Eagle's Nest direct in rubbers on a dry day. 'It does not', he complained, 'give the rocks a chance.' This is a hard saying, and suggests a grim doctrine; but I think we may find in it the clue to what really lies at the bottom of mountaineering conventions, or at any rate those which are worth discussing. They are the unwritten rules of the game. Our Spartan friend was adopting precisely the attitude of those others, who, in their several spheres, object to batsmen defending the wicket with their legs, or golfers using ribbed clubs, or sportsmen shooting at sitting birds; all things which tend to make the job in hand too easy, which fail to give the pitch, the course, the bird, or whatever animate or inanimate opponent it may be, a chance.'

Doughty further argued:

> 'Of course there are novices who learn in rubbers and acquire a bad style, just as there have been novices who learned in boots and acquired a bad style. Style depends on natural aptitude and good teaching. If one or other is absent, you won't make a silk purse out of either a piece of rubber or a clinker nail.'

R.S.T. Chorley, who in 1936 led Haskett Smith up Napes Needle on the fiftieth anniversary of its first ascent, also entered the fray:

> 'In fact, getting up easy rocks in rubbers is not climbing at all, and is valueless from the point of view of learning our craft, as is playing French cricket with a tennis ball and racket to the would-be county cricketer. In nailed boots however, it is always necessary to place the foot accurately, and the beginner realises this as soon as he gets on to the rocks. When the hold is smaller than a size which is soon recognised from experience, or steeper than a slope similarly learned, the foot must be placed with particular accuracy, and care must be taken in the raising of the body so as to give the foothold every chance. It is here that the importance of balance is felt and technique is born.'

What the champions of the nailed boot did not realise was that, with the increasing popularity of rock climbing, their footwear abraded many holds until a polished glass-like surface resulted, such as on Slingsby's Chimney on Scafell.

Kelly and Doughty wrote a Short History of Lakeland Climbing and in it they laid down ground rules for novice climbers:

> 'In earlier days the neophyte was expected to begin on the easiest climbs and work his way upwards methodically through the moderates and difficults. If he was sufficiently gifted he might hope, after some years of this patient apprenticeship, to lead a severe... Our young men of today would laugh at such elaboration. They start their training on Difficults and expect to be leading Severes within a year or two; after two or three years the best of them will be hankering after Central Buttress or something near that class. And whilst at times this speeding up may be overdone — to the learner's ultimate detriment — it is as unnecessary as it would be futile to demand a return to the more pedestrian methods of the past.'

Perhaps Kelly was influenced by the fact that he was in his mid-thirties when he reached the top echelon of climbers, whereas Herford came into his prime when he was still in his teens.

In 1923 Kelly produced the next Lakeland guide book, to Pillar Rock, with a style which was to be the forerunner to all future guide books. Bower's semi-humorous approach was given up in favour of bare descriptions of climbs and their whereabouts. Menlove Edwards, the great Welsh climber, a decade later provided the best comment on the Kelly style of presentation:

> 'The tiny narrow spotlight moving in a single line...the rocks might be any rocks and the conformation of the cliff and climb might be any conformation, might be any climb in mid-air, for the spotlight sheds no rays aside...'

This approach taken to its extreme could result in climbers being unable to find their way back on to a route if they got lost. But Kelly's guide had its strong points, for example the initial historical analysis and topographical description of the crag. As soon as he had finished his time-consuming duties on Pillar Rock he was able to turn his efforts to Great Gable and an unclimbed problem that had defeated him on several occasions — Tophet Wall.

The summer of 1923 was atrocious but fortunately there was one superb week which coincided with Kelly's holiday in Wasdale, and with the temperature in the eighties he set off for Gable's east wall, which impends above the scree-chute known as Aaron Slack. Kelly approached it with apprehension. A troublesome crack at the start had spurned him, so on his successful ascent he traversed in above it to produce Tophet Wall, a splendid Severe classic. At the top a friend brought him a basket of strawberries as a prize. However he still felt that the route should encompass the unclimbed wall at the start, including the elusive crack, so he went back and managed to thread the rope through the gap at the back of a tiny chockstone but still failed to get up:

> 'The sudden discovery of a miniature chockstone and the difficulty of holding on with one hand whilst the other forced — threaded would be too mild a term — a rope behind it as extra security. Security indeed! Experience had already taught him, on at least four occasions in his climbing career, that these safeguards were a snare. And this was the most snareful of the lot. Probably the energy expended in this operation, plus a little moral persuasion, would have got him to the top of the crack. But the rope stuck, as it always does, and the situation became hopeless. There was nothing for it but to retire. Then came the climax of the whole proceedings. Not being in a position to tell which was the right end of the rope to commence unthreading, and acting on what he thought was the advice of the second, he painfully worked twenty feet of it through the small hole only to find himself more firmly bound to the rock than ever, and almost at the point of exhaustion. He might have freed himself by cutting the rope — there would have been no disgrace in it under the circumstances — but even this was a physical impossibility. It looked at one time as if he would have to bite through it to regain his freedom. Actually the teeth were made use of though not in quite so drastic a manner, and with their aid the rope was eventually unthreaded.'

The major production in 1924 was the appearance of the guide book to Scafell by C.F. Holland, the last active survivor of the pre-war elite. He described himself as the

Frost leading Ash Tree Slabs (1920), Gimmer Crag in 1935.

Photo: C. Douglas Milner.

editor instead of the author because of the meticulous work of both Herford and Sansom, who had been working on the guide when the war broke up everyone's life. Holland summed up all hard climbers' attitudes when a new guide book appears:

'...the effect of the production of a guide, and incidentally the highest justification of its existence, seems to be the stimulus it gives to battalions of climbers to try and make it out of date as soon as possible.'

This was the third guide-book produced by the Fell and Rock Club in their imaginative scheme to provide detailed information on all the known climbs in the Lake District. More information led to an increase in the number of climbers, and Kelly and Doughty hint at social tensions which this brought about:

'Another outstanding feature of post-war climbing is the enormous increase in the number of participants, an increase which brings knotty problems in its train. Firstly there is a social problem. In former days we had among climbers a preponderance of the more fortunate people endowed with a certain limited degree of means and leisure. Never what would be called a rich man's sport, it was not a poor man's either. Nowadays all that has largely changed. The general movement towards outdoor exercise and more frequent holidays, increased facilities of transport, and various other factors have combined to produce a large influx of climbers of more limited means. That many of them do not find a natural and congenial home in the old-established climbing clubs is not in itself, perhaps, a matter of great moment.'

After the war British climbing did not keep pace with the developments made by the young German climbers on the steep East European cliffs and mountains; and even Kelly, who was in the front rank of English climbers, showed a stilted attitude:

'One or two features which have distinguished British from Continental climbing should also be mentioned here. One is the almost complete refusal of our own climbers to resort to artificial aids, apart from the rope. The continental climber, with his armoury of pitons (wall-hooks), hammer, and karabiners (snap-rings), has no counterpart in this country. Of course, our home crags offer a fair supply of natural belays, and do not call so imperatively for the piton (wall-hook) etc, as do the rocks of the Eastern Alps. And if the German, and Austrian, have perhaps been over-ready to rely on these adventitious aids, they have been led thereby to the development of new technical methods, enabling them to make attacks on smooth faces that could be surmounted by no other means. We may yet see such methods introduced in Lakeland as the supply of new routes gives out, but they will have to encounter the resistance of the strong prejudice.'

This philosophy seems inconsistent with Kelly's total-war concept of new climbs — top-roping, gardening, practising the hard moves on a rope, and even knocking in pitons.

It was inevitable with the increase in numbers that a woman would appear who was capable of the hardest climbs. Dr Mabel Barker did some of her hardest routes on Scafell. Her companion for her debut was C.D. Frankland, a teacher who had trained at Almscliffe and become very adept at hard cracks. Frankland's Green Crack on that cliff was regarded as a test-piece for many years. An expert on damp cracks, he sewed pieces of carpet to the knees of his breeches to improve the adhesion when backing

Opposite: Looking down Moss Ghyll Grooves (1926).   Photo: John Hartley.
      Inset: Harry Kelly.   Photo: Sid Cross.

up awkward chimneys.

Barker and Frankland started with the Girdle Traverse of Scafell main crag, but Frankland wanted to descend Botterill's Slab, so he decided to do the Girdle Traverse in the reverse direction, a fact that he artfully concealed from Mabel. She found the descent of the famous slab extremely hard, and at one point wished she had brought a pocket lens in her search for microscopic holds. The guidebook time for the climb was six hours but the pair did it in two and a half.

After this triumph, they spent a glorious fortnight climbing in Skye. They became extremely fit and returned to Wasdale resolved to attempt Central Buttress. On the Great Flake, Frankland led to the chockstones, tied himself to them, and brought up Mabel, who led the overhanging section in a unique manner:

> 'I do not really know what happened; except that I got on to and over my partner and off his head as quickly as possible. He says he felt for my foot to hold it if necessary, but could not find it, and I do not know where it went. Probably, being slimmer than former climbers, I got farther into the crack and chimneyed it. I faced out, and think there was a small hold far up on the inside wall. Almost at once I felt the top of the Flake with the left hand. "I've got it!" I said, thrilled with the realisation that the thing was virtually done, and there probably was not a happier woman living at that moment!'

There was some criticism of their climb by people who thought that they had taken unnecessary risks, but Mabel had found no serious difficulty, and the pair took only two and a half hours for the whole climb.

The following year the Fell and Rock Club surpassed themselves by producing two more guide books, one to Great Gable by Bert Gross and another to the Borrowdale valley by A.R. Thomson. Nobody could have been less physically suited to climbing than Thomson. He had suffered from infantile paralysis and was semi-crippled with a useless left arm, walked with a shuffling gait, and had slurred speech. This however did not stop him from climbing and doing other remarkable physical feats; more than once he exceeded 250 miles on a bicycle during a twenty-four hour period and for many years exceeded 20,000 miles on two wheels. Fortunately he was rich, had a chauffeur, and an appropriate lifestyle of leisure which enabled him to hire the famous Alpine guide Angelo Dibona to climb with him in the Borrowdale area.

On one occasion Thomson went to explore Piers Ghyll with his chauffeur. They discovered a man called Crump who eighteen days before they appeared had fallen, broken his leg, and been unable to move. It had been nearly thirty years since the previous ascent. The man had kept himself alive by drinking stream water and fortunately the weather was warm enough for him to survive. Thomson and the intrepid chauffeur carried him down to Wasdale, where he recovered and returned year after year to re-tell his escapade becoming something of a bore.

However Borrowdale did not become popular. It did not have any high mountain crags, the thinking of that time was against it, and the traditional areas remained the centre of attraction.

Kelly had another good new-route year in 1925 with nine fresh climbs, most of them on the Scafell group of cliffs. He was already forty-one and probably realised that there were not many years left at the top; and after seven glorious years of innovation 1926 saw one of his finest creations. Scafell had seen the start of his glory and provided one of his last major new routes.

Opposite: Top left: A.B. Reynolds stuck barefoot on slimy rock, B Buttress, Dow Crag. Ivan Waller is dropping a rope.
            Top right: A.B. Reynolds barefoot on the Monkey Movement in 1928.   Photos (including bottom right): Ivan Waller.
            Bottom left: Jim Haggas, 1948 style.
            Bottom right: Graham Macphee and Ivan Waller at the Monkey Movement, B Buttress, Dow Crag, in 1928.

It had been his keen-eyed rope-mate C.F. Holland who in 1919 saw the tantalising series of unclimbed grooves rising steeply out of Moss Ghyll:

'Also I still cherished a belief in the fact that the Central Buttress could be climbed by way of the grooves slanting out of Moss Ghyll, my fancy inclining with blind optimism to a most exposed line on the extreme left which would reach the easterly end of the V ledge.'

Holland had played a major part in the development of Scafell and thought strongly about new routes:

'The thought that gives me more pleasure than most is that of having been responsible for firing Kelly with enthusiasm for exploration on crags supposedly exhausted of new climbs.'

Gardening, top-ropes, struggles and frustration were evidence of Kelly's obsession with Moss Ghyll Grooves in the six-year period from 1919 to 1926. But 1926 saw a brave new world for him on Scafell. To remove any doubts he descended on a rope till he was only thirty feet above his previous highest point gained with so much gardening effort:

'...it certainly was a great relief to find some good holds hereabouts even though considerable gardening, under cramped conditions, had to be resorted to. The climb had unfolded itself in a delightful way and nothing now remained but to approach it from below.'

Enthusiasm rose as Kelly, Blanche Eden-Smith and J.B. Kilshaw had their lunch at the foot of the crag. A vicious thunder-storm sprang up and almost dampened their ardour, but just as quickly the clouds rolled away, the sun came out and they were ready for the fray again, to storm the last thirty feet of the redoubt which had repulsed Kelly for so long. Kelly nervously approached the unknown thirty feet and later described the solution of that difficulty:

'The holds, small from the first dwindled to none at all. A pedestal some six feet away looked hopeful, but it seemed hardly attainable, as the intervening space appeared devoid of even the minutest holds. A very close survey however did reveal something of the sort, I got across somehow. An upright but far from moral flake of diminutive proportions was used for the left foot, though it was high up and far away; and a still more immoral rugosity was found for the left hand. To balance, in transit, by the aid of these two points of attachment was a ticklish business, and a breathless moment followed, as a rapid change of hands was made, so that the left could search forward to the Pedestal and lodgement be gained thereon.'

Blanche Eden-Smith described Kelly's state of mind after he had done the crux:

'The earnest pathos in his voice, as he besought his followers to do their best when their turns came, was ominously indicative of what he thought of the place!'

It only took two hours to complete the whole climb:

'...seven years of intermittent hope and thought crystallised, almost unexpectedly into achievement.'

Kelly thought it a harder climb than Botterill's Slab, which was a correct assumption in the conditions he climbed it...It was so popular that the remaining grass and earth were soon removed and the standard later slipped to Hard Severe to give a delicate climb of outstanding interest. If any modern climber selected the four best Severes in the British Isles, Moss Ghyll Grooves would be one of them.

No one had been at the top for as long as Kelly. He did not quite reach the technical heights achieved by Herford and Roper but his output of new routes was far greater and his methods set the standards for future generations: in addition to guidebook layout and style, the use of rubbers, gardening and top-rope practising became part of the armoury with which future innovators overcame rocky problems. After Moss Ghyll Grooves in 1926 his output declined but he followed hard routes as late as 1938, when he was in his fifties then lived on into his nineties and eventually died in 1980. He had helped to sustain the position of the Lake District as the show-place of hard British climbing from its inception in 1886 for the next forty years.

Unfortunately triumph and tragedy clouded the scene the following year in 1927. C.D. Frankland was killed in August on Chantry Buttress on Great Gable. The route was Very Difficult and well within his powers. There were two happy parties on the climb that day, one led by Frankland, the other by Mabel Barker who had been with him on their successful ascent of Central Buttress.

When Frankland was twenty-five feet up the second pitch he came off without any warning. His body described a semi-circle as he fell and his head smashed into a rock after a forty-foot fall. When Mabel reached him he was unconscious and he died twenty minutes later.

He had not fallen due to incompetence; he had used a handhold which projected upwards from a ledge and inadvertently pulled it from its slot. He had been a careful brilliant climber, proved by his controlled descent of Botterill's Slab. In modern times he would probably have fallen harmlessly on to a running belay.

Frankland's death cast a shadow over 1927 but the year was redeemed a little when George Basterfield produced the first guide to Gimmer. The year before he had analysed the attractiveness of the crag:

'Gimmer seldom depresses with gloom. Its countenance south and west is frank and open, receiving the full benefit of the sun.'

He had been impressed with the upper unclimbed part of the North-West Face one winter's day when he climbed up the approaches towards the impending roofs crowning the cliff. Snow and ice coated the rocks and he had to do the final part with the aid of a rope, but he was convinced it could be climbed in better conditions and decided in advance to call it Hiatus because the most important part was still unled.

Triumph came the following year to George Bower. At the start of the looming overhangs a tenuous traverse left seemed the only feasible line to him. Fortunately there was a chockstone in a crack which he festooned with loops, some for belays, others threaded round the main climbing rope:

'...encouraged and morally fortified, the leader traversed to the left and started upwards.'

Hiatus received immediate recognition. It was the first Very Severe on Gimmer Crag and it still gets the accolade of a star. The modern guidebook mentions its 'magnificent finish'.

By 1927 there were nineteen routes of the middle grade of difficulty on Gimmer Crag. Bower had played his part with two excellent Severes — Pallid Slabs and 'D' Route — and Hiatus, a route done during his mature years, which helped the crag into a new world. Age creeps up on everyone and it was fitting that Bower, who was thirty-seven when he did Hiatus, had as his second, A.B. Reynolds, who ushered in the next stage of Lakeland rock-climbing exploration.

THE SCAFELL RANGE AND UPPER ESKDALE   (From the North)

Bill Smith leading the upper part of The Crack (1928), Gimmer Crag.

Photo: John Har

The Welshmen Cometh

In 1927 there was a spectacular development on North Wales rock by Fred Pigott, an ex-sniper with one hand deformed by a war wound. After making the third ascent of Central Buttress on Scafell, he climbed the pristine East Buttress of Clogwyn du'r Arddu after several determined attempts. It soon gained a reputation of awesome difficulty. In 1928 a crack was climbed in Langdale which although not quite its equal, was nevertheless a fine achievement considering the ungardened state of the rock and the lack of protection at that time. The local Lakeland climbers must have thought that the pendulum had swung in favour of hard Welsh climbs.

Tucked away on the North West Face of Gimmer Crag was the unclimbed crack which had already been named by George Basterfield in his guide-book to the cliff: 'The Crack'. (This crack is about 120 feet in length, vertical, rope climbed, but still unled).' It is not clear whether he meant that Bower had been merely safeguarded or helped using a top-rope, but it so impressed him that he doubted whether it would ever be climbed. This is surprising since his own creation, Hiatus, must have seemed just as daunting, although slightly easier; and one would have thought that Bower's experience on gritstone cracks would have made him an ideal candidate. However it seems fitting that the man who solved the complexities of The Crack, A.B. Reynolds, had been Bower's able second on the first ascent of Hiatus. He was a curious man as he liked to climb in bare feet, even to the extent of climbing Central Buttress without footwear.

It was on Scafell that there occurred one of the most bizarre accidents one could imagine. Reynolds was leading Tower Buttress, a Hard Severe and well within his abilities; he was seconded by George Basterfield. Suddenly without warning Reynolds fell off and although Basterfield fielded him expertly so that he was uninjured, during the fall a loop of the thin rope dropped over Basterfield's thumb and when the snatch came on the rope, the thumb was snapped off quicker than by a surgeon's knife The heat from the sliding rope on the thumb surfaces had been so great that it cauterized the skin flaps left and only a light bandage was needed afterwards. Reynolds was unhurt and they both set off to look for the thumb but couldn't find it.

A more macabre incident occurred to Reynolds whilst he was resting on the Esk Hause during a solitary walk over Scafell. A young man in his twenties, with blue eyes and fair hair, came and chatted to him. Eventually Reynolds realised that his fawn riding breeches seemed rather old-fashioned, and after talking for some time Reynolds got up to leave, took a few strides, then turned round — but the young man had disappeared. The event continually preyed on his mind until some time later, in the Wasdale Head Hotel, he noticed a picture on the wall which featured a fair-haired man. He immediately recognised him as the young man with whom he had talked on Esk Hause. It was Siegfried Herford who had been killed more than a decade before in the First World War.

Reynolds became one of the leading climbers in the Lake District in the Late Twenties and was ideally qualified to attempt the unclimbed cleft on Gimmer. At his first attempt Reynolds reached a turf ledge, which was the lowest point of Bower's top-rope explorations and is still known as The Bower. He had great difficulty finding a belay, so considerable time was lost until a thread was engineered underneath an overhang. These efforts so exhausted Reynolds that he persuaded his reluctant second, H.G. Knight, to try the overhang. He soon returned, and then realised that the sun was setting over the craggy western skyline. Fortunately a keen photographer who had recorded their efforts, was converted into a one-man rescue team but took 45 minutes to reach the top of the crag, during which time the stranded explorers had time to see the sun sink behind Rossett Ghyll and the moon come up over Langdale. The rope from above enabled them to finish the climb with the rock faintly whitened by moonlight.

Ivan Waller, a sprightly octogenarian who still rides a motorcycle and climbs Very Severes, remembers climbing with Reynolds on Dow Crag in the Twenties, when they did the Monkey Movement from Giant's Corner to Murray's Route. That day there was low cloud, a thin wind and arctic temperatures, with snow still lying deep in the gullies as Reynolds climbed the routes in bare feet, his usual practice. Later Reynolds returned to the attack on The Crack, this time with a rock-climber with a colourful background — Dr Graham Macphee. In the First World War he joined The Highland Light Infantry when he was 17, then transferred to the Royal Flying Corps, was shot down and became a prisoner of war. Subsequently he graduated in medicine at Glasgow University, then specialised in dental surgery in Vienna and was awarded the chair of Professor of Dental Surgery at Liverpool University.

In 1924 he started climbing and soon became one of the most proficient cragsmen in the country. Perhaps the most remarkable part of his personality was the wide range of companions he acquired from the top echelon of hard men. Consequently he was involved in major exploration in North Wales, the Lake District and Scotland particularly Ben Nevis. He drove from Liverpool to Fort William weekend after weekend collecting twenty first ascents in the process; perhaps it seemed natural to him to climb Ben Nevis, Scafell and Snowdon in a day and also to do the first descent of Moss Ghyll Grooves in order to make the laconic entry in the hut log book 'M.G.G.-G.G.M'. When he was sixty years old he climbed eleven Alpine 4000 metre peaks and when the President of the Alpine Club described him as 'a remarkable elderly gentleman', Macphee's cutting reply was 'that he was neither remarkable nor old.'

On May 5th 1928, Macphee was delayed getting to the Lake District and only reached Langdale at 4 p.m. During a hasty tea break he read a note from Reynolds which urged him to come to the west side of Gimmer Crag and to bring his Alpine line. Fortunately it had not rained for five weeks and this had completely dried out the cliff. At one critical point Reynolds protected himself by using several primitive running belays with loops tied to the main rope to protect himself and also to belay Macphee. Reynolds found the crux so exhausting that his laboured breathing could be heard seventy-five yards away. It took nine pitches to overcome its problems. It is given three stars in the 1980 guide book which calls it:

'...The best line in the valley and the classic climb of the Lake District.'

When the route description was published in the 'Fell and Rock Journal' it was described as 'Unpleasantly Severe'. A unique 'grade' which betrays the awe felt by climbers used to the more comfortable routes on Gimmer's South-East and West Faces. Macphee's article on the events leading up to its conquest had an introduction that puckishly describes the stages that a hard climb goes through as decades pass:

Opposite: Geoff Oliver on the top pitch of Devil's Wedge in 1959.   Photo: Geoff Oliver.

'An inaccessible crack — The most difficult climb in the Lake District —An easy day for an undergraduate.'

Unfortunately there were facets of Macphee's character which alienated some of his contemporaries and even now after a half century they will not elaborate on them. Perhaps a clue may be given in the waspish footnote to that article:

'It must be understood that in this expedition no artificial aids were used — a practice becoming deplorably prevalent even in our homeland climbs. No loops of rope were previously placed at strategic points for use as handholds, stirrups or possibly worse. Not a step was cut, not a piton was driven in, not even an artificial chockstone was inserted in The Crack.'

He was taking a swipe at the methods used by Pigott on Clogwyn du'r Arddu in Wales, where aid had been used to overcome short sections, conveniently forgetting that Kelly had used a whole battery of artificial aids to produce his climbs.

Macphee and Reynolds were proud of The Crack and as the autumn of 1928 dawned it was still unrepeated. George Bower who had been in Italy for some time, came to the Lake District and they re-introduced him to Cumbrian climbing by making the second ascent, which only took two hours. They were seen by two unknown climbers, who asked them if it was worth doing. With barely concealed annoyance they confirmed that it was. One of them was Ted Hicks, a Cambridge undergraduate who had already moved into the elite of Welsh climbers. The Lakeland trio stayed to watch the efforts of the two and A.B. Hargreaves described the bizarre trousers worn by Hicks as he nonchalantly overcame the difficulties:

'...the sartorial fashion then was to wear Oxford Bags — voluminous trousers with masses of material flopping around the feet. The Fell and Rock were able to observe, with something like horror, Ted proceeding up their new climb, rather nonchalantly, from time to time lifting the folds of his Oxford Bags from under the tips of his rubbers — which was hardly the seemly sort of procedure then followed by the Fell and Rock! Anyway Ted and Co. got up The Crack, casting down on their way a chock-stone which the first party had used on their ascent, much to their annoyance as they watched events from across the gully. The Crack became one of the most sought-after climbs by expert parties and has remained popular to this day.'

Macphee's restless urge for innovation resulted in his discovery of one of England's finest roadside crags, which also has one of the most romantic names — Castle Rock of Triermain. He wrote of its background, his own efforts to unlock its secrets and its profile which had been observed in the eighteenth century by a passing traveller:

'...a shaken massive pile of rocks, which stands in the midst of this little vale, disunited from the adjoining mountains; and have so much real form and resemblance of a castle, that they bear the name of The Castle Rock of St John's.'

He could hardly imagine his good luck when discreet enquiries amongst his rock-climbing friends revealed that none of them had ever heard of it. He arranged to climb there on no fewer than ten occasions with George Basterfield in the monsoon

Opposite: Melville Connell and Maurice de St. Jarre on Delphinus (Don Whillans and J. Smith in 1956). Raven Crag, Thirlmere.
Photo: Geoff Oliver.

summer of 1928 and on every occasion the rain foiled them. In the modern manner it was named 'The Secret Crag' and its jewels waited to be unearthed until Macphee climbed there with Mabel Barker. The main crag, which he described as 'an imposing central precipice' proved too much for them and they were forced on to the easier South Crag which rewarded him with four routes, one of them — Scoop and Crack, a Very Severe which still hides an awkward 5a move from which many have fallen over the years.

Another important contribution from the relentless Macphee that summer was again on Gimmer Crag where he led Reynolds up some very strenuous cracks to produce a strenuous V.S.-JOAS which translated into Just One Awful Sweat, and was even harder technically than the The Crack.

Macphee was again involved in the next surge of activity, in the beautiful and lonely valley of Far Easedale. Deer Bield Crag had a whiff of development in the Edwardian era and had then slumbered until 1930. Perhaps it was not surprising that Macphee was again involved. The climbing world was still then very small as the Depression still gripped the English economy, and recruitment came from the middle and upper classes. There was next to no representation from the working class, they were too busy surviving and could rarely afford transport to the mountains, although unemployed men were able to go for evenings to the gritstone edges of the Peak District.

Deer Bield Crag, a very steep buttress, had slipped away from the hillside and left prominent clefts on either side. The right-hand chimney had been climbed at Severe standard in 1908. The left-hand fissure had looked impossibly difficult and overhanging and had been left severely alone. It looked like one of the hardest gritstone clefts and it required the abilities of a top gritstone climber to overcome it — A.T.Hargreaves, or Bert as he was called by his friends. He was born in Rochdale and his teenage leisure years were spent on the gritstone crags close to his northern home. Soon he became one of the leading climbers on the outcrops and sprinkled them with his own inventions.

February 9th 1930 was a cold wintry day, Bert and Macphee tried the crucial overhanging chimney crack, and for two hours Hargreaves was precariously jammed in its diverging walls. Finally he retreated, but his failure gnawed, and the two were back again the following weekend:

> 'We again reached the foot of the chimney and again failed, this time through becoming so tired before reaching the last difficulty, that to have failed on it and descended would have been impossible...a trial on a rope proved it was possible to reach the stance without conking out, so we again joined forces and after much sweating reached the thread belay at the top of the chimney. The stance is only three inches wide, but as overhangs on the right wall had narrowed the chimney to about ten inches wide, the position was a comfortable wedge.'

After four hours they emerged at the top, tired but victorious. The climb is now graded Hard Very Severe 4c. It immediately acquired a formidable reputation which has diminished very little over the decades. Even Joe Brown twenty years later had a hard time overcoming it. A.B.Hargreaves summed up its position:

> 'Let us fix on Deer Bield Crack in Easedale. This is one of those that I rank harder than Central Buttress — a really fine climb of great difficulty and a very strenuous one at that. It has almost a Clogwyn du'r Arddu flavour about it and is perhaps as hard as Pigott's Climb or the Pedestal Crack.'

Opposite: Bridging up the infamous chimney pitch of Deer Bield Crack (said after the 1930 1st ascent to be Severe!).   Photo: John Hartley.

He was in a good position to make the comparison, as soon after the first ascent he repeated it with Bert Hargreaves as his second. A.B. being very tiny was able to wedge himself further into the crux recess and could jam his knee for greater security. However the final overhanging corner was almost too much for him and he thought he was going to fail until Bert made a Turk's Head bundle of knots and flung it to the top of the crack where it fortunately jammed. A.B. climbed up as far as his previous highest point, then, to Bert's astonishment, he seized the jammed rope and jack-knifed his body so that his feet reached the top first followed by the rest of him, Bert commented grimly:

"That's the most dangerous piece of climbing I've ever seen."

One of the reasons for Bert Hargreaves' far-flung activities was being a commercial traveller for Nestle's Milk, with a company car and therefore able to visit remote parts of the Lake District. Hargreaves carried on doing new climbs and remained in the top rank until his untimely death in a ski-ing accident in 1952. Deer Bield Crack was his first and most memorable climb. He then turned his talents to Scafell; but before that another young man broke through the pristine overhanging defences of the East buttress by climbing a slab which had brusquely rejected Kelly when he had tried it in 1919.

Colin Kirkus was the finest young climber since Herford. He had started by soloing almost everything: he knew no-one and didn't realise that it wasn't the way to start. Fortunately he fell in with A.B. Hargreaves who was an able and gregarious cragsman. One of their first routes together was Original Route on Holly Tree Wall in Wales, a precarious and mean V.S. which they nonchalantly climbed in nailed boots in the pouring rain. This so amazed their friends that they were promptly dubbed 'The Suicide Club'.

The following summer they had a holiday in the Lake District and did Eliminate B, Botterill's Slab, and North West on Pillar Rock, followed by the eighth ascent of Central Buttress and the fifth ascent of Gimmer Crack. Kirkus had also put up several new routes on Clogwyn du'r Arddu including Great Slab with the ubiquitous Macphee. No man was more qualified than Kirkus to take on the hardest challenges of those times and no man was so dedicated or thought about new routes so much:

'On a photograph of some cliff I would have all the known routes marked with dotted lines. The blank spaces in between fascinated me. Here was unexplored country; I longed to be the first to set foot upon it. I used to sit, pretending to work, with the drawer slightly open, so that I could see the photo inside. Then I would plan a route. Here was a chimney to start, but could I reach that little grass ledge 100 feet higher up? It might be possible; it all depended on the steepness of the rock. If I could find a way of connecting the next three ledges then victory would be mine. The first fine week-end I would put my theories into practice. Curiously enough, they usually worked. But it meant hours of suspense. I would go up, get stuck and have to come down again. Then I would try another way, until at last I found a route to the next ledge. Then the same thing would have to be gone through again, until finally I arrived triumphant at the top...'

On the great unclimbed slab on the East Buttress of Scafell all his talents came into play. One of Colin's support team was the Cambridge University rock gymnast Ivan Waller, who remembers that day over half a century ago and the man who made it so memorable:

Opposite: Colin Kirkus (inset) who made the 1st ascent of Mickledore Grooves (1931). Ivan Waller is seen seconding the pitch.
Photo: Ivan Waller

'Colin was a thin untidy-looking lad with wiry hair and slightly sunken features He looked neither strong nor athletic, and quite unprepossessing. In fact he was incredibly tough, determined and completely dedicated to the mountains. We had set off from Langdale and there had been the ritual swim in Angle Tarn...... On arrival at the foot of East Buttress, then unclimbed, Colin led the first two pitches just as if he was on a well-trodden route. Each pitch had a strenuous fingery move which I thoroughly enjoyed, but when I was taken up it again 43 years later I needed aid for both of them. For the main pitch the second man sits on a good ledge with an overhanging wall above, behind which goes the slab up which the pitch starts. After about a quarter of an hour Colin made an excursion to the left edge of the slab and his head appeared above me. He was happy and relaxed and assured me that all was going well. A further half hour all the rope was out, Colin was at the top and it was my turn to follow.'

It was the longest hard pitch in the Lake District at that time, soaring above the big undercut which guarded its base. Subsequently pitons were knocked into it by others not as bold as Kirkus, who condemned them in an article entitled 'The Ethics of Ironmongery'.

'It is hard to see how the use of a piton on an old climb can be excused. Any climb in part belongs to its pioneers; it should be climbed as they climbed it ...If an ascent has already been made it is safe to assume that there are some leaders who can repeat it in perfect safety, whatever the run-out. And the climber who cannot manage the long lead has no right to spoil it for those who can by sticking in his offensive ironmongery. He should choose a climb which is within his capacity.'

The modern guide-book gives Mickledore Grooves three stars and describes it as a classic of the district.

Kirkus fell off more than he should have done as the outstanding climber of his time. One of his narrowest escapes was with A.B. Hargreaves on Dow Crag's Great Central Route, in a fall from which he was lucky not to be killed:

'Above me was the overhanging South America Crack. The crack was terribly strenuous, and near the top the holds seemed to give out completely. My only support was my left arm jammed in the crack; I hung outwards from it and clawed at the rock with the other hand. I made a bad mistake here; if I had looked around I should have seen a good handhold up on the right. I squirmed up again until my head came against the overhang; my balaclava helmet dropped noiselessly to the bottom. I slipped down again and hung there exhausted. I was dimly conscious of a watching crowd of climbers, away on the left. There were good holds below me; I could still have descended. But I was too tired to think. I had to go on struggling — for ever and ever, it seemed. I jerked myself up again in a last despairing effort. I was so done that I could hardly see. Everything went black. The next thing I knew I was 30 feet lower down, hurtling head-first through the air. My arm had slipped out and I had fallen backwards. I passed about four feet outside Alan's stance. All fear disappeared as soon as I started falling. The struggle had been ghastly, but now it was all out of my hands; nothing I could do would make any difference. Now I'm in for a nasty smash, I thought; I knew I might be killed. All I could do was to wait and see what happened. Strangely enough it did not seem to concern me at all. My interest was quite detached. Somebody was crashing down to earth, but somehow it seemed to have nothing to do with me. I fell 70 feet. The first thing I hit was 50 feet below. I can still remember every detail. The rock rushed up and flung me out into the air again. The rope tightened and jerked me head uppermost, then ran out again and I continued on my downward way. I landed on the scree at the bottom, with my hips wedged in Hopkinson's Crack. I was conscious of no pain until I stopped; then my hips hurt fiercely for a few moments, and I thought something must be broken. But I could move, and I soon found I could walk. I seemed to be uninjured. I climbed straight up to A.B.H. so that I should not lose my nerve. The only injury was a broken toe. I limped down to Coniston and managed to climb for the remainder of the holiday, though I could not use the outside of my right foot. The toe went yellow and swollen, and each night I took great surgical interest in trying to set it with sticking-plaster. It was over a year before I dared to attempt G.C.R. again. This time I found the crucial hold and the crack went quite easily. I even managed to lead the wall above the Bandstand without a shoulder, which had not often been done before. So I had my revenge.'

Two more top Welsh climbers now became interested in Lake District exploration and in particular Pillar Rock: Maurice Linnell and Alf Bridge. Linnell was supposed to be the only climber in the Kirkus class, whilst Alf Bridge had acquired his strength as a steeplejack. He used to wear out the tops of his rubber plimsolls first, because he was so strong that he trailed his feet behind him like useless appendages. It was only after he climbed with Jack Longland that he started to use footholds in the accepted manner.

Linnell and Bridge met in a cafe in the centre of Manchester and over coffee decided that Pillar Rock should be explored. Linnell had had an austere childhood in a religious legal family in Kendal. He went to Stramongate School and when head boy founded a rock climbing club, which the headmaster refused to recognise. This did not deter Linnell. When he was only sixteen he did his first new route on Buckbarrow in Long Sleddale. He became an intense, brilliant climber, and when he went to Manchester University the gritstone outcrops honed his technique to perfection.

At Whitsun 1931, after looking at the guide-book to Pillar Rock, it dawned on Linnell and Bridge that there was no Girdle Traverse to the cliff. They realised that it would have to be over a thousand feet long and that it would not be possible to climb it in one push. Whit-Friday was wet, but they managed some preliminary investigation and returned next day to examine what they thought would be the crux, a formidable-looking section between North-West and the North Climb. It was Alf who solved the problem in probably the best effort of his climbing career, as described by Linnell:

'Bridge, who was exploring the almost perpendicular wall to my left, attracted my attention by suddenly jumping down the 15 feet or so which he had gained. However, he said that it would go, so we roped up and attacked it. After 15 feet on his unusually prehensile fingers he performed a neat mantelshelf movement, and looked a little better placed; but leaving the mantelshelf proved to be a very difficult problem owing to the grass and mud in the open crack above. He landed on a fair-sized grass ledge without any belay, where I was able with considerable difficulty, to follow him.'

Linnell too made a significant contribution to the solution of the difficulties:

'I took off my rubbers, and cautiously proceeded in stockinged feet. Some of the holds looked insecure, but the key holds, on testing, proved good, and I was rewarded by a view around the next corner. What I saw was a face of extremely steep, clean rock furrowed by irregular grooves and chimneys; I did not quite know what to make of it, but pushed on. With a slightly ascending movement I was able to work round the corner on to a lovely little stance with a perfect belay, from which point of vantage I could examine the face more closely. Only then did I see, not 20 feet away, the scratches of the North-West Climb. I shouted the good news, and Bridge came running round to see and to finish it off. By an extraordinary piece of good luck we had struck the North-West just where we had hoped to do.'

They were delighted at solving the main difficulties and when they got home they rang the ubiquitous A.B. Hargreaves to join them next day to gather the thousand-foot prize. Next day there was a heavy shower of rain whilst they were in mid-route and Linnell and Hargreaves had to climb in socks. The climb ran to twenty-eight pitches and despite being a trio they took only seven hours to complete it. However, they felt a twinge at the absence of one man who had done so much for Pillar Rock and whose last route there, Grooved Wall, had been so outstanding and gave the first 210 feet of their girdle:

'We had one regret, and that was that H.M. Kelly had not been with us. We had not seen him for some time and he knew nothing of our plans. We had hoped to work out the route and then get Kelly to come with us to Pillar for the first complete traverse. However to end a perfect day at Wasdale glasses were raised as Bridge proposed the toast — "To the man who made a girdle of Pillar possible."'

The climb in its final form is 1340 feet long, in 16 pitches, — the longest route in England and the truest girdle, since it encircles almost 270 degrees of the Pillar.

Linnell and Bridge became intrigued with the thought of Scafell, so the triumphant trio set out in the evening and slept out at Hollowstones in the tranquil moonlight. Bridge lay awake most of the night looking up at the Flake Crack, which he hoped to lead when the dawn broke. After an early start they all soloed to the foot of the Flake Crack where they all tied on. Bridge tried to lead the last overhang free, despite the fact that a fall whilst leading could have been fatal:

'I felt very confident that I could make my lead straight through, and I would not even hear of a thread belay at the chockstone. For the rest I have very little to say. I threw myself into a layback when I reached the chockstone, confidently braced my muscles for the last few feet, and then moved. Perhaps Hargreaves, who saw the whole of my movements, could explain what happened better than I can. All I know is that my feet just shot off the wall, and I made a hopeful grab for the top of the chockstone. There I made a happy landing and hung by my left hand, absolutely shot. That short drop had done quite a lot. I tried again but it had weakened my arm muscles, strained an old rugger leg muscle, and caused me to lose my guts. No words of mine can express my disappointment. I was beat. A few quick turns round the chockstone with my line and I rested. Linnell then came and climbed over me and then Hargreaves. My turn came, and I joined them at the top of the Flake with a great deal of help.'

As they rested on top of the Flake, three others appeared at its foot, Menlove Edwards, Marco Pallis (who had been with Kirkus on Mickledore Grooves) and Bill Stallybrass. Edwards was perhaps the boldest climber. He was a medical student at Liverpool University and in his leisure time trained hard in the gymnasium at the Adelphi Hotel and also on the sandstone outcrop of Helsby where he often made multiple solo ascents of the ferocious Flake Crack, which had resulted in a death not

Opposite: Engineer's Slabs, Gable Crag. F.G. Balcombe's 1934 route was not repeated for over 20 years.   Photo: Ian Roper.

long before Edwards's time. No man was more qualified than Menlove to free-climb Flake Crack on Scafell, which had defeated Herford and nearly caused the death of Bridge. Stallybrass remembered Edwards's epic ascent:

'At the foot of the Flake, Menlove quickly arranged some slings, called to Marco and me to change places on the rope, and brought me up to him. Our whole performance was hair-raisingly chaotic. I gripped hold of Menlove's shoulders and we both swung out from the rock; he seemed to be only very loosely tied in. My strength was by then running out. I seized hold of a spare rope which Menlove had secured to the chockstone and lowered myself until I could jam my body into the crack to take a rest, while Menlove made fresh arrangements with the rope. Suddenly he called out "I'm going to have a go." I was belayed, but not holding the rope. Next moment he was laybacking steadily up the crack and was soon at the top. It was an astonishing feat of courage after witnessing Alf Bridge's near-disaster. Marco and I both had ignominiously to be hauled up.'

It was a great effort and as soon as Colin Kirkus heard the news he wrote a sporting letter to Edwards:

'Dear Edwards, Congratulations on C.B. It was a most marvellous achievement to lead the Flake Crack direct. Herford did it on a top rope without, but even he failed to lead it throughout. I have sometimes thought of it but I expect I would have funked the beastly thing...'

In later years when Edwards's sanity was giving way and he started to turn against his friends, Kirkus was one of the few people for whom he still had a kind word.

Linnell carried on his good work in 1931 and teamed up with Bert Hargreaves to do the first descent of Gimmer Crack. Bert then repeated JOAS with its originator Graham Macphee. The Everest climber Frank Smythe was in attendance, but the brusque Macphee told him it was too hard for him and in the afternoon when Bert took Smythe up the pleasant Severe — 'B' route — the intrepid Everest climber fell off Amen Corner and was hauled up like a sack of coal.

Only a few weeks after Linnell's epic effort on Pillar he transformed the main face of the East Buttress of Scafell. His companion was Sid Cross who played a major part in Lake District climbing for the next three decades, in several different roles. In 1932 he was a cobbler and repaired the shoes of Linnell's family. One day a pair of climbing boots came in to be mended and he and Linnell came to know each other. Sid had already been climbing and had done The Crack and Hiatus within a few weeks of taking up the sport. Sid had started climbing with another lad from Kendal and Alf Bridge remembered the effect they had on him:

'We encountered the famous 'Charlie' and 'Syd' — two lads from Kendal, who, having begun to climb at Whitsuntide had done practically everything on Gimmer within 6 weeks! Not to mention a few odds and ends like Great Central! These two shook us up by preceding us up Hiatus (or what they said was Hiatus — it had actually a very severe direct finish discovered by themselves) using as belays, when they did use any, things like the 'coffin' at the beginning of the traverse...and eventually asking us when we reached the top, duly impressed, how to tie a bowline! However, I managed to get a bit of my own back on them for having to lead their new pitch by doing a super-direct finish from the last stance over some deciduous chockstones — mainly because I had got lost...That was an excellent day's fun and

I shall treasure the memory of overhearing our young acquaintances describe Hargreaves and myself as "a pair of doddering old devils".'

On the weekend of their climb together on the East Buttress, Maurice picked up Sid in his motor-cycle and side-car. They left the Old Dungeon Ghyll at 9.30 p.m. and two hours later arrived at the foot of Esk Buttress where they had a nap, Sid with a rug wrapped round him and Maurice in a sleeping bag. They rose early and were rewarded with a magnificent sunrise from the top of Scafell. Linnell looked at the virgin central face of the East Buttress and then set to work. The main face was described by C.F. Holland: 'the long line of cliffs on the far side of Mickledore with their formidable bulges and overhanging bastions.' Linnell followed a line of weakness which scythed rightwards and only hesitated once at the junction with a yellow slab. His creation was a five pitch masterpiece, Great Eastern, described in the guidebook as: 'a fine but wandering climb in a magnificent setting'.

It was a masterly pieces of route-finding that managed to pluck a crux which was 'only' 4b, surrounded by pitches of much greater difficulty discovered by future generations. They finished the route, then went to the foot of the crag where they had breakfast. Sid then led Linnell up Botterill's Slab, then Linnell traversed out of Moss Ghyll into an unclimbed groove above and parallel to Moss Ghyll Grooves. Sid belayed him, with the belay continually slipping off an indifferent blunt spike. Grass sods rained down on the unfortunate Cross.

A.B. Hargreaves was doing Moss Ghyll Grooves. When Linnell faltered on the last few feet A.B. dropped him a top-rope and with its moral support Maurice and Sid did the climb: a Hard Very Severe, later called Narrow Stand.

As the autumn mists started to swirl around Hollowstones, A.B. decided to try to lead Flake Crack by conventional means. He assembled a support team of mighty strength — Jack Longland, conqueror of the West Buttress of Clogwyn du'r Arddu — Ivan Waller and Alf Bridge. Bridge climbed up and lashed himself to the chockstone so that when the others followed they could use him as a ladder. Unfortunately as each man climbed over Alf his trousers parted company from him and they slid to his ankles. Suddenly Maurice Linnell appeared on the scene looking neat and immaculate as if he had just come from his tailor's. He viewed the bizarre scene with distaste and announced: "I'm not going to be buggered about by you lot."

He then soloed up Keswick Brothers, traversed on to Central Buttress and to their astonishment he soloed the virgin Bayonet-Shaped Crack, named by Ashley Abraham more than a quarter of a century before. It is still 5b but Linnell made light of its difficulties and produced the first pitch of that standard to be soloed on sight on mountain crags.

Just to show his excellent form Linnell then led Gimmer Crack in nailed boots in the pouring rain, a climb that only four years before was thought to be the ultimate in desperate climbing.

During the summer of 1933 Linnell was inexorably drawn back to the East Buttress of Scafell and its unclimbed temptations. He had noticed an unclimbed overhanging wall to the right of his previous route. Its start proved to be very strenuous and gave him some trouble:

'From here the fun begins, and on the first ascent several ways were tried without success before the objective on the right was reached. This consists of a formation resembling a gable-end, only that the roof ridge slopes as well as the tiles...Above there is nothing but

overhang and a few scanty holds; but to the right is a sort of scoop, with a holdless, vertical back-wall, and a quite inadequate crack at the far side to pull across into. There was only one thing for it, and it was an eventuality for which I had come prepared. I inserted a piton in the little crack, and inserted it well and truly with a hammer. Nor was it only put there as a safeguard; by pulling on it sideways, downwards, outwards and upwards, and finally planting a foot on it, I was able with a struggle to reach a little ledge. I offer no apologies; those who prefer to climb the place unaided are cordially invited to remove the piton and do so.'

Overhanging Wall, a Hard Very Severe with a problematical 5a first pitch, was just the start of Linnell's memorable 1933 campaign on one of England's highest cliffs. Three weeks later Bert Hargreaves decided that it was time to make a contribution to the East Buttress. To his surprise as he stood at the foot of his projected line through the frowning overhangs, Linnell appeared from round the corner. He was pessimistic about the chances of success but his joining the team ensured success:

'The first difficulty called for more artifice. This time I inserted a little chockstone in the back of a crack, tied myself to it and, so secured, allowed Hargreaves to stand on my shoulder and overcome the difficulty. Clegg and I both made use of a fixed rope when following. There ensued a stomach traverse which could be done with much more dignity and difficulty in an upright posture. The hardest part was a slabby bit a little higher up, which had to be climbed in order to reach the foot of a short chimney leading to a hollow. The section illustrates well the way in which angles are so commonly deceptive on this crag; it is obviously less steep than most of the surrounding rocks, and therefore appears to lie back at a comparatively easy angle; but actually it is its great steepness above which makes it difficult. I was deceived in exactly the same way at least half a dozen times on different parts of the crag, even sometimes when I thought I had made conscious allowance for the illusion. The perfect nightmare of a crack which rises above the hollow into which the chimney opens can fortunately be avoided by interesting ways on the left.'

Linnell thought it was the least difficult of the new routes on the East Buttress and graded it only Severe. The route was Morning Wall, now Mild V.S. 4c. The route was so-called because the early morning sunlight had warmed the unclimbed rocks for them.

As if he could not keep away Linnell was back on the cliff two weeks later in the company of Bert Hargreaves:

'On August 27th Hargreaves and I explored one of the great right-angled grooves to the right of the lower part of the Great Eastern route, but could make nothing of it, so went and climbed Mickledore Grooves.'

It is thought that they attempted May Day. It was climbed five years later by the master quarryman-climber, Jim Birkett, who used several pitons and a shoulder to overcome its difficulties.

One more streak of brilliance came from Linnell, as the autumn shadows of that year lengthened over Mickledore, when he produced his finest contribution to Lakeland climbing. The previous year, when he had pioneered Great Eastern with Sid Cross, he had paused at a huge yellow slab and reluctantly traversed right to finish the route. The unclimbed slab stayed in his thoughts and on 10th September 1933 he returned to unlock its secrets. This resulted in the superb three-star Yellow Slab, which the modern guide book grades Hard Very Severe 4c.

'Starting up the Overhanging Wall we tested the security of the piton, to our satisfaction. Pearson came straight up the final portion of the crack to stance three, cutting out the traverse right and return. This might not be so easy when the rocks were any less dry. From the base of the V we made for the White Slab, which gave a magnificent climb right up to the finishing point of the Great Eastern route. In spite of the drought the top pitch of the slab was running with water, but was successfully overcome in socks. This makes a far finer finish to the Overhanging Wall than the original chimney route. It is harder than the latter, but not so hard as the bottom part, which is common to both. Without unroping we set off down the Great Eastern route, following it as far as the top of the third pitch. Just to the left of this point is a line of drainage which is a sheer waterfall in wet weather, and which has washed the rocks to a curious yellow colour; hence the Yellow Slab. This day it was perfectly dry. Before the slab is reached there is a bulge and then a short vertical crack. I must confess to having used another piton to overcome the bulge; but once up I was not sure that I might not have got there without it, so I took it out again. Pearson stepped up from the point of the belay on the right of the bulge with the help of one little fingerhold, and traversed with great delicacy into the crack, which is itself also very severe...The following pitch is trying, to say the least of it. The leader runs out about 40 feet of rope on the slab itself, into a corner from which there at first appears to be no escape. However, by traversing out to the left a vertical crack comes into view, above a very fine drop. This is best started as a lay-back, but the top section calls for wedging of the arms and legs, and is very hard work. I only succeeded at the third attempt.'

Linnell's two great summers on the East Buttress had enriched the entire Lakeland scene; like a swallow on its summer migration he alighted on untouched ledges on the East Buttress and suddenly passed on.

He set off for Scotland on Good Friday 1934 on his motorcycle, with Colin Kirkus as passenger. On Easter Saturday they decided to do a snow and ice climb — The Castle on Carn Dearg on Ben Nevis where high up the route Linnell was belayed. Kirkus who was tackling the final cornice direct, fell, and as he plunged down a loop of rope wound round Linnell's neck and garrotted him. Kirkus suffered bad facial injuries and was unconscious for some time. When he climbed up to Linnell, he found that he was already dead, so with great difficulty Kirkus got himself off the mountain. He never pioneered a hard route again. It was as if a door had closed on an important period in Lakeland climbing.

A few months after the Ben Nevis tragedy another climbing meteor passed through the Cumbrian heavens. F.G. Balcombe came from Southport and as a boy had been to the Lake District with the Boy Scouts and had read O.G. Jones's 'Rock Climbing in the English Lake District' and started as a solitary scrambler with an ascent of Jack's Rake. Gradually he became more proficient and climbed with Bert Hargreaves and Graham Macphee on North West and South West on Pillar Rock. He then climbed Botterill's Slab with C.J. Astley Cooper who was engaged in writing the guide-book to Great Gable, and was so impressed with Balcombe's abilities that he invited him to help with the guidebook. Balcombe's response was astonishing. In two weeks he led six new routes and variations which started at Severe and finished at Hard V.S. 5a with Buttonhook on Kern Knotts. The route was so-called because he used a piece of wire to thread the rope behind a tiny chockstone. He had the sense to top-rope it first as he realised that it was going to be very hard. During this ascent he had an unnerving moment:

> 'The first pitch was rather strenuous and I did not notice the waist line had untied and it sailed away into space, but pendulumed back and I held it in my teeth in case I had trouble higher up. We didn't count that climb, but its memory has bitten much deeper than the formal lead that followed later that week.'

Later that day he and Astley Cooper went to Gable Crag to investigate a great unclimbed slab; however it rained and they had to retreat. It took six hours to garden the climb and remove grass and vegetation to make the ascent possible. At first they called it Central Route, then it was re-named Engineer's Slab. The route was not repeated for twenty years, and it became one of the classic Very Severes of the whole area. Balcombe returned again to produce Unfinished Arete, which was just that, but it was another Very Severe addition which helped to bring the crag two climbs further towards maturity on the last of Balcombe's astonishing few days' work on the Gable cliffs.

In the subsequent guide-book the historical introduction by Astley Cooper made no mention of Balcombe's name. This can hardly have been forgetfulness on his behalf; presumably he envied Balcombe's brilliance. Balcombe's final charge up unclimbed rock in that hectic fortnight was on Scafell, the cliff which had seemed to be all things to all men in the early years of the twentieth century. Menlove Edwards and Linnell had polished Herford's original creation — Central Buttress and transformed it into one of the most desirable hard climbs in the British Isles. Balcombe tried to lead the Flake Crack unaided but failed, then with the security of slings attached to the chockstone, decided on a bold leftward movement on to the smooth front face, but realised it was too hard and retreated. He then fell off but was saved by the slings. He had tried a pitch which is now an E3 5c pitch of Foxshooter, so it is not surprising that he failed. Later he returned to lead the Flake Crack by conventional means, and was then unsure of the way beyond as he did not have a description. The rock was wet and caused them to climb in socks. Balcombe then did a new direct finish, now the accepted normal finish, which included 5a technical moves. Jerry Wright, who was one of his team and a professional rock-climbing guide, commented later:

> '...but it was the finest bit of leadership I have ever seen and the greatest rock-climbing day of my life.'

It caused something of a sensation and even attracted comment from the Daily Telegraph. Surprisingly, Balcombe only made one more trip to the Lake District cliffs. He guided a team of top German climbers who were on a trip to this country, taking them up Central Buttress, including his Direct Finish. The conditions were wet and the second German team had to knock in a couple of pitons to get up Balcombe's finish. Later the Germans commented on the fact that it was too dangerous, but it had to be done.

Balcombe moved on to pioneer cave-diving and later became an honorary life member of the Cave Research Association, but he will always be remembered for his astonishing fortnight in the Lake District in 1934.

There had been an explosion of new routes in Wales too from 1927 onwards and it was felt by the Lakeland climbers that they had been overtaken by exploration of the high crags in lonely Welsh cwms, particularly Clogwyn du'r Arddu. A.B. Hargreaves

Opposite: An early ascent of Paul Ross's 1957 route, The Bludgeon, Shepherd's Crag.   Photo: Geoff Oliver.

was the most travelled hard climber of the Twenties and Thirties and shuttled back and forth between Wales and the Lake District; and was uniquely qualified to comment on the scene and the pessimism that pervaded the Lake District climbers when they compared their own cliffs with those in Wales:

'The principal advantages of the harder Welsh climbs over those of the Lake District are that they are usually longer, generally less artificial, and almost invariably better provided with natural hazards, such as quantities of grass, loose rock, bad rock and long distances between belays, requiring a really all-round technique. To some, of course, these are not advantages at all, and such are welcome to the comparatively clean, much smaller Lake District Crags, constructed of perfect rock and well sprinkled with belays. On the other hand, when once one has tasted the joys of negotiating, in conscious safety, pitches which in the Lake District would be written off as unjustifiably dangerous, one is inclined to be bored with climbs, the only reason for falling off which would be just letting go... The truth is that there is too much concentration upon one or other of the districts, and Welsh climbers who never come to Cumberland, and who profess to scorn the climbing there, are almost as open to criticism for being unenterprising and wilfully ignorant as those Lake District climbers who never visit Snowdonia and cling to the antiquated notions about the climbing there.'

Since the dawn of rock-climbing and its initiation by Haskett Smith Lake District climbs throughout Victorian times and the initial first years of the twentieth century had been harder than Welsh climbs. Although O.G. Jones and the Abrahams shared their leisure hours between the two areas their better innovation was reserved for Cumbria. The first Very Severe — Eagle's Nest Ridge Direct — put up by Godfrey Solly in 1892 came only six years after the ascent of Napes Needle by Haskett Smith. At the end of the First World War there was an explosion of new routes in the Lake District, whereas in Wales there was silence. From 1919 to 1926 different stars emerged from Lakeland. Then in 1927 Fred Pigott changed the status quo and allowed The Principality to raise its head again, with his victory on the unclimbed gritstone-type cracks on the East Buttress of Clogwyn du'r Arddu.

The following year Jack Longland climbed the untouched slabby sheaves of the West Buttress. While these great deeds were being unfolded Colin Kirkus started soloing then did five new routes on Clogwyn du'r Arddu which made him Britain's greatest climber.

By the end of 1934 new route actvity had slowed down in Wales and the Lake District and it seems an appropriate time to analyse the state of the art in the respective areas. Firstly in the Lake District:

	Technical Grading	Originator
Central Buttress	5b (unaided)	Menlove Edwards
Overhanging Wall	5a	Maurice Linnell
Yellow Slab	4c	Maurice Linnell
Black Wall	5a	Joe Roper
Great Central Route	5b	Joe Roper
Eliminate 'B'	5a	Bert Gross
Buttonhook	5a	Fred Balcombe
Deer Bield Crack	4c	Bert Hargreaves

Three of these routes were done by the Welsh climbers Edwards and Linnell. The routes by Roper and Gross had been produced just after the First World War and are no less because of that.

Up to 1934 there were 26 routes of V.S. and above in Wales, fifty per cent fewer than the climbs of a similar standard in Cumbria. Only three Welsh climbs rose into and above the Hard V.S. category — West Rib, Pedestal Direct, and the first E1 in the British Isles, Jack Longland's Javelin Blade.

This excess of harder climbs in the Lake District was to prevail for several decades, to the enrichment of Cumbrian climbing until new generations appeared to take over fresh challenges which had been left by those who had gone before them.

Opposite: Top left: Chamonix, Shepherd's Crag, Borrowdale, in 1946.
         Top right: The splendidly eccentric Millican Dalton.
         Bottom left: Graham Macphee with skis on Helvellyn in 1928.   Photo: Ivan Waller.
         Bottom right: Transport problems for the climber!   Photos: C. R. Wilson.

Millican Dalton

Hewers of Rock

In the mid-Thirties the first groups of working-class climbers emerged from Northern cities close to the gritstone edges, and some young Cumbrians also lifted their eyes to the hills. Their everyday toil was low-paid and it took a supreme effort after a hard day's labour to go out and learn to climb rock. During the years they were acquiring their craft two stalwarts of a previous generation carried on exloring the cliffs which had fascinated them for so long. Bert Hargreaves and Sid Cross had been leading Lakeland climbers for some years and still produced new climbs every summer, often with their wives Ruth and Alice. Alice became the first woman to lead Central Buttress on Scafell. Of course Sid and Bert did not have the cliffs to themselves, as other climbers were starting to reach the pinnacle of their abilities.

One of the most remarkable failures of this century occurred on Deer Bield Crag, the lonely cliff in Easedale, an hour's walk from Grasmere. The cliff is like a gigantic rock plate split away from the hillside with two great fissures. The left-hand cleft, Deer Bield Crack, which had been climbed by Bert Hargreaves, is bounded on its right-hand side by the smooth front face, which was thought to be unclimbable until a young South African climber Dick Barry, tried and only just failed to overcome its formidable ramparts.

Barry's credentials were impeccable, buttressed by one week-end in the Lakes in 1936 when he produced three new routes, one of which was to be the hardest route on Gimmer Crag for some years, a bolder and more direct finish to Hiatus, called Grooves Traverse, which is still Hard Very Severe 5a.

Wilfred Noyce who was one of the leading young Welsh climbers, commented enviously on his abilities:

'I envied his long looseness and the ease with which he seemed to caterpillar up Central Route. I wondered if all climbers I did not know climbed as well as he. For he seemed of another and more aggressively proficient school.'

J.R. Jenkins wrote of the determined efforts which he witnessed in 1936 on Deer Bield:

'Three of us gathered at the foot of the buttress and roped up with the Tiger in the lead, myself second, and Bob the third man. We had come well prepared for heroics and had armed ourselves with pitons, a hammer, half a dozen rope-loops, and 400 feet of rope and line... The Tiger gingerly pawed the slab. It was steeper than it appeared and offered no relieving excrescence between its upper limit — abutting against the base of a bulging wall — and its sloping outer edge, except for a very doubtful and very small patch of grass. The wall above was in two sections, each about ten feet in height. The first section bulged out awkwardly and was holdless except for a small wrinkle under the bulge. The Tiger described this as the limiting case of the mantel-piece problem.'

The climb Barry was attempting is now Deer Bield Buttress (E1 5b) one of the best of its standard in the area and not climbed until the early Nineteen-Fifties. Its technical

Opposite: Above: Len Muscroft, Jim Birkett and Charlie Wilson on April 1st 1939 after completing the 1st ascent of Overhanging Bastion, Castle Rock. Photo: C.R. Wilson.

Below: A.B. Hargreaves, Marco Pallis, Bill Dyson, ?, Alf Bridge and Colin Kirkus outside the Old D.G. in 1932. Photo: Sid Cross.

problems were just beyond the reach of Barry but his attempt was an epic:

'He got further and further each time, and eventually made an excursion round a corner where an incipient crack in the wall above was crowned by a small pointed chock-stone. Unfortunately the angle of the slab increased at this point so that the base of the crack was unattainable. After some deliberation a piton was tried to supply some hold and safeguard, and hammering one into a crack in the slab he attached his rope to it by a karabiner. On testing it he removed both the piton and a large section of the slab, and incidentally he nearly removed himself. We then decided that British rocks should remain undefiled by such sordid things as pitons. The end of the third hour found the Tiger hopefully trying to lasso the pointed chock-stone at the top of the crack, with both Bob and me arguing quite fiercely with him that the whole thing was getting rather beyond a joke. Then to our surprise he apparently performed the Indian rope trick and caught the rope-noose fair and square round the chock-stone. He tested it and it held...I watched, heart in mouth, while he applied the theory of the parallelogram of forces and succeeded in defying a sufficient number of Newton's laws to overcome the mantel-piece problem. This was not easy as weight had to be carefully distributed to prevent both the pieces of crag from coming away and the loops from dropping off them. From the mantel-piece a sitting position at the foot of the second wall was reached and for a while it seemed difficult to make any headway. The Tiger succeeded in attaining a precarious standing position.This he consolidated with such a cat's-cradle of rope-loops and safety ropes that I felt rather like the driver of a four-in-hand. Eventually the second section was vanquished with comparative ease by the aid of a small tree, a few bearded tufts and some grassy handholds. Ahead the groove which we had seen from below sloped up at an easier angle and in twenty feet he reached a good belay and lowered me a fixed rope. The Tiger was given a shoulder by Bob to enable him to get a start on the groove above, which at this point was becoming quite steep. He was soon forced out on to the right and came to a full stop some fifteen feet higher standing precariously on the pointed bulge at the apex of the buttress. The limit came at last when the rocks under his feet moved slightly in a most disconcerting way, causing him to shout loudly for a rope from above. This had proved too much for even the Tiger's nerves and he was later heard to utter in a very small voice, "It's a pity I ever came up here." His moments of anxiety ceased when he had the supporting rope from above round his waist and he rejoined Bob at the belay below. A spectacular hundred-foot abseil landed them both on terra firma after seven and a quarter hours of climbing.'

It was one of the most determined and noble failures in the history of Lakeland climbing, and the line had to wait until 1951 before Arthur Dolphin overcame its ferocious problems.

Barry who had seemed as if he might lift British climbing to even greater heights was killed in the South African mountains shortly after.

Noyce became one of the best Welsh climbers in the late Nineteen-Thirties and was helped to this high level by climbing with Menlove Edwards, who had done the first clean lead of the Flake Crack of Central Buttress. During the summer months they often joined Oxbridge climbing parties which spent part of their summer vacation at the Buttermere house of a Cambridge Don, Professor Pigou. It was common practice to award 'The Brass Medal for Distinguished Incompetence' if someone had been particularly inept that day. Edwards was perhaps the strongest climber in the country at that time and was just as much at home in the water as he was on unclimbed rock. A.B. Hargreaves remembers some of his aquatic excursions:

Opposite: Top left: Jim Birkett and Joe Page.
             Top right: Jim Birkett on the scoop during the 1st ascent of Overhanging Bastion in 1939.
             Bottom left: Jim Birkett on The Tarsus (1937), Dove Crag, his first new route.
             Bottom right: Jim Birkett on White Ghyll Traverse.
                                                                                      Photos: C.R. Wilson

'I could tell many more stories of Menlove. For instance, as an incredible swimmer; who thought nothing of plunging into roaring torrents and bouncing about amongst the boulders, or systematically swimming across every sizeable piece of water in the Lake District during a short holiday.'

It was inevitable that Noyce would be drawn to the East Buttress of Scafell as Mickledore Grooves had been pioneered by his cousin Colin Kirkus who had guided Wilf's first faltering steps when he had started climbing on the lonely Welsh cliffs. The weather was poor whilst Edwards and Noyce stayed at Pigou's house. Time was running out, so on September 21st, although conditions on the high crags were not right, they set out for Scafell. Water was dripping from the lower overhangs of the East Buttress, and some of the upper corners were wet too, including the one which contained the climb. Noyce needed a shoulder from Menlove to start the climb, then Edwards looped the rope around an indifferent belay. Noyce made slow progress and as he neared the top of the critical pitch he tried to ease his inner tension by announcing that he would need a lot of beer the following evening. Almost immediately he fell from the final moves. Later he wrote a graphic description of the fall:

'I remember nothing from that last belay to the pain, three days later, when I started to dim consciousness in Whitehaven Hospital: nothing but a distant chaos of lights and voices and jolts and operating tables. But enough had happened. The ledge had come away, loosened perhaps by former feet and by weathering. The belay had failed to hold. I had fallen clear, for some 100 feet above Menlove and 100 feet below; while the rope stretched another twenty feet. Two strands parted, so that I dangled just above the ground. Two ledges, hit as I passed, had knocked an eye and a jaw out of shape; my face was not pretty to look at. Menlove had been severely tugged. It was lucky that he was so strong, competent, and elastic. There had been difficulties of getting the body down, of transport in the valley, and anxiety at Lower Gatesgarth and at home. I awoke only after the first skilful patching of the bleeding face. It was about two months before anything of plastic surgery could be begun.'

Noyce had four huge falls during his climbing career and followed his painful Scafell tumble with another crash on Ben Nevis in 1938, followed by another unfortunate accident on Great Gable after the Second World War.

'But before you go you glance up, shall we say, into these misty ridges of Great Gable, the peak of Cumberland that most resembles your well-loved Tryfan. You clamber up, roped. The rock is firm, but the wind blusters about you. However, the climb is soon finished. There remains one pinnacle, high on the left. It should perhaps be climbed, too. You are up it quickly. No, you are not. Around its top corner hurls a suddenly gust of wind, unexpected. It tears you straight away, throws you out and down, in a somersault. Again you sit up on a ledge. Again your leg is broken and bent under you. Again it is a miracle, and seems a bitter miracle, that you are alive. Again you are waiting for your companion, giant of strength that he is, to bring up the rescue party. Light snow falls, again. And once more you must look forward to Whitehaven Hospital, to the nursing and the injection and the bed and the pain.'

Noyce died in a fall a quarter of a century after his trauma on Scafell on an expedition to Russia, together with his roped companion Robin Smith, the young great hope of

Opposite: Above: R.J. Birkett and C.R. Wilson on left in May 1937 below Gillercombe Buttress.
Below: Jim Birkett (middle front) and the 'orphans of the storm' on Pillar mountain in a freezing gale.

Photos: C.R. Wilson.

Scottish mountaineering.

Leading rock-climbers are not often killed while climbing up hard rock. It is usually when they change over to mountaineering that death begins to loom, particularly if they participate in Himalayan mountaineering, where the death-rate still averages between ten and twenty per cent. No amount of mountaineering skill can dodge a well-aimed lump of ice and even a fit man can die from illness high on a Himalayan mountain with no hospital facilities. The survival rate amongst top rock climbers who have rock-climbed only in this country has been very high despite the almost complete absence of protection for a leader before the Second World War.

Even while Noyce was having his epic trauma on Scafell, a young quarryman started to become interested in the Cumbrian hills where he lived. Jim Birkett had begun his working life in a slate quarry at the age of fourteen and every day he split slate blocks and so in time became immensely strong. His first introduction to the high fells was when his uncle took him fox-hunting, but the rocky cliffs soon became his playground and in 1937 he produced his first new climb, The Tarsus, on Dove Crag. Jim had been interested in birds from an early age and built up a large egg collection. His first new route was named Tarsus after the shin-bone of a pigeon killed by a peregrine falcon and eaten on a ledge. Jim Birkett often in those days climbed in his working footwear — a pair of clogs which had a thick rim of iron.

'You had to be a precision climber to use them, rubbers would stick on anything when it was dry, but when it was wet they were useless.' He never smoked and if he went out for an evening with his mates he drank grapefruit juice.'

He worked for a while in the quarries on the flanks of Honister Pass. A measure of the strength needed by workers there was provided by a Victorian predecessor, Joseph Clark, who one day carried two hundred-weight loads of slate on a sled on his back forty-six times during one working day, a staggering total of more than 10,000 pounds down steep slippery ground. Apart from Jim's enormous strength he had athletic suppleness: when his friend Charlie Wilson told him of a gymnast who had done a back somersault, Jim responded by doing a perfect back somersault although shod in heavy nailed boots. It was on the East Buttress of Scafell that Birkett moved into the forefront of his generation of climbers. Charlie Wilson had noticed a superb unclimbed line and persuaded Jim to have a look at it. There was an expanse of overhanging rock between Mickledore Grooves and Overhanging Wall which had a huge diedre high on the face guarded by a formidable initial wall. Jim set off with a bunch of pitons which had been made by Charlie's uncle who had a forge at Thirlmere. The start of their projected new climb looked ominous, a steep smooth inviolate slab. Charlie Wilson led up to a narrow sloping ledge fifteen feet up the pitch where he knocked in a belay piton. Jim stood on Charlie's shoulder and carried on until the holds became microscopic and following him Wilson had to use the second piton for aid. The pitch is strenuous and still graded Hard Very Severe 5b. Birkett had not used the pitons for aid; this factor was ignored by Bentley Beetham who wrote:

'To-day almost everyone is agreed that our English rocks must never be mutilated and defiled by Continental ironmongery; pitons are unthinkable; absolutely taboo, and yet...Peep round the corner of our most famous crag, look on what I have heard referred to as the gentleman's side of Scafell, and you will see not one piton, but three within almost as many yards of each other, and this at the very commencement of one of the newer climbs. It is,

Opposite: Above: Jim Haggas on Overhanging Wall, Scafell East Buttress,1938.
            Below: Jim Haggas (left) and Robert Clough about 1947.
                                                                        Photos: J. Haggas collection.

John Hartley on Jim Birkett's 1938 May Day Climb, Scafell East Buttress.

Photo: John Har

therefore, not a question of whether we should or should not allow these things to be hammered into our rocks; the piton has already arrived and is firmly driven in.'

One cannot help thinking that the reference to the gentleman's side of Scafell was a swipe at Birkett's humble background. Climbing had been the exclusive reserve of the middle classes since the days of Haskett Smith; and Birkett's May Day climb may have seemed to the Lakeland hierarchy as a threat to their previously exclusive hold over the Cumbrian cliffs.

Another great climber, Colin Kirkus, made the most sensible comments on the use of ironmongery to protect new routes:

'On a new climb, however, the situation is rather different. The pioneer party has a certain right to choose its tactics and if it seems probable that the full length of the rope will be used without any belay being reached, then a piton may be justifiable. Also, if a very desperate move has to be made, it may be very desirable to have the second man close at hand in case the leader meets an unforeseen obstacle higher up and is forced to return. This argument applies of course only to routes of great difficulty.'

Birkett was fortunate to live in the Langdale area; he could wait for good weather weekends to ensure good conditions for his exploratory work. Close proximity to the cliffs, extraordinary strength and daily working on rock faces gave him many advantages over his predecessors. At one stage he worked in the quarries at the summit of Honister Pass and during the week stayed in the barrack accommodation provided by the company. On summer nights he often did a couple of climbs on the cliffs close to the barracks and certainly was much closer to the modern style of climbing than anyone before him.

In the late Nineteen-Thirties almost all the gullies and wide-crack climbs had already succumbed to the tread of rubber footwear. Birkett ventured on to steeper, less obvious lines of weakness, more dangerous because there was still only minimal protection for the leader.

May Day Climb had been a wonderful spring bonus for Birkett, but even on that day the consequence of a leader fall was tragically outlined. A young Scots girl fell 250 feet to her death when she slipped during a hard move. Her second tried to grab her rope as she hurtled past, but the scything rope burnt his hands to the bone during her fatal plunge. Birkett and his friends carried her body down to Wasdale. The following weekend a close friend of Birkett, Dunbar Usher, fell from Stand Crag because of a loose hold and died from a broken neck.

Birkett's exceptional physical abilities helped to overcome pre-war class barriers and soon he climbed with enthusiasts from all strata of society, although occasionally they did not come up to the mark. One keen young undergraduate climbed for a short time with his group until the young man was climbing above Jim and unfortunately dislodged a large rock which Jim thought passed too close for comfort and cuttingly said:

"If ye can't climb without knockin' stones doon ye can booger off."

Jim's right-hand man in his initial exploration had been Charlie Wilson, but they were soon joined by Len Muscroft who was just as strong as Jim. He could do a one-arm pull-up with ease and would amuse his friends by taking two six-inch nails together

Bob Allen nearing the top of the gangway on Overhanging Bastion, Castle Rock.

Photo: Ian Rc

and bending them till they broke.

Birkett was not obsessed with new routes and it was inevitable that he would have to do Central Buttress which had been such a corner-stone in the reputation of previous generations. As if to make his own mark, he led it in nailed boots. He and Muscroft soon realised that between them they had an unrivalled knowledge of the Cumbrian crags and that this knowledge could be commercially useful. On 1st January 1939 they formed themselves into the Cumberland and Westmorland Guides. One of its conditions was that its members had to be born and bred in one of the two counties. One of the climbs available to clients was Central Buttress. The standard daily charge for such a route was £1.50 per day with a maximum of three in the party.

In 1939, as the war clouds gathered on the European horizon, Birkett made a monumental new climb on a cliff quite close to the blacksmith's forge that belonged to Charlie Wilson's uncle. The crag was Castle Rock of Triermain, one of the most romantic names of any cliff; Charlie became intrigued with it during one of his holidays at his uncle's house. He hand-traversed along a huge flake until he found himself in the middle of the face and noticed an inviting gangway which slanted steeply up leftwards. On April Fool's Day 1939 the assault took place with Jim, Charlie and Len Muscroft ready for the fray. The line proved to be an overhanging bastion and that was the name that Jim gave it. John Wilkinson commented on the climb:

> 'Overhanging Bastion, the crux of which took the line of a narrow gangway slanting across the main face and sandwiched between overhangs, was impressively exposed, sensational, and lacking in protection. Birkett showed how far ahead of the times he was regarding the use of protection when, on one of the lower pitches, he inserted pebbles in a crack and threaded them with thin line to provide a running belay of sorts. (The line was Jones's Gold Seal, sold at three pence a foot. Birkett once remarked "I wouldn't trust my mother's washing on it.")'

Overhanging Bastion placed Birkett amongst the top echelon of British climbers, and has remained a classic for nearly half a century; it is awarded three stars in the current guidebook and is described as 'The classic route of Thirlmere.'

Three weeks later Jim and his friends returned to the cliff and produced another starred Very Severe called Zig-Zag because it traced out a swastika-shaped line. Jim and his friends were ecstatic about their achievements, but were unwise in talking to the press about it, as their comments were wildly exaggerated and Overhanging Bastion was reported as the Lakeland Everest. The press also failed to point out that the summit of the crag could be reached quite easily from the fell on either side of it. The three triumphant climbers were depicted as guides whose main aim in doing Overhanging Bastion was for monetary reasons. The local paper proclaimed:

GUIDES' BID FOR FAME TO BEAT PROS

> By Our Special Correspondent.   Local-born mountain guides in Cumberland and Westmorland have started a drive against professionals from outside areas. Their first move to gain recognition was the first ascent of Castle Rock, Triermain — the "Everest of Lakeland." This was accomplished on Tuesday by three members of the newly-formed Cumberland and Westmorland Local Guides Association. "It is time we were recognised as the best guides in our own mountains," 'Mr C.W. Hudson, one of the guides, said to the Daily

Herald yesterday. For a long time we have taken a back seat to professional guides who come to Lakeland from other areas for the season. Our new association has as members only local-born men and there are some first- class guides and climbers among us. R.J. Birkett, who led the ascent of Castle Rock on Tuesday, is probably the most courageous climber in the country.' 'It was the third new climb to his credit inside twelve months. The local guides will try more new climbs during the season. We are out to prove if any proof is necessary that local men can't be beaten on their own mountains.'

There were other professional guides who took exception to the newspaper reports, Stanley Watson who was then chief of the British Mountain Guides was particularly incensed and although he was not a Cumbrian he shrewdly addressed his comments to the Editor, which were published under the heading of Thirlmere's Everest:

'Sir, A report appeared recently in the columns of the daily Press that the Castle Rock in Lakeland had been climbed for the first time. In common justice to the scores of people who have been visiting this rock since 1928, I wish to correct this inaccuracy. The first ascent was made by those superb mountaineers, Miss M.M. Barker and G.G. Macphee, both members of the Fell and Rock Climbing Club of the English Lake District, on 31st March 1928. During the same year, four other climbs were made up the rock. I myself led a party on the second ascent of the direct route. Indisputable evidence of these earlier ascents appears in the Journal of the Fell and Rock Climbing Club for 1929. Details of the climbs are given. It is grossly unfair to the real pioneers of the Castle Rock that the recent reports have been published. One cannot blame the Press, which has to rely on outside sources in specialised technical matters. One can, however, blame those irresponsibles in search of notoriety who hand spurious reports to the publicists who accept them in all good faith. Damage to my guide organisation, British Mountain Guides, will undoubtedly ensue and may have to be assessed. I trust that the publication of this letter will help to put matters right.'

The misleading comments in his letter were swiftly rebuffed by Birkett in his reply which was published under the banner: Climb on the Castle Rock of Triermain. Guides Chief's challenge:

'Referring to certain letters which have been published regarding the climb on Castle Rock of Triermain as reported in last week's "Cumberland News ", Mr R.J. Birkett, chief of the Cumberland and Westmorland Guides, has issued the following statement:- "Firstly, in justice to the Cumberland and Westmorland Guides, I should like to say that Mr Stanley Watson should be sure of his facts before making such statements in the Press. Any variations of the article headed 'Lakeland Climbing Feats' which appeared in the local newspaper, were made by newspaper correspondents in search of saleable 'copy'. The heading 'The Lakeland Everest' is some journalist's stretch of imagination and is entirely ludicrous, for anyone can reach the top of Castle Rock by easy walking. I know of and have done all the known routes on this crag: in fact, I have checked the proofs for the new Fell and Rock guide for the outlying climbs.' OVERHANGING BUTTRESS. The climbs to which Mr Watson refers, made in 1928 by G.G. Macphee and Dr Mabel Barker are the Yew Tree (130 feet), Slab Climb (80 feet) and Scoop and Crack Climb (145 feet) whilst our route, which has been named Overhanging Buttress, is some 240 feet high. This can hardly be confused with the Direct Route which Mr Watson mentions, as it is quite 300 yards away and some 220 feet higher. "C.R. Wilson had also climbed with Dr Mabel Barker for some years

Opposite: Rigor Mortis, Castle Rock first done by Paul Ross with 5 points of aid and later freed by Martin Boysen.   Photo: Al Phizacklea.

and has several times heard her version of Castle Rock explorations. In fact, only three weeks ago he told her of the projected attempt on the central unclimbed face by the overhanging buttress, and she remarked that Graham Macphee and herself had attempted that face without success and had gone to the South Face where they had made their routes."
"Those 'irresponsibles' whom Mr Watson mentions in one paper, have no more wish for notoriety than people who climb Kern Knotts Crack blindfold, as did Mr Watson in his film 'High Hazard'. While we deplore competitive climbing, we think that if Mr Watson still doubts the accuracy of our report perhaps he would lead the second ascent of this route."

The dust soon settled and Birkett and Muscroft carried on to pluck more rocky fruits from Castle Rock of Triermain culminating in Harlot Face (1949) whose crux moves may be said to represent the first Extreme climbing ever done in the Lake District.

Less than a month after Birkett's Thirlmere triumphs another man, Jim Haggas, breathed life into a formidable crag whose frontal face had repelled all aspirants. Dove Crag is perched menacingly high in Dovedale above Brotherswater. Haggas was from the classical mould of Lakeland climbers and a keen member of the Fell and Rock Club. During the early months of 1939 snow had cloaked the fells and crags with a white shroud. On one fine cold weekend Haggas had kicked steps up a snow-filled gully next to Dove Crag and noticed that the main face was so steep that it had resisted a white mantle except for a small slab sprinkled with snow. Would it provide a possible key to the first new route on the main face?

On a fine May day, when the snow had melted from the rock and there were just a few snow-fields in the high gullies, Haggas solved the complex problems of the main face and named it appropriately Hangover, a two hundred-foot Very Severe which had to be broken into seven pitches to overcome its problems. Arthur Dolphin, leading climber of the next generation, was so impressed with it that he wrote of it as:

'...the only possible line of ascent and must rank as one of the purest lines in the country.'

In 1986 John Wilkinson commented:

'He took the easiest line up one of the most impressive pieces of virgin rock in the whole of the Lakes.'

Hangover gave Arthur Dolphin some anxious moments when he came to lead it:

'A long swing to the left on a rather doubtful handhold gave me some misgivings. A violent arm-pull was then followed by a delicate traverse on small, mossy holds to a very strenuous overhanging corner giving access to a chimney. This was easy, but very loose, particularly near the top where some massive blocks seemed to lean longingly towards their comrades down in Dovedale. I was careful to give them no encouragement ...the right hand grasps this ledge and the left soon afterwards: a pendular movement follows as the legs and body swing over to the right to hang in the void beneath the nose: the arms struggle to change a cling-hold into a press, but the ledge is narrow and legs can give no assistance; the pendulum is revived and the footholds far to the left regained with difficulty. The descent is continued to the resting place and the problem reconsidered...'

Next year whilst the R.A.F. and the Luftwaffe were shooting it out over the sunny skies of southern Britain, Haggas and two of his friends discussed the possibility of a

Opposite: Esk Buttress with late afternoon sunlight picking out a team on The Red Edge. High up a climber on Central Pillar is silhouetted against the sky.   Photo: Al Phizacklea.

formidable-looking line to the right of White Ghyll Chimney in Langdale. The first pitch was relatively simple leading up to the cosy recesses of a cave but the view of the second pitch filled Haggas with apprehension:

'The traverse right from the cave is extremely exposed and looks likely to crumble at the touch, being composed for the most part of thin projecting shelves of rock covered with loose blocks, spillikins and the like... The left hand lets go of the flute and hastily takes a press with fingers pointing right, while the legs swing to the pendant position: the right hand grasps the edge of the ridge and the right foot is raised until the toes can touch the extremity of the ledge at the tip of the nose. This movement is rendered very difficult by the ledge sloping downwards to the nose and this, combined with the side-pull on the ridge, tends to swing the body to the right and off the crag; the legs hang free and so cannot resist this tendency much, but as the right leg is raised the knee may be kept in contact with a shallow vertical groove in the face of the rock and this just gives the friction required.'

Such is the famous crux of the Gordian Knot, the first of White Ghyll's many knots and nots.

There were other new route developments during the summer months of 1940 on an unlikely-looking cliff. Boat Howe, at the head of Ennerdale had been discovered by T. Graham Brown the renowned explorer of the Brenva Face of Mont Blanc in the Nineteen-Twenties. Sid Cross and Bert Hargreaves with their respective wives quixotically named their route Prow of the Boat and it was a fine Hard Very Severe and a good addition to the climbs they had done over the previous ten years all over Lakeland. The family climbing-teams of Sid Cross and Bert Hargreaves produced many inventions on five different crags, often with their wives, Alice and Ruth. Sid's climbing career spanned over four decades right from the rudimentary days when he had used bull's nose rings for abseiling. After the war Sid and his wife bought the Old Dungeon Ghyll Hotel in Langdale and the bar became the focal point for all rock-climbers who came to the valley. He combined the hotel business with mountain rescue duties over several decades. On one occasion while in his sixties he reached a casualty at the foot of Pavey Ark in thirty-five minutes from the valley floor, to ensure that he could return to the hotel in time to carve the joint for the evening meal. The one-time apprentice cobbler eventually retired and carried on living in Langdale at Clappersgate and richly deserved the award of an M.B.E for his devotion to the Lakeland Mountain Rescue organisation.

As the Second World War increased in ferocity Birkett, Cross and Hargreaves were joined in the new route business by another artisan, Bill Peascod, who eventually made a whole new climbing scene on the Buttermere cliffs. He too, like Birkett made his living from hewing rock, but Bill's working day was spent hundreds of feet below ground down a coal mine. Even to get to the coal face he had to walk three miles each way from the pit cage which plunged him to his workplace. He worked shifts and as black night gave birth to the dawn, he joined his fellow miners who clattered down the village streets in their iron-rimmed clogs. One day after work he decided to ride into the unknown Lake District on the bicycle that his father had bought him for twenty-five pence. Soon he had reached another unknown world:

'As I breasted the hill the whole panorama of the beautiful valley began to unfold. Below me Loweswater and the hazy fells slept in a gentle dawn. From high up on Fangs Brow I could hear the Valley sounds — voices of man and beast — the 'clip clop' of a draught-horse. Apart

from them all was still and totally at peace. After a night spent in the darkness and turmoil, amongst the sweat and stink of stale air, pit ponies and one's own pit shirt, my discovery of Western Lakeland set my senses in a whirl. From that moment my thoughts and needs took wings. All my spare time was given to extending the limits of my world of discovery on my bike, on foot and in dreams. I explored throughout the summer and the winter.'

He bought some boots which he studded himself with clinker nails and fifty feet of manila rope with three red strands woven into the core to show that it was safe. On the crags he met the President of the Fell and Rock Club, silver-haired Gustave Robert Speaker who proposed him for his club, at a time when a working-class member was as rare as fine Lakeland summer weather. Bill scanned his membership booklet for local members who might be climbing partners and so met Bert Beck, the English master at Workington Grammar School, who later wrote:

'Just as Marshall had met Snelgrove and Crosse met Blackwell it was perhaps inevitable that Peascod should meet Beck...'

Peascod was twenty years old and in the full physical maturity of a miner. Shod in flimsy rubber plimsolls bought from Woolworths he and Bert Beck were ready for their first major challenge on the front face of Eagle Crag Buttermere. The main face was unclimbed. Peascod and Beck carried out a thorough investigation by girdling it before they launched their attack on a major line right up the face. On the hard pitch Peascod had trouble, and Beck even greater problems following:

'A ten-foot slab had only tiny ledges which sloped outwards and tilted the body in that direction, and I found that the rope, which Bill had threaded through a snap-ring loop halfway up this 90-foot pitch and was now running horizontally to me, was threatening to pluck me backwards. So I had to stand poised with my rubber-shod feet on the sloping gangway, retaining my balance by means of two finger-tips inserted under one tiny undercut hold, while Bill descended a little to flick the loop off the small point. A slight shower of rain began and I meditated on infinity and the mutability of human affairs.'

This crux pitch tested Peascod's abilities to the limit, as Beck related:

'The most difficult part of all came next. Even the optimistic Bill, as he just succeeded in establishing himself on the rock bulge above and desperately strove to move up it, was suddenly constrained to exclaim "Look out, I'm off any moment!"'

With the problems solved they were able to take their ease on the top breathing in the sweet Buttermere air:

'We sat there, together, in the sun. The evening was still; we were completely alone in the Combe — in the world! The War, the pit... they didn't exist. We didn't say much. What was there to say? Each of us was drenched in his own emotions, dreaming his own dreams and experiencing that most exquisite of sensations — the elation of success at having climbed something really worthwhile. We called the climb Eagle Front.'

Eagle Front was one of Peascod's finest creations, even more remarkable because he and Beck had not done any routes of Very Severe standard up till then. Bill carried on

Opposite: Terry Parker finishing the crack of Jim Birkett's fierce F Route (1941) on Gimmer Crag.   Photo: Ian Roper.

to produce a total of five Very Severes in 1940, and the following year just before Beck joined the Royal Artillery, the pair attacked the last big unclimbed Lakeland gully, Y Gully on Haystacks, which had repulsed the timid attempts of earlier explorers. It is steep, loose and wet and is very rarely climbed in summer. It required all Peascod's skills acquired underground on loose coal faces to deal with its concentrated dangers. It took two tries to overcome it. They took three ropes in case they had to abseil off, together with three slings and karabiners; they felt that they were overloaded with gear. However Beck summed up their elation at their ultimate triumph:

> 'I joined Bill at an extremely uncomfortable position where everything sloped the wrong way, nothing was secure, and there was neither definite belay nor strong stance. Immediately above was an awkward bulge, and higher still the cleft became much more deeply-cut and narrow between smooth sheer walls. And the back of this chimney bore out our worst fears by curving forwards, so that it was necessary to bridge and work upwards and outwards. And, to crown all, the rock was still bad. I do not think I have ever been in a more hopeless-looking place.'

During that Battle of Britain summer Jim Birkett was also very active on Dow, Gimmer, and Great Gable where he produced his finest route of that year — Tophet Grooves, on the gloomy steep wall overlooking Great Hell Gate: it had to wait seven years before it was repeated by the next great man, Arthur Dolphin, who struggled with its mixed pleasures:

> 'We had heard of no second ascent when, on a wet and misty afternoon in June 1947, the tyrannies of Guide-writing demanded an inspection. The rocks looked singularly uninviting as Des and I roped up below the overhanging nose up which the climb commenced. A shallow, grassy groove about twelve feet above our heads was obviously the first objective, but the method of attaining it was less obvious, holds being conspicuous by their absence. 'Shoulder useful' was the laconic comment of our notes. Des, being lighter, made the first attempt, but soon had to retire — boots, overhanging rock, and slimy finger-holds proving too powerful a combination. With the double advantage of socks over rubbers, and a longer reach I managed to force an entry into the groove... A shattered pinnacle seemed a useful take-off point for the awkward move into the crack. I was stepping up, pleased at having found an easy solution to the problem, when, with a rumbling noise, the whole world seemed to fall apart and before I knew what had happened I was dangling on the rope. A loud crash signalled the arrival of the pinnacle on the screes. Somewhat shaken, but otherwise undamaged, I started off again. This time I tested every hold. The grass, in particular, felt most unsatisfying!'

Jim Birkett was finding the hardest routes to date on traditional crags whilst Peascod was putting up new lines at all grades on crags which had been left almost untouched even after two generations of Lakeland climbing. Langdale, Ennerdale and Wasdale had been the popular places whilst Buttermere and Newlands had been left in peace. The vegetated Borrowdale had also been ignored. Now Bentley Beetham transformed them by fire and ice axe. He had done the second ascent of Central Buttress in 1921 and this buttressed his credentials as a candidate for the Everest expedition of 1922. Afterwards his public school and university background made him an ideal member of the Lake District climbing establishment. Beetham's tenacity produced over ninety routes in Borrowdale, but as a qualified naturalist it seems strange that he

ill Peascod on the 1st ascent of Resurrection Route, Birkness Combe in 1941.

Photo: Austin Barton.

castigated Birkett for driving in three pitons when he had removed many tons of soil and rich Lakeland flora. Later in life he became a delightful eccentric and a friend remembers meeting him at Dow Crag. He was rather indignant at the failure of a companion to appear, and asked him to join his rope, then at the end of the day Beetham suddenly remembered that he should have been potholing with the absent friend. Trevor Jones remembers meeting Beetham in the early Nineteen- Fifties when both were staying at a Fell and Rock club cottage in Borrowdale. Beetham asleep in an armchair with a copy of that day's Times covering his face. It rose and fell as he breathed in and out in deep sleep; eventually he woke up, introduced himself and said abruptly: "Equator last week, North Pole today, what do you think of that?" Jones was not sure whether he was being stupid or in receipt of a fundamental truth so tried to put on a look of deep understanding. Eventually it appeared that the old man had been to Africa a few days previously and that day had repeated one of his own climbs called The North Pole.

Beetham's climbing career had never been the same after a horrific fall in 1942 from one of his own climbs, Cock's Comb on Raven Crag in Combe Ghyll. As he pulled up on a flake it broke off; he called out "Gosh" as he fell fifteen feet on to his head. His skull was fractured in six places, his right wrist was broken, and he was unconscious for three weeks. He slowly recovered but never remembered the circumstances of the fall. That same year G.R. Speaker was killed on Eagle's Nest Chimney on Great Gable. He was in his seventh decade when he died; he felt suddenly ill on the day of his fall and remarked: "I don't seem to be in my usual form." He too fell on his head and died; and it was left to Beetham to commment on the drawbacks of rock climbing in later life:

'I have always thought, and still do think, that one of the great advantages of mountaineering is that it can safely be indulged in from youth through manhood far into old age, whereas most other active sports last for but a brief period in our salad days. Yet it is obvious with advancing years, strength and agility lessen, as do probably, though less patently, balance and the power of recovery; but to offset this loss, experience, judgment, caution and possibly technique increase. In old age, we may, in some cases certainly do, enjoy our climbing as much as we ever did in youth, but we may unconsciously be taking greater risks due to an unfelt, unappreciated lack of ability. If there be any truth in this reduction in the coefficient for recovery with advancing years then these recent accidents may at least, serve to warn some of the old guard that they are not as good, as quickly and efficiently responsive to potential catastrophe, as they were and as they take for granted they still are; and that therefore, with advancing years they need to climb with an ever-increasing margin of safety.'

Beetham recovered to do nearly sixty more new routes right up to 1952, most of them solo. When his Borrowdale guidebook came out there was scepticism about certain of his first ascents claimed to have been climbed when he was over sixty years of age. His new climbs with other people had been of a Mild Severe standard or below, yet two of his routes, namely Devil's Wedge and North Buttress, are still graded Hard Very Severe; no-one before or since has soloed new climbs of such a standard in their sixties and it was widely felt that he should not be credited with their first ascents. North Buttress on Shepherd's Crag did not have a detailed route description in Beetham's guidebook and was properly climbed by Peter Greenwood much later in the summer of 1954.

While Beetham was beavering away on the Borrowdale cliffs Jim Birkett was active too and in 1941 he turned his attention to Gimmmer Crag, a cliff like half a giant grey

Opposite: Bill Peascod on the 1st ascent of Slabs Direct, Birkness Combe in 1942. He then lowered his rubbers down to the second man.
Photo: Austin Barton.

wedding cake perched high up on the fellside. It is one of the first magical sights of the
Lake District cliffs from the road alongside Windermere. High on its West Face is a
fierce-looking rightward-facing corner crack which cuts into the bounding edge of the
face; it had already been named in advance 'F' Route in the alphabetical Gimmer
tradition, but it had rejected the timid advances of previous explorers, until Birkett
provided the muscles necessary for the strenuous layback moves. Later that year
Birkett did another route on Gimmer — appropriately named Bachelor Crack
because soon afterwards he got married. He continued to be an all-rounder of the fells
as appreciative of and knowledgeable about the Alpine flora and peregrines as he was
about the steepest cliffs. Winter too, opened up other challenges to him and when the
first frost of winter whitened the hills his thoughts often turned to frozen cataracts and
one in particular, Inaccessible Gully on Dove Crag, where he did the first winter ascent
cutting steps up its steep first pitch with a long-shafted ice-axe. (It is now a classic route
recommended in Dave Alcock's 'Cold Climbs'.)

Peascod and Birkett were not in the armed forces and were able to carry on creating
new routes throughout the war years. However, in Wales rocky inspiration dried up.
The sole Welsh climber to equal the Lakeland leaders, Menlove Edwards, produced
three superb creations in the early part of the war, Bow-Shaped Slab, Brant and
Slape; the latter two names being Cumbrian patois for steep and slippery. After these
routes, the Welsh cliffs remained untouched by inventive hands and had to wait for the
next generation. Edwards, the last active link with the pre-war Welsh generation,
whose powerful arms had plucked the rope fetters from Central Buttress was first
admitted to a mental hospital in 1944, after trying to kill himself. Despite climbing
occasionally he eventually comitted suicide in 1958.

The gap between climbing in the Lake District and in Wales seemed to be widening
even further as it had been for the previous six decades, until an unknown commando,
Chris Preston, changed the face of British climbing with Suicide Wall (E2, 5c) in Cwm
Idwal. His commanding officer David Cox, himself a distinguished climber, said it
would not have surprised him if Preston had jumped out of an aeroplane just to savour
the experience. Suicide Wall had defeated Kirkus and Edwards, and was the first E2 in
the British Isles. Jim Birkett almost certainly knew nothing about it in those days of no
climbing magazines; but almost at the same time he made his only visit to Helsby, a
defiant sandstone crag which juts out of the Cheshire plain. It houses a ferocious-
looking upper slab which had repelled all boarders. It had been named Morgue Slab,
and even defeated the redoubtable Arthur Birtwistle who had done the painfully thin
slab climb Diagonal on Dinas Mot in the Llanberis Pass.

One day during the war-ravaged years after the Luftwaffe had unloaded their bombs
on Liverpool, strange things happened to Morgue Slab. A visigoth drilled a hole in a
critical position,then wedged a piece of wood into the hole just above the overhang.
Fortunately, even with this aid he failed. The piece of wood fell out and the scene was
set for Birkett, who came, saw and conquered, even though a fall from the slabs could
have been fatal, and produced Morgue Slab, still thought to be 5c and which proves
by implication the high standards Birkett was setting in the Lake District. Like Preston,
the commando climber, Birkett had ushered in a harder level of climbing, the first
increase over the 5b standard which had been initiated three decades before in 1914
by Herford. In 1944 as the Allied forces stormed the Normandy beaches Birkett
returned to the high crags of Scafell where he had started his new route six years
before. Initially he was attracted to a vicious overhanging groove on the East Buttress
first noticed by Charlie Wilson and named by him Hell's Groove, but it was one of

Opposite: Above: Esk Buttress seen in early morning.
            Below left: Richard McHardy and Martin Boysen high on Medusa Wall (1947) in the 1960s.
            Below right: Richard McHardy on Central Pillar (1962).
                                                                    Photos: Bonington collection.

Birkett's rare failures and it had to wait for the lead team of the next generation, Dolphin and Greenwood in 1952. Not disheartened Birkett produced a clutch of thirteen new climbs during 1944 and 1945 on the East and Esk Buttresses, the most challenging of which was Great Central Route on Esk. He tried to overcome the awesomely steep central pillar, but realised that the final overhanging defences would need pitons; since Mayday climb he had not used them, so he veered off right and produced a four-hundred-foot Very Severe Great Central Climb.

By this time Charlie Wilson had been drafted into the Royal Air Force and was stationed near Harrogate. On a day's leave he went on his bicycle to Almscliffe and met a flaxen-haired youth who asked Charlie to climb with him; Charlie was amazed at his elegance and skill and afterwards wrote to Len Muscroft that he had met a young man who was as good as Jim Birkett. Muscroft replied loftily that no one was equal to the great quarry man, but Wilson's assessment had been correct. The youth was Arthur Dolphin and he was about to usher in a new era in Lakeland climbing.

Opposite: Above left: Eric;'Matey' Metcalf   Photo: R.B. Evans.
           Above right: Ginger Cain and Peter Greenwood on the wall at Wall End Barn in the early 1950s.   Photo: P.J. Greenwood.
           Below left: Nat Allen temporarily out of action.   Photo: Norman Rimmer.
           Below right: Ike Myers, owner of Wall End Barn.   Photo: P.J. Greenwood.

The Yorkshire Gazelle

Dolphin was in an entirely different mould from the seasoned Cumbrians, Birkett and Peascod. Fleet-footedness was in the family, and eventually he became a Yorkshire cross-country runner. His grandfather, the celebrated Wilfred Rhodes, has often been referred to as England's greatest cricketer. Dolphin was to carry on the great tradition of Yorkshire climbers such as Slingsby, Botterill and Frankland. His prodigious memory enabled him to gain a degree in metallurgy at Leeds University and he once won a bet when he memorised forty verses of 'The Rubaiyat of Omar Khayam' and repeated them word perfect.

At the tender age of fourteen the steel showed in him, when he led Deer Bield Crack in clinker-nailed boots, a route which had struck terror into hard men only a few years earlier. In 1944, the same year that he had so impressed Charlie Wilson at Almscliffe, he went to the Lake District with John Wilkinson, who was destined to be a future president of the Fell and Rock Club. John had borrowed a karabiner from a friend, and together they climbed Eliminates A, B and C, on Dow, followed by the thousand-foot girdle traverse, all in two days with the one karabiner between them and eternity if the leader fell. John remembers that they climbed past spike after spike, wondering if the hardest move was still to come, and often arrived at the next stance without using the precious karabiner.

In 1944 Dolphin started his new-route career with a modest Severe, Demon Wall, on the Tophet Wall of Great Gable, then the next day he did the Tophet Girdle, which was nearly four hundred feet long.

Those were difficult war-time days and it was another summer before Dolphin was able to get back to the Lakes, with Nocturne a pleasantly exposed Very Severe on Pallid Buttress, the best of four routes that he climbed in the year in which the war ended. By this time he was producing a torrent of routes on Yorkshire gritstone. That was still in an era when the high summer was expected to be a time for Alpine adventures. Unfortunately Dolphin suffered from mountain sickness which spoilt his trips above the high snowline and although restrictions were removed on travel to the continent soon after the war, he was also unlucky enough to be hampered by one of the most nauseating mountain complaints, and therefore became a rock specialist.

Athletic genes had been passed down to him via his cricketing grandfather, and his own physique was ideal. In addition his continual running helped his brilliance as Yorkshire's hardest climber. His feet were small, so when his tall frame was poised on small holds, the mechanical moment was reduced to a minimum. Some friends organised a finger-tip pull-up competition and eventually two of them, with difficulty, managed three. Arthur nonchalantly did seventeen. There were few climbers just after the Second World War, probably only a twentieth of today's numbers, and only a select few were able to follow the flaxen-haired Yorkshireman, so he started to solo climbs during rare Lakeland weekends when he had saved his meagre supply of petrol ration coupons for his large motor cycle. One wet day, wearing nailed boots, he soloed Gimmer Crack. There was a strong wind and, as a consequence of wearing a cycling cape, a gust of wind inflated the cape and blew him off. Somehow whilst still in mid-flight he managed a convulsive pirouette and landed on a small ledge. After composing himself he nonchalantly completed the ascent.

In addition to all his physical activity, art was important to him as an integral part of his life and he often went to the Halle Orchestra concerts and ballet. The Times Crossword was a daily challenge for such an active brain and not surprisingly names for new climbs were produced only after careful deliberation, often in a punning way:

'Gone forever are those carefree days of Route 1, Central Buttress and the North Ridge when a man could break new ground and enjoy himself secure in the knowledge that the route would name itself.....An occasional flash of genius stands out. Routes 1, 2 and Zero on Scout Crag were magnificently followed by 'J' — the root (or route) of minus one. Route 1.5 on the same Crag suggests dreadful possibilities, however! Another delightful example is Godiva Groove on Gimmer — a rather exposed route! On Raven Crag East we followed a similar line of least resistance with a Sherlock Holmes series. A hound which followed us up from the New Hotel, provided the inspiration for the first climb, Baskerville. The route which followed was comparatively elementary and naturally became Watson Wall. Mamba and Speckled Band were added later. We even sank to the 'Numerical' level of Routes 1 and 2, though we did use the Greek equivalents Protus and Deuterus. A weakness for feeble puns has been the basis for most of the rest. The name Kipling Groove (or wall or what have you) was long preserved for some route which could justly be described as ruddy ard; 'Whit's End was appropriate in more ways than one, but 'Garden Path' has been most inapt since the famous fire removed every vestige of vegetation from the Crag.' (White Ghyll)

He was no elitist and would climb with anyone, whatever their standard, even young boys such as Dennis Gray, who first saw him on a boy scouts' outing to Ilkley Moor. There Dennis became separated from the main group and wandered into Hanging Stones Quarry where a group of people was absorbed in watching Arthur climbing:

'A tall, athletic, white-haired man was balanced on what appeared to me a vertical holdless face. Nonchalantly he pulled a handkerchief out of his trouser pocket and blew his nose, to the delight of the watching climbers, and reminded me of a stage acrobat. He began to move upwards and this was somehow immediately different from a stage show; his ability, grace of movement, control and, above all, the setting high above ground, with no apparent safety devices, sent a thrill through my young body such as I had never before experienced. I had read about mountain climbing but my reaction hitherto had been indifference. One of the group whispered to a newcomer: "It's Dolphin!"'

Peascod was still pioneering in Buttermere and in 1946 he made an important discovery near the top of the Honister Pass, where a cliff reared above the waste from an abandoned slate quarry. Birkett had lived and worked in a quarry just a few hundred yards away but hadn't noticed it. Buckstone How had nearly three hundred feet of untouched rock, with elegant curving ribs, great bridging corners and alarmingly-embedded flakes. He started his probes on the last day of March 1946 with Bert Beck, who had just abandoned his khaki uniform, and the two of them unlocked the first gem which Peascod called Sinister Grooves, 'a climb distinguished by a smooth-walled dark-coloured corner which makes a perfect challenge for any V.S. leader'.

Two weeks later he discovered another important cliff. Eagle Crag is set in the hillside, high above the junction of Greenup Ghyll and Langstrath, where two tumbling rivers and connected crystal-clear pools meet. It is a lumpy cliff made of giant blocks split by sensuous cracks, waiting for Peascod to breathe life into them. Grassy

Opposite: The Hobbit (1969), Pavey Ark, seen in 1976.   Photo: Alan Hinkes.

eye-lashed ledges, whose fronds hung down to hide their virginity.

Bill's first inroad produced one of his best classic fissures, Falconer's Crack, which combined a strenuous struggle with delicate and bold face-climbing; and it was one of Peascod's major contributions to Borrowdale.

Birkett was far from idle and if anything the quality of his routes was increasing. He was attracted to the central upper mass of White Ghyll where overhangs sprout in profusion. Nearly six years had passed since Haggas had struggled to force Gordian Knot through its left-hand end, so Jim repeated it, and his quarry-trained muscles enabled him to pause on the crux to find an unused hold, which helped him to move with greater ease to better holds above. His own creation was White Ghyll Wall, which added another Very Severe to the cliff.

There followed the most bitter winter since 1895, when the River Thames had frozen over and bonfires had been lit on it. In early 1947 snow fell day after day, and trains became trapped on the line running over Shap Fell.

During that awful winter an old man died. During his life Millican Dalton hadn't been a good climber but he had loved the Lakeland crags and fells and gave up his job to be amongst them. He called himself the 'Professor of Adventure.' He had become a rock-climbing guide as early as 1905 and scandalised Edwardian climbing by introducing mixed camping on his guided holidays to the Lake District, Scotland and Switzerland. His home during the summer in Borrowdale was in a cave on the East side of Castle Crag where his friends could pinpoint his domain by the smoke from his wood fire. He gathered nuts to help his vegetarian diet and entertained his visitors by shooting the rapids on the Derwent on a home-made raft. In the winter he retired to Epping Forest and camped out there. He made his own clothes, which were held together with a red plaid and he crowned himself with a slouch hat pierced with a jaunty pheasant's feather. He climbed until his eightieth year and his cave can still be seen. Dr Mabel Barker described his philosophy of life:

'He did things on the rocks, as everywhere else, to please himself, but not for self-seeking; to fit in with his theory of life, and of earth and his relation to it. He believed that people (astronomers included) were 'shutting their eyes to the foundations of the universe'. Perhaps he was wiser than most of us, and his long and happy life indeed trod a pathway to the stars.'

In late March the icy stillness ended in Lakeland. Billions of tiny ice crystals collapsed, and the valleys were flooded. Melt water filled the becks to flood-level and the greenery of the fells appeared once again, still flattened from the crushing effect of deep snow. Throughout the spring the temperature kept rising until in the high summer it was so hot that the tar melted on the Kirkstone Pass road, forming sticky rivulets that flowed imperceptibly towards Ambleside. It was that rare year when even the wettest places dry out and hitherto damp cracks become climbable. On the first day of May, exactly nine years after Birkett had entered the hard league, he went to Castle Rock of Triermain, eight years since his last new route on the main crag. His objective was a natural vertical gutter, which was normally damp and smelly but a natural line that had to be climbed. The dry spell enabled him to produce May Day Cracks. Twenty-one days later during the Whitsun weekend, there was intense activity in Langdale; firstly, Birkett was drawn back to White Ghyll where he produced Slip Knot, then just across the valley on Side Pike, Dolphin was hard at work on a new route followed by yet another the following day. He completed the trio with a typically-named Dolphin creation on Gimmer Crag — Whit's End. It was parallel to and strenuously similar to

Opposite: Rick Graham on the crux bulge of Fallen Angel (1972) Pavey Ark, first done in 1972 by Ed Grindley and Ian Roper.

Photo: Al Phizacklea.

Birkett's 'F' Route. It was with this route that Dolphin really started to stamp his name on Lakeland rock tablets.

Peascod was not left behind during that glorious summer, and was drawn back to Buckstone How where he produced Groove Two, an uninspiring name, but an excellent production. Its ninety-foot hard pitch gave Peascod cause for concern and this sentiment was echoed by many leaders who came after him, in the days before the advent of modern protection.

'Upward progress was noticeable by its total cessation for a while. I picked at the fine pebbles jammed in the base of the groove, searching enthusiastically for a handhold; and finally my determination was rewarded by the unearthing of a tiny fingerhold, above the bulge, just big enough to take the tips of two fingers. With a heave I pulled on the tiny hold and got a knee jammed into the bottom of the main groove proper; an awkward shuffle or two followed and then I was standing up at last in the groove. It stretched up above me for another unbroken, unprotected seventy feet. But even though it was steep and somewhat strenuous, the climbing was straightforward until I reached the very top of the groove — and there on the sloping ledge, at which the groove ended abruptly, was a mass of fine quarry debris. Give me grass or heather any time on which to debouch but may the Mountain Gods protect me from landing on masses of small stones — or thick mud.'

In August 1947 Birkett and Dolphin both went to Esk Buttress each thinking what could be moulded from its buttresses. The cliff faces south-east and when the Scafell cliffs swirl in mist, Esk buttress, much lower, can be lit up by the sun and will dry quickly. Dolphin did two routes there, Gargoyle Groove and Medusa Wall. The latter a three-hundred-foot high quality route, was an exposed Very Severe. A week later Birkett produced Square Chimney, and had a look at the unclimbed central pillar; but it was fifteen years before it succumbed. Finally he signed off the year on Dow Crag, with his precarious Leopard's Crawl, his first new route on the cliff for seven years. The pockmarked wall has a frightening lack of protection and in the Sixties it was usual to put up to six karabiners on one sling to protect the precarious moves up the scoop, as there were sharp-edged rocks waiting not far below.

In 1948 Dolphin came, saw, and conquered. The head wall of the North-West face of Gimmer Crag is bounded on the left by the piece de resistance of the Thirties, Gimmer Crack, and on the right by Birkett's test-piece layback 'F' Route. There was an obvious entry under an overhang. Birkett had abseiled down, cleaned away some of the loose rock and vegetation and talked about its charms to Dolphin, who then top-roped it several times. During Whitsun weekend 1948 he did three new climbs in three days, the first on Pavey Ark, which broke through The Barrier in a Very Severe way, wandered about for three hundred feet and was finally called Alph for reasons which he described:

'The magnificent weather of Whitsuntide '48 enabled us to do three new climbs in as many days. The first was up a corner on the left of Asterisk. It looked such an obvious route for it to have been by-passed for so long that the name Samaritan Corner was an obvious choice. A wandering route on Pavey Ark the following day had us baffled until we remembered the river of Kubla Khan; 'five miles meandering with a mazy motion,' and made the climb its namesake. The holiday reached its climax with the ascent of Kipling Groove, and on the final day we were even content to sunbathe in perfect weather. We couldn't have climbed anyway — we had exhausted our stock of names!'

Opposite: Arthur Dolphin and J.R. Lockwood making the historic 1st ascent of Kipling Groove, Gimmer Crag, in 1948. Photos: M.F. Blake.

Kipling Groove (so-named because it was ruddy 'ard) was one of Dolphin's most courageous leads; he was criticised for top-roping it, but there were many precedents. He was climbing new routes on rocks steeper and more continuously difficult than previous hard climbs. Central Buttress, Black Wall, Moss Ghyll Grooves and Gimmer Crack had all been top-roped by stars of previous generations. Dolphin's own guide-book description of Kipling Groove summed up its problems:

'Extreme severity and a high degree of exposure combine to make the route the most serious undertaking in the district.'

At the same time it was probably the most serious climb in the Lake District. One of the problems of the Nineteen-Forties was that all the hard climbs were bracketed together under the Very Severe umbrella and there were no technical gradings, so Dolphin decided that in his guide-book he would include a graded list, and Kipling Groove was at the top of it.

The previous week Birkett had revisited the upper wall of White Ghyll, to produce Haste Not, an incredibly undercut traverse with an unusual crux which entailed a slide down a holdless rib, which later caused even the mercurial Don Whillans to adjust the rim of his cloth cap several times before he managed to do it.

Three months later Birkett went back up to Scafell where he had started producing new routes a decade before. Slab and Groove was his last masterpiece, an immaculate face which angles leftwards out of the upper reaches of Moss Ghyll. Until small wired nuts were invented its main pitch was unprotected.

As the quarryman walked down the scree he could not have realised that his new routes on the high crags were over. The man who had done a backward somersault in nailed boots was soon to be afflicted by his family complaint of arthritis.

1948 was just as remarkable for Bill Peascod, as he had just passed his colliery management exams after seven years' study. He was appointed ventilation manager at Whitehaven Colliery and two years later started teaching at Workington Technical College, where he met George Rushworth, an ideal partner in both strength and sense of humour.

In 1948 he produced a dozen new routes in Buttermere and Newlands, far more than either Birkett or Dolphin. On Eagle Crag in Buttermere an unclimbed fissure split the cliff from top to bottom. It had even attracted the flying Scotsman — Harold Raeburn, who had tried and failed as early as 1918. Peascod had two failures before his successful foray with Bert Beck, the third man being George Rushworth. They gathered for the final attempt with Peascod travelling on a bicycle and carrying his nailed boots. He later described their epic:

'Without incident we reached the major problem (or so we thought). This is a steep chimney, with the left wall overhanging badly and the right wall cut away about half its height into a small sloping ledge. The top of the chimney also leans out, and at that time a large cannon of rock stuck out at the top of the cleft, barring progress. After ascending on to the ledge on the right I managed to work onto the groove formed by the left wall and the back of the chimney, and with difficulty and considerable thought for those below I worked over the cannon which was dangerously loose. After climbing above it I sent it hurtling down to the screes below, to join the rest of its companions. Above this the chimney was still steep, but in ninety feet it eased off, and a comforting belay was reached. We were now in an overhung cleft, with a narrow exit between the overhang and the right wall. The exit, guarded as it was

Opposite: Slab and Groove, Scafell Crag, Birkett's fine final contribution to the crag, done in 1948. Photo: Ian Roper.

by an intimidating bulge, proved to me to be the most awkward section of the climb. This pitch is also an anxious one for the leader because of its tricky landing, and ascent of rounded slabs to a corner. The pitch is eighty feet long and the belay is reached thankfully. Once there, however, all is over.'

The route is rarely climbed now from the bottom to the top but if it is approached via one of Peascod's harder routes, Fifth Avenue, its upper pitches make a storming finish on the summit plateau of the mountain.
Peascod's new responsibilities for mine safety influenced his thinking about safety on the crags. When he and his group were storm-bound in a barn at Gatesgarth they used to discuss better rope techniques and the barn with its roof trusses and stacked hay bales below provided an excellent indoor test facility whilst the weather raged outside. They jumped off, simulated unconsciousness and, as a result of their investigations, devised the Gatesgarth Sling which Peascod described:

> 'It was made out of one continuous piece of three-quarter weight nylon rope. It comprised a waist loop and braces which crossed at the back between the shoulder blades; the braces then passed over the shoulders and were attached to the waist loop through 'eyes' spliced into the rope ends. The assembly was held together at the front by a screw-lock karabiner and the leader's rope was attached to a second karabiner (which clipped over the braces where they crossed) by means of a Tarbuck Knot — a sliding knot which permitted some give or elongation in the rope, in the event of a fall. (This is achieved, these days, by using ropes of greater elasticity.) The difference between hanging from a waist-loop and the Gatesgarth Sling was tremendous.'

The Gatesgarth Sling was really a prototype body harness and Bill used one for several years; its modern equivalent was not developed for another twenty-five years, when Don Whillans thought along similar lines.
Peascod carried on climbing throughout the year and one winter night, bound for Wasdale he stopped to shelter in a coalhouse of a farm to have some soup. This was contained in a self-heating can, a relic of war-time army rations. When it was ready he discovered that he hadn't a cup and as the tin was too hot to use he decided to put the contents into a new rubber plimsoll. However, not surprisingly, the combination of hot soup tainted with fresh rubber proved to be rather repugnant and was not to his liking.
Near the end of his Buttermere career, as he began to think of trying to go to Australia for better pay and a freer life, he was drawn to an imposing unclimbed face on Buckstone How, next to Groove Two. The weather was good, he was feeling in top form, and the climb was one of his best creations despite some problems:

> 'Suddenly, I thought of 'combined tactics'. With Brian standing on the bracket and a now utterly useless belay underneath us I climbed on to his shoulders, made a couple of airy moves, then got the hold. It stayed secure. With a whoop of delight I was up the difficulty and I hung on to decent holds whilst Brian climbed down off the top of the bracket to get himself belayed again. Then I moved on. Up the wall the third overhangs were reached easily and I traversed under them to the left to a good belay. The stance to accompany the belay was rudimentary but adequate — and I called for Brian to join me. When he reached me I moved out up the wall to the left then, in about twenty feet, moved back once more to the right, via a delightful, though short traverse, into the shattered groove immediately above the third line of overhangs. The left hand wall of this groove led straight to the top of the crag — it was all

air and light and joy. We called the climb 'Cleopatra'. The date was 18 May 1951. It was one of the best new climbs I ever did...What is it that Shakespeare said about 'Age cannot wither her nor custom stale her infinite variety...?'

Peascod emigrated to Australia the year after, and when his educational career came to an end began to paint as an artist full-time. Thoughts of his beloved Buttermere gnawed at him for nearly thirty years, until he returned to live in the Lake District with his second wife and took up Lakeland climbing with all his old gusto. He put up six new routes in Buttermere between 1981 and 1984 and died in 1985 on the Great Slab on Clogwyn du'r Arddu in company with Don Whillans and Bill Birkett, Jim's son.

After Peascod's efforts in 1948 the scene was set for an even bigger explosion of activity in 1949. There was a six-week conquering surge by Jim Birkett in May and June, when Lakeland is at its best. It was his last flourish, on one of his favourite crags — White Ghyll. In the boulder-filled gully at the foot of the crag, his eyes were drawn to an obvious leftward traverse line crowned at its end by a shallow corner. This was Perhaps Not, which made even Arthur Dolphin comment in his guide-book that 'faith in what may be above is required when the holds disappear'. Thirty years later the phrase is still used to describe the precarious chimney pitch. It was listed as the sixth hardest route in Langdale when Dolphin's guide-book came out. Just a month later, in a seven-day period Birkett did his last two hard climbs; the first, on White Ghyll, Do Not, followed an unknown prow to the right of his Slip Knot. On the crux, the rope dangled clear from his waist for dozens of feet, and needed steady nerves to deal with a lack of runners, danger and not least the difficult sequence of moves.

A week later on Castle Rock of Triermain he put up his last hard route — Harlot Face (E1 5b), the first climb of that standard in the Lake District, whose main difficulties consisted of grappling with an overhanging groove, followed by an even more alarming series of ape-like swings round an undercut rib. It seems right that the tough quarryman bowed out of his leading role with his hardest route. He never fell off, climbed neatly in nailed boots, and left only the faintest scratch on the rock after using a small hold. He retreated in good order from such major lines of the future, as Gimmer String, Extol, and Sidewalk when, as he put it, 'things got a bit out of hand.' He also knew that Heron Crag in Eskdale had superb unclimbed lines but peregrines nested there, so it never occurred to him to disturb them.

Perhaps dealing with rock in all its colours and shapes, both at work and play, caused a friend to say that he had 'rock in his blood', which Jim took as a compliment. Harlot Face is like the man who put it up — as it is hard, has uncompromising steepness and should be treated with respect.

In the autumn attention focussed on an independent start to Birkett's flying top pitch of Do Not, at the steeply-grooved centre of White Ghyll's lower crag. There is an ugly-looking curving open groove. Dolphin top-roped it, then failed to lead it and instead held the rope for one of his friends, fleet-footed fell-runner Ken Heaton, a previously unknown climber who produced the first E1 5b pitch in Langdale. Heaton carried on doing new routes, particularly on the Neckband Crag, a gloomy and steep little cliff high up on Bowfell; but none of his routes was equal in difficulty or significance to his epoch-making pitch in White Ghyll. Eventually he became even more proficient at fell-running and in 1961 became the holder of the Lakeland 24-hour record, and covered 51 summits in 22 hours 13 minutes, striding 82 miles and 81000 feet of ascent in the process. Sadly, as with Birkett, but more acutely, his limbs were seized by arthritis and running and climbing are no longer possible for him.

In 1950 Dolphin was heavily involved in work to produce his Langdale guide-book. In its historical section he mentioned only one of his own routes, Kipling Groove, but lavished praise on Birkett's achievements in the valley. A year later, 1951 was to be the year when a great change came over Lakeland climbing.

Far away in Wales, a short dark-haired Manchester plumber — Joe Brown was transforming Welsh climbing after having set new high-standard climbs in the Peak District. His first new route in Wales was Hangover (E1 5b) on Clogwyn y Grochan, which was repeated three weeks later by Peter Greenwood, supported by the Drasdo brothers, Harold and Neville. The three of them were part of a small Yorkshire group which came to be known as the Bradford Lads. They were a happy-go-lucky bunch of young working lads, who were all keen on climbing. The effect of Greenwood and Harold Drasdo on Lakeland climbing was profound. There had been working-class climbers before, but never as cohesive a group as the Bradford Lads. Several factors influenced them; petrol rationing ended at Whitsuntide 1950, so that there were more vehicles on the roads to the Lake District and a better chance of hitch-hiking there. Just as important was the introduction of the five-day week. By leaving on a Friday night from Bradford, two full days were possible in the Lake District. The Bradford Lads became aware of Brown's brilliance on rock and his relentless new-route drive, as he narrated his hair-raising exploits in mesmeric flat Mancunian tones, punctuated with frequent smiles. There are few people who automatically entrance an audience, Brown is such a person.

His enormous output of new routes has not been done by strength alone. He was one of the weaker members of the original Rock and Ice. Joe (Mortimer) Smith could do fifteen press-ups with a girl sitting on his back whereas Joe Brown was unable even to move with the same burden and was only able to do three pull-ups. However he could hold himself in a one-arm locked-off position for one minute, a far more important attribute on hard climbs. The most brilliant leader of the Bradford Lads was Peter Greenwood. As a teenager his main interest had been ballroom dancing, until one night a girl he fancied took more interest in some climbing photographs of another youth. Greenwood sniffed contemptuously and said there was nothing to it, so the climbing youth took him to Ilkley Quarry and took Peter up several V. Diff. climbs, then asked for a top-rope on a Very Severe — Josephine Super-Direct, which Greenwood then promptly soloed to the astonishment of the watchers, including sundry members of the Bradford Lads. The youth who had climbed with him gained reflected glory by announcing, 'my protege!' Paul Ross who later often climbed with Greenwood named him Rubberlegs because of their remarkable suppleness in severe situations. Even thirty years later he can still fold them into the full Lotus position, rock over on to his knees and walk around the floor.

Greenwood was to turn into a brilliant climber and became a regular member of the Bradford Lads. When he heard that Kneewrecker Chimney was the hardest climb in Langdale, he immediately did it, even though it was winter, with snow on the ground. Next day he met Arthur Dolphin, who told him that Kipling Groove held the ultimate accolade. They became firm friends and climbing companions, one of the most powerful post-war teams in the Lake District. In the winter of 1950 Joe Brown made the third ascent of Kipling Groove, the second ascent having been done by George Shields, a Scots climber. Brown knocked in a piton to protect the crux moves, on the grounds that the run-out was unjustified.

The Bradford Lads met every Sunday night in Tommy's Cafe in Otley, where they related their weekend's deeds. The scene was set for one of climbing's greatest stories.

Opposite: Above: The masterly Haggas solution — The Gordian Knot. White Ghyll.   Photo: C. Douglas Milner.
                Below: John Hartley leading Do Not (1949). White Ghyll.   Photo: J. Hartley collection.

One Sunday evening Harold Drasdo burst through the door and dramatically announced; "Joe Brown's done Kipling Groove and put a peg in." For a few seconds there was a stunned silence then Greenwood said grimly, "Something's got to be done."

Next weekend a large audience watched Greenwood redeem the honour of White Rose climbing. As he reached Brown's illicit piton, he paused, spat on it, then efficiently finished the climb. Far below, the watching crowd clapped and cheered and thus brought to an end a dramatic episode which was one of Brown's very few errors.

The protection available to Dolphin was still sketchy by modern standards as John Wilkinson has pointed out:

> 'In the immediate post-war years, however, more climbers were beginning to realise the value of the running belay for protection, and karabiners were at last becoming available. The ex-War Department karabiners proved of doubtful value as they had a tendency to open up under strain, but karabiners of improved quality imported from Europe were gradually becoming available. Even by the end of the decade, however, leaders were still carrying only a pitifully small number of slings and karabiners. Most climbers were reluctant to use pitons, and their single hemp ropes had inadequate strength, so it is scarcely surprising that the number of high-standard routes climbed during this period did not rise appreciably: the leader simply could not afford a fall. Indeed it is a remarkable tribute to the ability and courage of climbers of the period up to 1950 that so many hard routes were made with such poor protection.'

The start of Arthur Dolphin's renaissance was on Deer Bield Crag, where Dick Barry had fought so hard before the Second World War. Dolphin produced Deer Bield Buttress (E1 5b), which had a much greater concentration of difficulties than anything which had been done before in the Lake District. The technical grade was thought to be 5c by the star of the Seventies — Peter Livesey.

Dolphin realised that the new working-class climbers, who although adopting a Rabelaisian life style, were as determined as he was in new-route exploration in both Wales and the Lake District. He became more dedicated, and the quality and difficulty of his new routes gradually increased. It is fitting that Harold Drasdo should make the logical analysis of Dolphin's Deer Bield Buttress:

> 'Deer Bield Buttress ranks as one of Dolphin's best half-dozen climbs, but it ought not to be taken as his monument. In a curious way, though, it imitates almost exactly something personal in his style of climbing, an athletic series of transfers and re-establishments between strenuous moves and delicate positions: at the same time it catches a less open aspect of his nature, lonely, separate, puritanical, uncompromising.'

Just afterwards Greenwood was waiting at the Old Dungeon Ghyll to get the bus back to Ambleside when Dolphin appeared, pushed a piece of paper into his top pocket, smiled and said, "Try that". It contained a description of Deer Bield Buttress. Greenwood was eager to try it, and even though it was a wet day for his attempt he was not discouraged. On the first pitch a block which Peter was using for a layback move, became more detached, just missed the second man Fred Williams, and chopped twenty feet off the rope. Still, Greenwood persisted and later described his traumatic ascent:

Opposite: Above: Deer Bield Buttress, Dolphin's 1951 solution to an outstanding problem.   Photo: Ian Roper.
           Below: Arthur Dolphin (seated wearing white rubbers) and Peter Greenwood with a somewhat casual group.
                                                                                    Photo: Peter Greenwood.

'What we should have done is what you do today and said "Bugger this." On the overhanging corner (the first crux, and of a technical grade as hard as anything then climbed in Britain) I'd my legs stretched out across the walls. My socks were worn out by now, I couldn't get a grip, I needed to get up and I needed to get down. This solution came to me. Take off the dirty wet sock, hold it in my teeth, take off the plimsoll, hold it in my teeth, put on the plimsoll, put the sock back on top. Which I managed to do. And I did the same procedure a few moves later with the other one...On the second crux a block had come out and formed a gangway with a roof on it. Somehow you had to get a hold on this shiny, slippery roof to reach up to these good holds above. The more I tried the more my bloody hands were slipping off until I was going 'Pfftt' and passing down the crag. No problem, Freddy held me all right. I collected my wits and said, "Are you going to have a go, Fred?" "Am I hell!"

On the last hard moves there was an awkward roof. Greenwood managed to use his rubbery legs to jam a knee in the exact place where he had fallen. A final mantelshelf, then success. They danced jigs and sang all the way back to the Dungeon Ghyll and brewed up on a primus stove in the bar. The landlord, Sid Cross, came to throw them out, but when he learned what they had done, told them to carry on. Much has been made of Joe Brown's abilities in awful conditions. Greenwood's efforts that day, on the second ascent of Deer Bield Buttress, were just as remarkable.

Greenwood gave up climbing more than thirty years ago, he has drunk twenty thousand pints of beer and smoked five hundred thousand cigarettes, but this has not crippled his prehensile legs or his twinkling anarchistic sense of humour. He recalls that he once 'acquired' a cafe sign in Ingleton and produced it proudly to the Bradford lads on the bus they had hired to take them to the Lake District. Inevitably the long arm of the law caught up with him and a court appearance the following Friday in the Lake District got him to Langdale many hours before his law-abiding friends.

At the end of the 1951 season Dolphin did another E1 5b — Babylon, on East Raven Crag in Langdale. He did it with his girlfriend, Marie Ball, who was the first woman to be on the first ascent of a climb of that grade; a fine celebration of her twenty-first birthday. She had a struggle on the crux until Arthur gently pointed out that she was still clipped into a running belay below her. In typical Dolphin manner the name was inspired because of hanging gardens of vegetation below the overhangs through which the route cleaves. Dolphin couldn't have been more different than Greenwood; he had a schoolboy sense of humour, and a love of classical music and poetry which might have made him an object of fun to hearty climbers. In fact Greenwood idolised him because of his climbing achievements and when the year after Dolphin's death, Paul Ross decided to solo Kipling Groove, Greenwood seized him and snarled, "You leave Arthur's routes alone". He had no intention of letting another tear-away like himself sully the memory of his dead hero.

Another autumnal E1, Rubicon Groove, had been discovered by Dolphin on Bowfell. It was the third high-standard discovery of the year. The Lakes climbers were responding to the brave new climbing world that the Rock and Ice stars were fashioning in Wales. 1952 was equally productive, and on a very hot day in May, Greenwood and Dolphin went to try a tempting exposed traverse leading high across onto the East Buttress of Scafell. Dolphin thought for a brief period that he had found the first Severe on the crag, but then his routes got harder and harder, until he had to put in a piton with a long sling for aid. When Greenwood followed he was able to dispense with the aid. The name was in the best Dolphin tradition; and as the climb was peg-assisted the route came to be called Pegasus.

Opposite: Above: Nat Allen (standing left) on a typical Wasdale weekend in 1950.   Photo: J.R. Nat. Allen.
            Below: Wall End Barn and climbers.   Photo: Harold Drasdo.

Next weekend they were back on the East Buttress to try the overhanging crack which had been named Hell's Groove by Charlie Wilson, and which had defeated Jim Birkett. On the overhang near the start Greenwood clung on with a knee-jam as on Deer Bield Buttress, while he felt for handholds above. When Dolphin got to the same point he was unable to rest and although harrassed managed to lead the next pitch.

There was still a lot of daylight left, so Dolphin suggested a look at Esk Buttress's unclimbed Central Pillar. He abseiled down to inspect the line of the route, having told Greenwood that he would tie onto the abseil rope and climb up the untouched section. Unfortunately the rope did not reach a ledge, communication was impossible, and Greeenwood had no idea that Arthur was dangling in space at the end of the abseil rope, frantically trying to tie a bowline knot. After what seemed to be an eternity he climbed up to join a puzzled Greenwood. They both liked Esk Buttress and decided on the second ascent of Birkett's Girdle Traverse. Dolphin made the journey to Eskdale on his Gold Star motorcycle, one of the first in Yorkshire. He found that it would only reach 98 mph, took it to pieces, polished the vital parts which others hadn't reached, reassembled it, and consequently reached 105 mph. Despite this tuning the bike would not even take a passenger up Wrynose Pass, and Don Hopkins had to puff up the steep road behind, whilst Greenwood ran to the cliff from Langdale. It was November so they led through quickly. The climb was nearly six hundred feet long, and not surprisingly darkness started to close in while they were on the last pitch. Greenwood was anxious to get back to the Langdale pub and asked to lead, then promptly unroped and galloped off. When it came to Dolphin's turn, shod in nailed boots, it was completely dark and he and Hopkins were benighted. Greenwood comfortably esconced in the pub, became more concerned the later it got, and drank on and on. He was greatly relieved when a chilly Dolphin turned up the following morning.

One day in the summer of 1952 Greenwood went to Bowfell and saw a large area of steep unclimbed rock on the north-east-facing crag above Flat Crags. He returned with Dolphin to try a line on the highest of its three grooves. Its main feature was a slender jammed flake, which led Dolphin to call the climb Sword of Damocles (E1 5b). Unfortunately the slender pinnacle crashed to the rocks below during the early 1980s leaving the scabbard bare, but still climbable. The following year the Everest Expedition was selected and Dolphin's name was not amongst those who were chosen. Greenwood was incensed that his hero had not been included and proclaimed in Tommy's cafe in Otley that he had just left the best British climber in the bar of Dungeon Ghyll. On the day Everest was climbed, by a Sherpa and a New Zealander, Greenwood put up a new route on Raven Crag, Thirlmere and called it Anarchist as an anti-establishment gesture.

A fortnight later another of the Bradford Lads made a major contribution to Lakeland climbing. Harold Drasdo is an intellectual and could not have been more different from Greenwood. Drasdo has thought deeply about the contorted thought process of climbers and mountaineers, their failures, deceits and triumphs, and written about the resultant behaviour patterns. In September 1952, however, he was still in the bloom of youth with thoughts firmly fixed on new Lake District rock. He had done a new route on Castle Rock of Triermain, Barbican, and noticed that jackdaws kept disappearing behind a flake, on an awesomely steep wall. He reasoned that the flake would supply a superb running belay and might provide the key to a route. He and his brother returned to garden the climb and managed to get up the first two pitches. Then Harold returned with sixteen-year-old Dennis Gray who had just bought

Opposite: Above left: Joe Brown in the early 1950s.   Photo: N. Rimmer.
            Above right: Joe Brown laybacking up a free-standing pole at Wall End, Langdale in September 1951.   Photo: George Kitchin.
            Below: Merrick 'Slim' Sorrell supporting Joe Brown and Peter Cargill, September, 1951.   Photo: George Kitchin.

a new nylon rope. They stayed in a scout hut the night before; where Harold tried to impress the young teenager with gripping tales of adventure of Anderl Heckmair and Giusto Gervasutti to indoctrinate themselves for the forthcoming struggles.

The following day all went well until the middle of the third pitch, where a sturdy yew tree reaches up to a line of overhangs. Harold sprang from its topmost twigs, seized the overhang, and was up; but Dennis was so small that he was unable to reach any holds. Harold instructed him to sway the tree, and at the point of maximum arc to project himself up to the overhangs. Dennis complied, clung to a hold, and reached Drasdo, who then lay-backed up the jackdaws' flake, draped it with a running belay and stepped on to a narrow gangway. The top part led round an arete to a superb traverse crack, then to a niche, where he banged in a piton with a stone. North Crag Eliminate (E1 5b) is probably his finest creation in a long line of new routes all over the Eastern fells. It became one of only eleven Cumbrian routes picked for the classic book 'Hard Rock', and was always crowded on a good weekend. Recently two young Scots did it, and when the leader got to the jackdaw flake, he was unsure of the next moves. Unbelievably and with some difficulty he pulled 'Hard Rock' from inside his shirt, nearly one hundred cubic inches of climbing literature which had been jammed against his chest. He consulted it, pushed it back in place and finished the climb, convincing at least one spectator that care with money was still important to young Scots.

Drasdo is one of the few people to analyse stress in association with rock and mountains in general, and has contributed numerous essays on this theme:

'Now at one time, the threat of a fall was a very serious one and almost always involved a risk to life; but, with the development of pegs, nuts and tapes for aid in one type of climbing, and for protection in another, there are now many climbs in which the chance of falling means no more than the chance of a short and harmless drop. At the same time, such climbing offers the satisfaction of the most dramatic situations in which a man can find himself. And, since even the shortest and most painless fall is an exhilarating and stimulating experience, these routes can purge the 'worry-potential' of a climber perfectly. So a sort of substitute has been invented to replace the climber's historical exposure to real risks, although he may, of course, still carry out climbs of great technical difficulty.....it might be claimed that cliffs and mountains are facades without shape or dimension until they are floodlit by human effort. Just as the Prince wakes the Sleeping Beauty so the climber's touch brings the cliff to life. The more it is worked over, the more aspects are revealed and the more secrets suggested. And this mystery is never diminished. Every storm, every change in the weather resurrects and reasserts it.....Climbs interpret mountain faces. A climb is the most human relationship possible with a mountain face. Climbs amplify the persona of a mountain. The more effort has been expended, the more increment to the mountain's character. The Hornli Ridge is not desecrated by those half million climbers who have ascended it. It is hallowed. The mountain might even be considered a holy place, as in many cultures it has been. The climber reveres each detail, he knows it as a monk knows his abbey or as a curator of an historic monument knows the parts of his building. Even on the meanest gritstone escarpment on the darkest foggiest winter afternoon he tells off the buttresses, corners and gullies one after the other, name by name or presence by presence as he passes underneath them. And every feature is charged with meaning...British climbers use the expression 'cheating' in two ways. First, we joke that we are cheating when we use more assistance than is usual; but by this self-accusation we resign from the contest and clear ourselves. Second, we cheat when we don't tell the truth about the aid we've used. The opportunities for this on smaller crags have become less with population pressure. But even on British cliffs there can

Opposite: George Smith at full stretch on Rob Matheson's Holocaust (1971/75), Dow Crag.   Photo: Al Phizacklea.

be few leading climbers who have never found themselves with a foot 'caught in a sling', 'whilst gardening holds', maybe. And if any essential aid has been admitted to, dispensable aid is less likely to be recorded.'

1953 was to be a year of extremes in more senses than one. Dolphin had always suffered from altitude sickness and in 1953 was determined to overcome it. He went to work on a glaciological project high on Monte Rosa and the lengthy time he spent at altitude suggested that he had at last overcome his problem. To prove it he did the Gervasutti route on the Petit Capucin, then the first British ascent of the South Face of the Dent du Geant, graded T.D. and one of the harder climbs in the area. On the descent he slipped on an easy ice slope and was instantly killed.

Dolphin like many Lakeland stars, died an early death. As with Dolphin O.G. Jones had died in the Alps, whereas Linnell had died on Ben Nevis. A.T.Hargreaves on the other hand was killed ski-ing. Of those who did not die whilst in the hills, Herford was killed in the trenches, Botterill was poisoned with T.N.T. and Bert Gross committed suicide. It is very unusual for top climbers to meet their deaths on high-standard climbs.

For the next year or two there was no front-rank team based in Cumbria and some of the most notable leads were made by the Rock and Ice. The formidable trio of Brown, Whillans and Moseley went to the Castle Rock of Triermain, to look at the vicious-looking groove that Birkett had attempted when he had done Harlot Face. He had made a few moves up it, then decided to make the big swing out to the right. Joe had the first try, and inserted chockstones combined with running belays, then retreated when he was tired, and Whillans took over. This was to be the style of many of their joint first ascents, first Brown then Whillans, whose phenomenal strength enabled him to stop and rest in the most exacting conditions. Inserted chockstones had been used before, but the Rock and Ice had brought it to a fine art. Whillans led the climb, but when it was Joe's turn a hold broke off. The rock was so overhanging that he swung into space and had to be lowered back to the belay ledge. He then climbed it in its entirety. They called the route Triermain Eliminate (E1 5b) and the guide-book description might well describe its originators rather than the route — 'uncompromisingly fierce'.

Because Brown had fallen off the climb it acquired a tremendous reputation. Their next effort was an awe-inspiring expanse of rock to the left of Haggas's Hangover. On Dove Crag Harold Drasdo, supported by Dennis Gray tackled an obvious groove, but failed. Soon after Gray told Joe Brown about the exciting possibilities. Once again it was Whillans who led the pitch after using a sling on a flake on the left wall of the initial groove. Unfortunately the flake broke off and others who tried to repeat it by using a sling in approximately the same place, were brought face to face with a dangerously-poised block. Joe and Don called the route Dovedale Grooves (E1 5b) and a decade went by before it was repeated by the leaders of the next Welsh wave of exploration, Peter Crew and Barry Ingle.

Ron Moseley did Pendulum on Deer Bield Crag, using novel techniques involving a rope pendule from a piton placed by abseil. When the Rock and Ice came back from their Alpine holidays in Chamonix, Moseley started with Dight (E1 5b) on Gimmer Crag, which is short, hard and exposed. A fortnight later, Brown, Moseley and Tom Waghorn tackled a deep right-angled corner to the right of Do Not, on White Ghyll. It was roofed by overhangs and Brown had to tension out right to get round them. When it came to Waghorn's turn he was ordered to remove the sling and swing into space; when he objected the only response was peels of laughter, hence the name — Laugh

Opposite: The Graduate (1971/79). Deer Bield Crag.   Photo: Rob Matheson.

Not.

Next day Whillans and Moseley rounded off the Rock and Ice Lakeland year with a girdle traverse of Deer Bield Crag which included Pendulum. Lakeland climbing had never had so many new Extremes in one year solely due to the Manchester-based group.

The Lake District had dominated British climbing since the inception of the sport by Haskett Smith seventy years earlier. A comparison of the Extreme climbs in Wales and the Lake District up to 1953 suggests how standards were evolving:

WALES

1930 Javelin Blade	E1 5b	Jack Longland
1945 Suicide Wall	E2 5c	Chris Preston
1948 Overlapping Wall	E1 5c	Mervyn Hughes
1951 Hangover	E1 5b	Joe Brown
1951 Vember	E1 5b	Joe Brown
1951 Cemetery Gates	E1 5b	Brown/Whillans
1952 Black Cleft	E1 5b	Brown/Whillans
1952 Pinnacle Flake	E1 5b	Joe Brown
1952 Bloody Slab	E2 5b	John Streetly
1952 Cenotaph Corner	E1 5b	Joe Brown
1953 Surplomb	E1 5b(aid)	Brown/Whillans
1953 The Grooves	E1 5b	Joe Brown

LAKE DISTRICT

1949 Do Not	E1 5b	Ken Heaton/Jim Birkett
1949 Harlot Face	E1 5b	Jim Birkett
1951 Deer Bield Buttress	E1 5b	Arthur Dolphin
1951 Rubicon Groove	E1 5b	Arthur Dolphin
1952 Hell's Groove	E1 5b	Greenwood/Dolphin
1952 Sword of Damocles	E1 5b	Dolphin/Greenwood

Tony Greenbank, one of the Yorkshire Austin team on Langdale rock.

Photo: R.B. Evans.

1952 North Crag Eliminate	E1 5b	Harold Drasdo
1953 Dovedale Groove	E1 5b	Don Whillans
1953 Triermain Eliminate	E1 5b	Don Whillans
1953 Dight	E1 5b	Ron Moseley

There was almost the same number of Extreme climbs in both climbing grounds with just the edge of difficulty in Wales, but with a much greater abundance of climbs in the Very Severe bracket in the Lake District.

Opposite: Nearing the end of the exposed traverse of Ron Moseley's 1953 route The Pendulum, E2, on Deer Bield Crag.   Photo: Ian Roper.

Brian Evans crossing Kipling Groove on the Gimmer Girdle.

Photo: Tony Greenban

The Good Guys versus The Bad Guys

In the middle Fifties there was still development in Langdale, but it slackened off with the death of Dolphin and the departure of Greenwood to Keswick for work and night life. The Rock and Ice Climbers were too busy with acres of untouched rock in Wales to devote much time to the Lake District crags. Brown and Whillans were the best climbers in the British Isles but their future new routes in the Lake District were few in number, although they usually had a profound influence on each crag that they visited. Joe Brown once said, in a moment when he felt like goading the local climbers, "I like the Lakes," then paused, "the fishing's great". He went to Wales for preference, and there became famous, although its demands, such as crowds watching him climb, often forced him to go to remote places. His need for a private life once caused him to refuse a £1000 lecture fee.

Whillans went to work tunnelling for the North West Water Board near Haweswater, and developed a liking for la dolce vita of Keswick. This brought him into contact with Greenwood who was working on the Woolworth's site in Keswick. There had been a haze over the North Buttress climb on Shepherds Crag, since Beetham had claimed it, but without a description. Greenwood solved the problem and capped it with a 5b direct finish supported by the wedge-shaped Whillans who got on well with him and later wrote:

> 'Pete Greenwood was a fine climber who was always slightly competitive in his approach. He has many fine routes in Britain to his credit. Pete's home ground was the Lake District and the tales of some of his falls from those friendly crags are now part of climbing folklore. Pete, brought up in the traditional aid-free spirit of British climbing, firmly refused to countenance the presence of pitons on British rock even in their accepted role as protection. On occasions, he would jump for a hold. Brave it may have been, hair-raising it certainly was. Luckily it was never actually disastrous.'

Greenwood didn't stay entirely in Borrowdale and went back to Langdale to repeat Dolphin's girdle traverse of Gimmer Crag. When he traversed out of The Crack, a sling caught under a spike and jammed. He couldn't untangle it before his strength ran out and he fell. The second burnt his hands to the bone, and Greenwood fell over a hundred feet and broke his arm.

Just a few weeks after Greenwood's triumph on North Buttress another young man started climbing — Paul Ross, a forestry worker, who lived in Keswick. He found fifty feet of rope in a coal shed, and with another novice went to Round How, a cliff close to Keswick. Ross fell off, thudded into soft ground at the foot of the crag and was fortunately unhurt, much to the astonishment of his second, unbelayed dozens of feet above him. Neither knew anything about belaying. He was only sixteen and soon to become one of the best-known names in post-war Lakeland climbing. Despite his Round How shock he went to Shepherds Crag and soloed up to a jackdaw's nest, to the disgust of a Fell and Rock climbing group, whom he humorously labelled the Fell and Frock Club. Athletic ability and nerve soon promoted him to the front rank of Borrowdale climbers. He put up two new climbs that autumn — one of them,

Troutdale Pinnacle SuperDirect, a delicately strenuous Hard Very Severe. On its third pitch he was seriously committed, with the second badly belayed. When Ross announced that he was coming off, the second screamed, "You'll kill us both." Ross's immediate thoughts were:

'"Bloody hell, it's Saturday." That was the first thing that came to me. "I'm going to miss the dance." Even if I survived the fall, I wasn't going to be in any shape to dance.'

Fortunately he managed to grab a small hold and saved himself. It was inevitable that Greenwood and Ross would be drawn together — birds and booze on Saturday night, new routes during the day. They went to Castle Rock of Triermain, one fine June day in 1955 and added another eliminate. On the crux, Ross traversed left above the overhang and Greenwood was pressed to follow it. Ross described his experiences on the crux of Thirlmere Eliminate (E1 5b) as follows:

'Above us was a frightening-looking bulge, and above that extremely steep rock. Peter climbed a few feet up the right wall and, after almost exhausting himself, planted a peg halfway up the bulge. I offered to have a go and, unfortunately, he agreed. With the aid of the piton, and after much struggling, I managed to pull over this obstacle. Going quickly a few feet to the left, I made one upward move, and not to my surprise, found the crux of the climb. The next two or three moves were of the 'up or off' variety, mainly due to my rubbers on the rounded and very lichenous holds. With great relief I reached a belay. Peter followed and, after the bulge, said he had used enough energy for one day, so a quick pull soon got him over the worst. Then we set off in search of cigarettes as on such climbs these tubercular tranquilizers soon diminish.'

The details were entered by Ross in the new-route book in the Old Dungeon Ghyll Hotel. The only other place to record new climbs was in the Fell and Rock Club's, hut log books and club journals for the general climbing public. The Old Dungeon Ghyll book was the only other source of information.

Ross's ultimate ambitions were Alpine; he had been influenced by Guido Magnone's tale of the first ascent of the West Face of the Dru, and the liberal use of pitons; and he started to use pegs to complete new routes in a day. He invariably gardened a route as he went up, and declared anything used for aid. Sometimes he repeated a route with less aid, but did not amend the original description. Paul summed up his light-hearted attitude to life:

'When you're in a good mood, why bother to go climbing? I can easily be distracted when I'm having a good time. Whillans used to call me Holiday Bollocks for that reason...I reckon Greenwood was better than Dolphin. The thing is, Greenwood was a bad guy, like Allan What-do-you-call-him can't do anything wrong. It doesn't matter how many pitons they use or how much cheating they do. A good guy will always beat a bad guy at climbing no matter how good the bad guy is! Greenwood was a bad guy. They call me the climbing Teddy boy and he was a bit like that.'

The use of pitons clouded some of Ross's routes. The fact that his climbs were recorded in the Old Dungeon Ghyll log book was used against him. His base was in Keswick, so his Langdale detractors were quite happy to read of the climbs on which pitons had been used, not knowing the weather conditions on the first ascent and of

Opposite: Top left: Fred Williams and Peter Greenwood after the third ascent of Kipling Groove.
            Top right: A youthful Peter Greenwood (2nd from left).
            Bottom: Peter Greenwood making plans.   Photo: P.J. Greenwood.

Bentley Beetham on Shepherd's Crag, Borrowdale.

Photo: Austin B

Ross's ethics which made him complete routes in a day in line with his Alpine principles. In contrast even Joe Brown used eight points of aid to get up November, which violated his own limit of two points of aid per pitch on a new route. It was rare for Ross to exceed the Joe Brown ethic of two points of aid in his early career and as he later commented:

'We climbed there for fun, we never dreamt that people would complain about the 'ethics' of these routes later. At that time, any peg we put in, we mentioned whether it did us any good or not, any runner or peg. You had to mention everything and there wasn't any great onus the way there is today that leads to cheating and omissions. We were doing a lot of these climbs with tremendous hangovers. On Bludgeon it started to rain on the top pitch. I thought, screw it, I'll just get up the thing, and you never thought what people would say later. Of my eighty new routes in Britain, what they criticise is about three of them. The Horror for one, and bloody If. We did If as a totally provocative route, up an incredible piece of rock. I find it very rewarding to climb the most impressive part of the cliff.'

If on the front face of Gimmer, took the line now followed by Eastern Hammer. Ross wanted to do a new climb on the East Buttress of Scafell and it was obvious that the huge groove above the start of May Day Climb was a tempting prize. It usually glittered with water. He got two-thirds of the way up it and was only a couple of steps from easy ground, but a wet streak barred the way and so he decided to put in a piton. The second man objected, so Paul abseiled off and left the sling in place. Ross never did finish it. The second couldn't keep quiet and told Geoff Oliver, who went up and completed May Day Direct. Ross never forgot the loss of this route and right at the end of his career he got his own back on Castle Rock of Triermain when he did a route with Chris Bonington that Oliver had gardened, and called it Last Laugh.

Ross had many escapades. One of his most alarming happened in Langdale, when he hit a flock of sheep. A girl who was riding pillion was hurled through the air by the force of the impact. In court the farmer said that during her trajectory she struck a flying sheep with such force that it was killed. On another occasion Ross arranged to meet Greenwood on Scafell. When they met Paul developed acute abdominal pains and thought he had appendicitis. He was carried down to Seathwaite on a stretcher by the Mountain Rescue, but when he reached the road he miraculously recovered and went back to Keswick on his motor-cycle.

1955 could be said to belong jointly to Ross and Greenwood. Ross did his first two Extremes in Borrowdale, The Fou and Porcupine, then Greenwood during an active weekend in July, produced Irrawaddy, Hard Very Severe 5a, on Castle Crag, then stayed sufficiently abstemious on the Saturday night to produce Obituary Grooves with Ross on Black Crag. Both said separately that the other was the better climber, but the important thing was their excellent tally of new routes and their equality as a team.

It was the era when big cracks were being climbed. The art of climbing such formidable problems was developed to a fine art by Brown and Whillans; and although steep wall-climbing has progressed enormously, Joe Brown considers that their methods for strenuous wide cracks have not been bettered. One unclimbed wide crack on Eagle Crag Borrowdale attracted Whillans's attention. A big jammed chockstone blocked it at a critical point low on the crux pitch and in the ensuing struggle Don got his knee inextricably wedged just below it. The minutes ticked by and still he couldn't wrench himself free. After twenty minutes struggling the knee unexpectedly popped out and he fell backwards, fortunately onto a deep bird's nest on a ledge below. Ross tried it the following weekend with a new partner, the strong and fitness-conscious Peter Lockey. On the first pitch, as Lockey followed up a steep flake crack, a large six-foot pinnacle slid out of it and started to grate its way downwards. Fortunately Lockey made a grab for a handhold and swung his feet off as the stone monolith plunged down in a shower of sparks and sulphurous smells.

On the main pitch Ross climbed up to a jammed chockstone in a wide awkward crack, then came down for a rest after attaching a sling. Lockey climbed past it, knocked in a piton on the right wall, for protection only, then he too retreated. Ross took a rest at the chockstone then led the rest of the pitch, with just two pieces of protection. Paul called the route Post Mortem. At E2 5c it is one of his hardest routes and is a milestone in Cumbrian climbing. Even with aid at the chockstone, it is still a 5c pitch — the first in Lakeland to go beyond the 5b standard which had reigned since Herford set it in 1914.

Although the spotlight was on Borrowdale, Harold Drasdo rekindled interest in Langdale after several years at college. He returned to Wall End Barn which was still owned by Ike Meyers who regularly used to appear at 7 o'clock in the morning shaking a small bag, shouting "Shekels" to make sure that no-one left without paying his dues. A three-foot bed of bracken carpeted the floor; and most climbers were still sound asleep on a cold January morning in 1956 when Drasdo decided to tackle a new route on Deer Bield Crag. A deep groove on the right of the crag had long, loose caterpillars of grass and vegetation weeping over sparse rock-holds. He used one piton on the first pitch and two more on the second, and called it Hubris, which is a much steeper route than it looks. Brown and Whillans repeated it, used some aid and removed more vegetation, but thought it a good route. Later the Langdale guide-book writer Allan Austin climbed it free, having the benefit of warmer weather and previous vigorous gardening. He wanted to claim it for himself but after a chilly chat with Harold, Drasdo's name remained. The next month, February 1956, in freezing conditions Don Whillans made the second ascent of Dolphin and Greenwood's Sword of Damocles. Later that year Allan Austin announced in the bar of the Old Dungeon Ghyll that he himself had done the second ascent of the route. Tucked away in a dark corner Whillans listened keenly to Austin's breathless tale biding his time. As silence fell he said drily: "Oh aye, I did second ascent in't winter." He paused for maximum effect then added, with a puff on his cigarette: "I 'ad to chip ice off't holds wi' a penknife."

Joe Brown also had a dig at Austin after he had failed on a route with Brown watching:

> "I always said you were the best climber to come out of Yorkshire, but then they're never any good are they?"

One day Greenwood looked out of the Old Dungeon Ghyll bar window and saw Drasdo doing a new route on Raven Crag which was to be called Holly Tree Direct. It was a steep smooth way up to the holly which used to grow out of the central chimney; and later the same day Greenwood repeated it, as he put it 'while the rock was still warm'.

However Drasdo's real love was the Eastern Fells which were far from piton controversies and mundane roadside crags. He wrote later about a climb that he did with his brother Neville, called Sforzando on Gowther Crag in Swindale — a lonely

Opposite: Modern climbers on Hell's Groove, Scafell East Buttress, following in the steps of Peter Greenwood and Arthur Dolphin (1952).

Photo: Ian Roper.

unspoilt dale which reaches out eastwards towards Shap. His article 'Extremes and Excesses' analyses all that goes through a leader's mind in the development of a new route — with the subtlety that has made him one of the best of rock-climbing writers.

'I started to let fall the cliches of the uncertain leader, drawing neither encouragement nor acknowledgement, other than subtle adjustments in the tension of the rope. I said that if I could just get my feet where my hands were...; that it was no use; that one good hold would take me to the resting place; that the holds all sloped; that I was going to fall off; that I was not going to fall off; that I would have to move back for a rest; that we were all wasting our time; that I would have one final go. I had it; and several more. Another half-hour slipped by. "Its no good," I said. "I'm coming down. Right. Take in."

When the leader was in a resting place, these struggles rewarded, an excess of pride took him and he stood there in a composed but dramatic attitude, surveying the next problem coolly, as if his fumblings of the last two hours were somehow negated by the simple act of standing in that arrogant pose above them. Taking myself very seriously, I had a suitably tense rest and after prevaricating with running belays as long as I decently could I moved up to the next problem; but it stopped me, as, indeed, I had seen it would. We changed places and Nev had a go; he too came back agreeing, to my extreme annoyance that it was flatly impossible. Unfortunately it was. But as he was descending I noticed that a slanting flake a good way out of reach, showed a tiny step that might just take quarter-weight nylon. I urged him to flick a sling over it but he wouldn't believe me. However, I knew, and began to try; once, twice — he was grinning sceptically — and the third time, there it was. I pulled up and stood high in a short sling with difficulty against a tilted wall. Until, finding that time and intention had gone, I came down resolving never to come back.

A half-hour later I believed that we would climb it the following day; my mind mauled the little corner, I could not eat or sleep, I recognized a grand infatuation.

There we were again. Rather apprehensively, I set off. Perhaps the thirty feet to the resting place, two hours' work yesterday, took a whole minute. I adjusted myself for the sling-flicking whilst Nev watched with admiration and interest. I swung; again; and again; and again and again and again; probably fifty times, maybe a hundred. Sometimes I climbed up within six inches of the tooth but could not spare a hand; sometimes I tested extravagant and intermediate positions, making futile gestures with the sling whilst holding myself in precarious balance. Theories were advanced: I had not got the optimum length of the sling; Yesterday's was older and less springy. The heavy arm went monotonously backwards and forwards, the sling rebounded consistently occasionally squatting idiotically on the edge of the notch. Nev called out in wonder remarks about unicellular organisms, made explanations not listed here, jeered and advised. Clearly, I had been wrong all the time. Yesterday's success had been a pure accident. I said "You were right" I prepared to descend.

Then it was easy. But, counting resting time, we had spent about four hours on that sixty-foot pitch. We had used ourselves, we had climbed a towering Extreme, I said. And look at it now, the holes all cleaned out the methods noted, a solid piton in place; a Medium Very Severe; the reward of the devotee of these vegetation ceremonies.'

Drasdo set about transforming the Eastern Fells into a modern climbing area, one so remote from the crowds that eagles returned to nest after a gap of a century and Eagle Crags took on a proper meaning again. It was Scrubby Crag with its unsavoury name which gave some of his best new routes. It faces south-east and scoops up any available sunshine, on its sound steep rock. There were four hundred climbs in the 1979 guide-book. Only four had the three-star accolade, and Harold's Grendel on

Opposite: Above: Allan Austin, Jennifer Ruffe, Brian Evans and Aileen Evans, in about 1959.   Photo: N. Drasdo.
            Below: 'Beer revives mountain courage' in 1950.   Photo: Sid Cross.

Scrubby Crag was one of them, a sheer hundred-foot corner which offers classic wide bridging on tiny ledges.

Drasdo's companion from the Bradford Lads, Peter Greenwood, gave up climbing in the summer of 1956 whilst on holiday in the Dolomites with Whillans, to whom he gave his climbing gear. He had done thirty new routes all over the Lake District with a variety of partners starting with Dolphin, then Ross and Whillans who both spoke of his agility and fearlessness. He was in the vanguard of the working class lads who transformed Cumbrian rock with routes on crags big and small all over Lakeland. Dave Cook summed up these trends:

'The members of clubs like the Rock and Ice were not inhibited by prevailing attitudes about what was possible and appropriate. Existing clubs, like the CC, the FRCC and the SMC, were not only the preserve of a certain type of climber, but also of a certain type of attitude — an attitude that in an important way was not competitive. The very exclusiveness of the established clubs led the new working-class climbers to form their own clubs and groups, and unconsciously to assert their own attitudes. In complete contrast to the old middle-class clubs, the new ones were most definitely competitive. Let me be clear: I'm not talking about competitiveness between clubs, but within them. After 1950, when climbers became good they became good in relatively big groups — not in very small ones as had previously been the case. The new sort of competitive, primarily working-class club, coming to the sport disrespectful of the accepted way of doing things, acted as a type of hothouse, forcing the growth of those within it. And obviously it was not only internal competition that was at work here; mutual reinforcement also played an important part.'

One day Ross was bouldering in Grisedale with a group of friends and he climbed a fierce crack with consummate ease. A six-footer with large feet attributed his success to his tiny feet. Ross promptly put on his size ten boots and still floated up it. A new man appeared on the Lakeland scene, Allan Austin, from Yorkshire. Austin was parochial and viewed anyone from across the Lancashire border with suspicion; and still says 'brass is brass'. His nickname 'Tubby' was given to him as a result of wearing several layers of tattered woollen pullovers, which combined with a round bespec-tacled face and Billy-Bunter-like appearance to conceal a rare ability. He could do a one-arm pull-up which helped on Yorkshire gritstone and Cumbrian granite climbs. His start was on new routes was a Hard Very Severe — Stickle Grooves on Pavey Ark with Brian Evans. Over the next decade, Austin made Pavey Ark a great cliff. He was involved in his father's woollen-waste business, and had the use of the firm's van at weekends. Dennis Gray remembers being given a lift to the Lake District when his share of the total petrol bill was thirteen shillings and eleven pence halfpenny, with a ha'penny change. Austin ransacked his house for the elusivse coin, despite Dennis's protestations, then Allan borrowed the coin from his father down the road to settle his debt.

Austin had been on a novices' rock-climbing course. In a few short hours he made a meteoric rise and was sent to the star instructor. In his early days he was obsessed with the repetition of Dolphin routes and particularly the Girdle Traverse of Pavey Ark, as Brian Evans remembers:

'We had an epic on the Girdle. When our team was strung across the most heavily vegetated part of the crag at a time of summer drought, fire broke out on a juniper ledge below, probably caused by a carelessly dropped cigarette. The flames spread, with alarming rapidity

causing a spectator to shout "Get climbing, you fools!" I had unroped and soloed back whilst Allan and Jenny, and Brian Fuller and Alison, had split into two ropes and were climbing parallel ways up unclimbed rock, with flames licking the second's stances. Alison's ledge collapsed but Brian managed to fetch her up just in time.'

Austin's dominance of Langdale was to last from 1956 to 1974, with a final total of nearly forty new routes.

In 1957 the Rock and Ice made more forays into the Lake District, and Joe Brown produced the second E2 in Cumbria with Eliminot, which breaks through the overhangs below the Perhaps Not traverse and finishes up the very steep rock right of the final pitch of Haste Not. Although it was one of the hardest climbs that he produced in the Lake District it was not up to the quality of his other climbs. However the third man of the Rock and Ice team, Ron Moseley, produced the piece de resistance of the year with Phoenix (E1 5b) on the East Buttress of Scafell. The 1984 guide-book was later to comment: 'Although not realised at the time, this climb was a full grade harder than anything else on the crag'. Moseley continually lived in the shadow of his charismatic clubmates. He was a slower climber and he constantly felt that he was overshadowed by Brown and Whillans. Soon after his Scafell triumph he gave up climbing for good, not realising that after all, he really had made the grade for which he had been striving so hard.

Next year Austin did five good new routes. One of them Golden Slipper (Hard Very Severe) turned out to be one of the more delightful slab climbs in the area. It was set high on the crag above Jack's Rake and was accentuated by the gloomy corner crack on the right. But the great event of the year was the invasion of Cumbria by the young Scottish climber Robin Smith, who had crowned his brief career with Shibboleth (E2) on the Slime Wall of Buchaille Etive Mor in Glencoe, whilst still an undergraduate at Edinburgh University. That summer he went to Chamonix and was hit on the head by a rock. The hospital patched him up with a large pad on top of his head, held picturesquely in place with a bandage tied under his chin, which gave him a Florence Nightingale look. A few weeks later he did the second ascent of the West Face of the Blaitiere with Trevor Jones. During the second bivouac, Jones noticed that Smith didn't appear to possess a down-padded duvet. He explained rather testily that it was Haston's turn for it that week. On the East Buttress of Scafell Smith did two superb new routes in a day, Chartreuse (E1 5a) and Leverage (Hard Very Severe 5b). He was not a crack climber and failed on Hell's Groove but returned to go high on Gimmer Crag and link the cave stance on Kipling Groove with the rib high above The Bower on The Crack, a crucial part of Gimmer String, which Austin completed a few years later.

On North Crag Eliminate he paused for some time to the delight of fellow Scot Patsy Walsh one of the best Creag Dhu climbers, who shouted up to him "Wait till I get hame and tell' em ye failed on a wee English boulder". Smith was galvanised into action and shot up the pitch like a rocket.

Smith's efforts were followed by a deluge of new routes from a variety of people. The main activists were from the small Alpha Club whose members were mostly from a trans-Pennine axis based on Manchester and Sheffield Universities. The first to make an impact was Les Brown, a physics graduate, six feet four in height, with thick spectacles and an academic air of detachment. Les's adhesion to rock in challenging situations is masterly and it made him into a climber who was described as 'one of Lakeland's master craftsmen'. His first new route Inertia (Hard Very Severe 5a) was on

Opposite: Late evening sunlight on the superb wall pitch of Saxon (1976), Scafell Crag.   Photo: Bill Birkett.

Gimmer Crag and the reason for its name was that Les was recovering from a broken ankle caused by a fall from the tricky gritstone cleft, Chequers Crack. Despite becoming one of the leading Lakeland climbers, his summer months were mainly concerned with the Alps and the higher ranges. He climbed Nuptse, the third peak of Everest, in an expedition of all the top talent of that time which included a youthful Chris Bonington. In the Alps too, Les made his name and with Don Whillans made the second ascent of the Walker Spur on the Grandes Jorasses, although he was handicapped by the loss of all his clothes, and had to beg and borrow a complete outfit for the climb, topped by a decrepit hat which someone had found in the rafters of the Chalet Austria. Despite his mountaineering ambitions, he produced a number of excellent new routes which rapidly became classics; probably because of the criteria that he set himself for a new climb. The first requirement was that the line should follow a sequence of naturally connected weaknesses and preferably be inescapable; and the second requirement was that it should have a mountaineering setting. Les was one of several newcomers who were to take a prominent part in Cumbrian exploration. Apart from Allan Austin who held the Langdale fort, the newcomers tended to make Keswick their base and joined in the Bacchanalian pleasures orchestrated by Paul Ross.

One of Les Brown's new route peers was Geoff Oliver, the leading climber from the North-East, who also gravitated to Keswick. He started climbing with an old sisal rope from a coal mine and soon developed an elegant climbing style that made him the envy of many. One of the factors which improved his standard was a revolution in footwear. The cheap rubber gym shoe had been used by hard men ever since Kelly, half a century before. The new boots were known as PAs after their inventor, a leading French climber called Pierre Allain. They looked like a hockey boot and had a stiff sole which made it easier to stand on tiny holds. The first recorded use by British climbers was on the first British ascent of the North Face of the Piz Badile by an Oxford University party in 1956. By 1958 every hard climber in the U.K. had them and they made possible a full grade increase in top standards.

5c pitches were climbed on Cumbrian cliffs by several top climbers; Les Brown, Ross, Austin, Geoff Oliver and Whillans. Walter Pater wrote 'Nothing which has ever interested living men and women can wholly lose its vitality.' The hard good climbs that the five pioneered were soon repeated, and some of them were even hailed as masterpieces.

Geoff Oliver took advantage of the exceptionally dry summer of 1959 to attack the East Buttress of Scafell and scooped the prize of May Day Direct, on which Ross had been defeated by a streak of water. The route became Oliver's first E2 new route in the Lakes. Only seven days separated this from his next effort, Goth on Pillar Rock. It was the first major route there for nearly twenty years and was a grade harder than any previous climb on Pillar.

Another of Oliver's friends who did a new route, Vandal, on the same day was Maurice Felix de Saint Jarre, who with such a name was almost bound to make an impression of sorts. He had come to the North-East on a college sandwich course, and as part of his study went down a coal pit. The Geordie miners of course were utterly fascinated by his middle-class accent and in turn he responded by imitating them.

The fine 1959 summer enabled Les Brown to overcome a normally wet line, Moon Day (E2) left of Overhanging Wall on the East Buttress which had dried out for once. As if he was aware of the determined newcomers, Paul Ross produced one of the best climbs of the year on Castle Rock of Triermain. During his ascent of Thirlmere

Opposite: Phoenix (1957), Ron Moseley's big lead, which was a full grade harder than other routes on Scafell at that time. Photo: Ian Roper.

Eliminate with Greenwood, he had noticed a vertical cone of light-coloured rock. They tried it and were repulsed but the line stayed in his thoughts and he returned to conquer it. His inevitable ascent was not without trauma

'We were now below the unscaled cone whose upper section appeared particularly savage. I started up its left-hand side which here formed a small corner. The first 25 feet went fairly easily, then everything started to bulge. Swinging onto the right-hand edge, I reached a spike for a sling and by standing in this a few more feet were gained. Progress seemed impossible now as far as free climbing was concerned. Up to the left I noticed another slight projection, but it was not until after much strenuous swinging and chipping that this became suitable for a single line sling. Transferring myself to this sling — my perch for the next hour — was no mean feat as it needed very little encouragement to roll off. Eventually I managed to jam a piton into a wide crack to steady myself and started to hammer at a knife edge up to the right, trying to find a weakness to make some sort of spike on which to hang yet another sling. After a great deal of banging a chunk flew off, just missing Bill, but leaving a beautiful sharp spike. I now lifted the jammed piton (which was no longer necessary), out of the crack and, using a stiff sling, managed to hook it over the spike and transfer myself; I then felt a lot safer. About 5 feet above this I succeeded in knocking in what looked like a secure piton.

Bill had been on his belay for about 2 hours and was feeling very cold and stiff and probably thinking of his previous day's long, unfruitful wait. The problem now was a smooth vertical groove which, after everything had been tried, did not yield an inch. I looked to the left which seemed the only way out. Here was a slightly overhanging wall which, after 8 feet, would bring me into a mossy-looking groove. I decided on my plan of attack and asked Bill to tension me out from the piton and across the wall.

Once again I started to chip; this time I had to be extremely careful as only in one place, towards the middle of the wall, did there appear to be anything that could be made into a hold for a sling. When I had finished, there were three minute projections within the space of an inch, the largest being about half the size of a thumb nail.

A very delicate operation was necessary to move into this sling and, once there I realized, after both the smaller projections had broken with loud twangs, that this was not a very healthy situation. I quickly swung into the mossy groove and, after two very trying moves reached the ledge of the second pitch of Thirlmere Eliminate ...We named the climb Rigor Mortis, as we thought it a rather stiff problem.'

Les Brown started off 1960 on Heron Crag in Eskdale. Many had thought of its possibilities, but Les lived less than twenty miles away and was ideally placed to make an assault. The previous winter he had leafed through a Fell and Rock Journal and read:

'Beyond doubt the best is yet to be. The main nose, with a remarkable flake half way up seen in profile on the way from Taw House, and the whole right wing of the crag, overhanging by several feet at the bottom, remain untouched, waiting for some V.S. pioneers.'

Brown responded with Gormenghast (Hard Very Severe 5b), described as 'A classic climb of great character' which was one of his finest creations. On the second pitch he launched out from the foot of a steep corner onto a wall with a widely spaced sequence of flat holds perfectly suited to Les's height, but at the top he was confronted by a tricky traverse back into the corner and arrived at a ledge and a piton belay. Forgetfulness occasionally overtakes Les. Although he threaded a hefty braided nylon belay sling

Opposite: Above: Norman Rimmer, Ray Greenall, Pete Greenall, ?, Eric Price, Don Whillans and Les Wright at a Rock and Ice dinner.
Photo: J.R. Nat Allen.
Below: Geoff Oliver and the lads outside the Old Dungeon Ghyll Hotel.
Photo: P.J. Greenwood.

Allan Austin's 1957 route Cascade, Pavey Ark.

Photo: Ian Rope

Oliver Woolcock on Agony (1959), Castle Rock in the 1960s.

Photo: Rosemary Soper.

through the piton he only clipped into one loop and when the second, Ackers Atkinson, fell off, only the knot prevented a plunge to their deaths. The quality of the route was soon apparent, then Whillans added a direct finish and Allan Austin produced a direct start.

Les's next production on Dow Crag started deep in Great Gully. A step off a pedestal into gnawing exposure, then a hand-placed piton to steel his nerve for the next awkward moves, and finally Sidewalk (E2) one of his most sustained lines. His next route was on the East Buttress of Scafell, Armageddon, which strikes across diagonally from the foot of Overhanging Wall. Just over a month later, Geoff Oliver did a climb that others had coveted. Les Brown had abseiled down it, then decided it would need too many pitons. Greenwood had named it Ichabod in advance from C.F.Holland's introduction to the 1936 guide-book

> 'And so we leave the history of Scafell at a time when the future is bright with the possibility of great developments, a time when there is no danger of the call of Ichabod, a time when we may well feel that the best is yet to come.'

Oliver originally wanted to call it Harpie but decided on Ichabod in deference to the history of the name. He did the main pitch on the Saturday, but didn't complete it, abseiled off, and returned next day to finish the line. Austin proclaimed the route as being ten years ahead of its time. It was not however entirely straightforward as Oliver made clear when he wrote about all the troubles he had:

> 'A short overhanging corner crack followed and this led to a large niche below a roof. Ten feet to the right was the corner I hoped to attain, and this was the immediate problem. On a rickety flake in the corner of the niche I arranged a line runner and tensioned to the right to reach a handhold at shoulder height. The hold was not big and the angle bulged slightly, but it seemed as though it might be just possible to mantelshelf on it. One hour and 10 attempts later I realized it was not feasible, so I called in science in the form of a thin-bladed piton. At the side of the crucial hold was a crack, and a few gentle taps of the hammer pushed home the peg, jeopardizing the existence of the hold by widening the crack. With a sling on this flimsy support, I straightened up to reach a good hold for the step across to the corner, and the first obstacle was overcome. The going was easier for 10 feet, then the angle steepened and I had to leave the corner for a diversion onto the right wall ...My route from here was dictated more by the position of the holds than by my own wishes and I progressed diagonally right by a succession of delicate mantelshelves. My objective was the foot of a V-chimney above and 20 feet to my left, but the few holds available still led to the right. However, the prospect of reversing the moves I'd just made was appalling, so the only possible course was to push on. Eventually I came to a crack with reasonable handholds and here I rested after a fashion. The rope snaked down for 70 feet and dragged abominably through the pitons, but I was cheered by the sight of the V-chimney with which I was now level. The approach to it was via a narrow sloping ledge with no handholds at all in evidence. I dearly wanted a piton in the shallow crack which I was about to leave, but the best I could arrange was a combination of two pegs jammed side by side. The rope running through these helped to hold me in balance as I inched across the traverse. On reaching the chimney I found an ideal thread belay and the gravity of the situation disappeared completely. I was not at all surprised to learn that the ascent of this 110-foot pitch had taken three hours.'

Opposite: George Lee, Geoff Oliver, Frank Carroll, Geoff Arkless, ?, and Len Willis below Falcon Crag in May 1960, the same month as Ichabod was
                   done.
        Below: Wilf, Lou, Don Laws, ?, Frank Carroll and Geoff Oliver.   Photo: Geoff Oliver.

It was a great 1960 Easter for Don Whillans, who was staying with the Rock and Ice at Dale Bottom Farm near Keswick. In an incident in the town a foolish drunk stroked Audrey Whillans's hair. Don's fist speared over Audrey's shoulder, knocking the drunk to the floor and tearing his face open, before he was eventually carried to hospital. It was the famous 'Dob of dobs'. The details were soon exaggerated and reinforced Whillans's reputation as a man 'not to be trifled with'.

Whillans was drawn back to Dove Crag. At the back of his mind he had remembered a huge unclimbed corner that he had first tried in 1953. On that occasion he had traversed into the middle of the face until surrounded by menacing overhangs he had decided to retreat — but marked it down for future attention. It was certainly the main feature to be climbed. At 8 a.m. on an Easter morning, he made a start on his motor-cycle with a reluctant Colin Mortlock as pillion passenger and second man. Later on when Whillans started up the line he could not have realised that he was about to produce a masterpiece, possibly the finest pitch in Lakeland at that time. Mortlock, who must have had an unnerving time waiting for the outcome described the situation:

' A large, black, sunless corner containing a hundred feet of nearly vertical rock and steep slab, topped by about forty to fifty feet of mostly overhanging rock. It was rather like a double-sized Cenotaph Corner topped by overhangs and without a crack in the corner. There were no escape lines and no place for a stance below the top. It took Don two and a half hours to climb this pitch. It must be the finest piece of rock climbing I have ever seen. I sang rock to relieve the tension (mine as well as his!) Don smoked incessantly.

This final pitch turned out to be just as long as our rope (150 feet). It began well with a short vertical traverse which revealed good holds, then a steep forty- foot wall where holds and grass sods were again adequate. A runner here protected the next fifteen feet. It needed to (Don fell off here on a previous attempt). The slab was not only steep but greasy and minute ripples accounted for all holds. Don cracked it by patience and magnificent skill...
Above this another runner and straightforward slab and groove climbing for thirty feet. Then the corner overhangs forced one diagonally rightwards towards a small overhang forty feet above. Progress at this point was made by small flakes which were so situated that all the handholds were on the left and all the footholds on the right. The result was a sideways progress — itself out of balance and accentuated by the vertical to overhanging rock.'

The pitch was one hundred and fifty feet and Mortlock had to start climbing although Whillans had still not finished the difficulties. A faint Whillans voice carrying down from far above seemed to imply that he was belayed, as Mortlock started to grapple with the difficulties.

'Trying to climb too fast I grabbed a flake which reciprocated by breaking off. Tired and out of balance I came on the rope — in space. By swinging I grabbed the runner and rested (or tried to). After five minutes I moved up, still finding it very hard. Just above the overhang, in a shallow groove, was a peg (for protection only, said Don). I said something else; grabbed the peg, swung clear and pulled up. Of course even the last twenty feet up the groove were pretty holdless. By now, however, I was not worried, for there was Don and the top a few feet away.'

It was a magnificent end to the Rock and Ice contribution to Lakeland climbing and Extol (E2 5c) became one of the finest pitches in Britain, marred only by the rather

Taylor on Les Brown's fine route, The Centaur (1960), Scafell, East Buttress.   Photo: Ian Roper.

loose and evil chimney which leads up the big pitch.

A few days after, Don met Les Brown in a Keswick pub and bemoaned that he had 'buggered it up' by putting a piton in Extol. Lesser mortals would have needed more help and therefore Extol helped to set the tone for 1960.

The next climb by Allan Austin to achieve classic status was on Pavey Ark. Unlike many, Austin believed in truthful reporting of first ascents. If people used aid and then failed to declare it in the route description, the guide-book writer was then faced with the difficulty of whether or not aid had been used. Perhaps the best comment on Austin's ethics was made by Peter Livesey:

> 'It was Austin's ideology that had profound effects on the later history of Lakeland climbing; so dogmatic were his ethics that their effect on the total British climbing scene is still gathering weight. As a spiritual head of the Yorkshire purist movement, which is like saying whiter than white......'

Austin carried on making Pavey Ark into a rock-tigers' playground and added three more routes, Rectangular Slab, Red Groove, then the superb Astra, E2 5b. A quarter of a century later, it is still described as 'the best climb in the valley'. It took several attempts and a piton to overcome its grudging wall pitch to produce one of the great modern Lakeland classics. Not long after Paul Ross invaded Austin's Langdale fiefdom and cheekily put up his piton route If, left of 'F' Route. He admitted that it was to annoy Austin and it is a gross understatement of the situation merely to state that he succeeded.

Next month Les Brown went up to the East Buttress of Scafell to try a line which had defeated Ross, who had knocked in a piton, then retreated. The line was awesomely steep, bending round the corner between the right and left flanks of the buttress. Brown climbed up past successive overhangs, then managed to sidle round whenever he reached an impasse. Any expert would have said that an Extreme route would be needed to overcome its problems. Les, the master craftsman, managed to fashion Centaur (Hard Very Severe 5a), one of the best climbs of that standard in Britain. Although it was three hundred feet long, he finished it so early that he followed it with Central Buttress, then Moss Ghyll Grooves and still managed to reach Wasdale Head for a lunch-time pint.

Two of Les Brown's fellow Alpha club members, Peter Crew and Barry Ingle, also took a passing interest in the Lake District that summer and did Odin on Pillar Rock, the prelude to a new approach to Cumbrian climbing. Crew was utterly obsessed with the idea of toppling Joe Brown from his pedestal, where he had perched for so long. Crew's fierce competitiveness inspired him to feverish activity. Competition was his watchword and by 1960 his new routes in Wales had made him a major force.

Austin now built on his previous efforts and went to Heron Crag. His companion was Eric Metcalf, who was universally known as Matie; it was a curious nickname as he was certainly anything but gregarious. They were poles apart in their climbing technique. Austin wore an aura of grim determination and was nimble, even in bizarre footwear such as vibram-soled shoes, which caused him to be dubbed 'The Yorkshire Shoe Champion'. Matie was technically better and always looked at ease, but did not quite have the dash of Austin. Matie's climbing skill was not impaired after an accident with railway detonators, and an even worse accident occurred when he was demonstrating his agility by hanging from his toes from the parapet of a railway bridge...he slipped off...and landed on his head in front of his startled friends.

Opposite: Moving out across the steep slab of Ichabod, Scafell East Buttress. Inset: Geoff Oliver.   Photo: Ken Wilson.

Chris Bonington on the big pitch of Extol, Dove Crag, put up by Don Whillans in 1960.

Photo: Chris Boning[

...eth (1962), Crew and Ingle's big line on Dove Crag.

Photo: R.F. Allen.

Austin had things much to himself in 1961, mainly on account of the fact that Les Brown was away for seven months on the Nuptse Himalayan Expedition and the other main opposition, Geoff Oliver, got married. It was left to Austin to develop Heron Crag in Eskdale with Spec Crack (Hard Very Severe 5a) with Matie. New routes are never straightforward and even the hardest men sometimes get paralysed with fright. Austin wrote of his doubts and his ecstasies:

'Matie loitered and tried to get a runner. Then he announced that it was too steep so he had better have a piton. From my stance on my comfortable ledge I was well placed to administer a stern warning on the degenerate ways of ironmongers, but he ignored me and planted one. It belonged to a well-known variety of piton, probably the commonest and best known of all. It was a 'Manky Piton'. And there he stayed perched on the wall like a kitehawk. Presently he dropped something, but it was only a threader, deserting like a rat from a sinking ship, to hide away in the bracken at the bottom. Presently he announced his retirement and seconded me for the job, and said he was coming back. At this I got all crafty and thought I would like the piton tested, so I offered to lower him off. But he declined. Then it was my turn to mess about on the bulge and examine the piton, a poor specimen indeed. It was hammered lengthways along a horizontal crack and the way it flaunted its vital statistics would have amounted to indecent exposure anywhere else. But I was the only one there and I wasn't impressed. So I chipped, threaded and wedged till I got a single thread. Our immoral piton pulled out without a blow being struck, a cowardly act.

I became wedged in a wet greasy crack-cum-niche with my hands on top, or what should have been if it had been more permanent. Laid across the top of my crack like a lid was a stone, a loose one. I began to shake a bit. As the hard men say, I had got muscle fatigue and started the long involved process leading to a retreat. It begins with some words such as

"It's a bit loose up here" or "It's so slimy it's like trying to catch a frog," closely followed by "and its too steep to rest".

But there were no encouraging sounds from below, only a stony silence. A hard taskmaster my mate. So I turned back to my stone. Now it's well known that I am a coward so although the stone was only half my size, it will cause no surprise when I say I was frightened. Anyway to cut a long and pitiful story short I girded up my loins and made my summit dash.'

Austin had tried to repeat Dovedale Grooves, but failed and it was left to the leading Welsh predator Peter Crew, supported by Barry Ingle, to scoop the second ascent prize of a hard Rock and Ice route. Crew was not the best technician, and certainly he could easily be burnt off on boulder problems, but when it came to a big unprotected lead, combined with extreme difficulty, he had no equal. Nobody climbed as fast as Crew and perhaps Hugh Banner made the best comment on the manner of his climbing, 'He's got a neck like a giraffe'. Crew wrote of the three memorable days he and Ingle had on Dove Crag:

'We expected Oliver and Brown, L or Ross to come rushing round in the night to steal a march. Even though they didn't come we got up early just in case they crept over from Dunmail. Flogging up to the crag he kept moaning about the bloody long walks up to the Lake District crags, even though this one was only half as far as Cloggy. And then we were there and he was impressed ("Nearly as good as the East") and I was even more impressed because I would get the first pitch since it was my idea. Anyway there was no one else around so I talked him into doing this Dovedale Grooves route which hadn't been repeated for ten years ...So I grabbed his spare slings and climbed over him and stood on his head. And he

Opposite: Rob Knight and Steve Swindells on Equus (1976), Ed Cleasby's fine open line up the front face of Gimmer Crag.

Photo: Al Phizacklea.

started moaning so I said the block above his head was loose to make him moan more. Then I rushed up and grabbed the block and there was this big thrutch and a long step onto a slab on the left. But one of the ropes got jammed so I had to untie it and I was dead chuffed because it's always he that messes the rope up and leaves me in desperates. And he came up the chimney with the rope pulling him off but he didn't fall off, so I was dead sick. There was a lot of spare rock above for a direct finish but we reckoned we would just make a dinner-time pint so we leapt past this raven's nest and rushed off down the valley.'

Next day the two went back to try a new route in the middle of the crag, to make a trinity along with Dovedale Grooves and Whillans's Extol. At a critical point they constructed a running belay, using a large nut they had picked up from the track of the Snowdon Railway during one of their many successful treks to Clogwyn du'r Arddu.

'The wall above was full of overhanging grooves but he couldn't do any of them so he traversed right and descended to a stance about five feet above me and several feet out and passed the buck. But though the overhang was easy for me I got gripped on this queer slab that would be even harder in normal damp conditions. We looked down the top bit of Extol and I persuaded him to save it for tomorrow and we got down dead on opening time. We decided to call it Hiraeth because we were longing to get back home again to Wales.'

Hiraeth is Welsh for 'a longing for Wales' and at E2 5b was surprisingly the easiest of the three routes that they did during their memorable three days. The following day they completed the triptych with the second ascent of Extol, even though the weather was menacing. Afterwards they rushed down to Keswick to goad the locals and enjoy the doubtful pleasure of scoring off their fellow climbers, who didn't really care as much as they did:

'Black clouds were rolling over on Monday but we reckoned we might do Extol before it started raining so we rushed up even faster than ever. The first pitch was a rotten narrow chimney that he couldn't get into so I had to give him a tight rope again. But he got his finger out on the big pitch and was up in under an hour which seemed good going considering its reputation. The last overhang was a bit dicy and he kept the ropes slack to get his own back for Dovedale Grooves. If I had come off I would have ended up in Ullswater but I didn't and we were dead chuffed and got back to camp with the black clouds chasing us hard. It rained so we went to Keswick and they were all dead sick because we had swiped their routes but they bought us some beer and we bought plenty more for a party. But the clumsy fool dropped the case in Lake Road and broke half the bottles. Still, the empties made good missiles to throw at the tents in the next field.'

One of Crew's best friends and a crucial companion in the production of the hardest Welsh routes was geologist Jack Soper, who had a dual nationality as he was a member of the Fell and Rock as well. He became intrigued with the unsolved problem of the Central Pillar of Esk Buttress, which had defeated Greenwood and Dolphin. Soper abseiled down and levered off some loose blocks at a critical point, then rushed down to the Old Dungeon Ghyll bar to tell Sid Cross of the great prize that was within his grasp. Unfortunately there was a Crew informer in the bar who immediately told Crew of Soper's plans. It might have been thought there would have been a bond of loyalty between Crew and Soper after all the new routes that they had done in Wales

The splendid main pitch of Astra (1960), Pavey Ark.

Photo: R.F. All

dney Valentine leading Gimmer String (1963).

Photo: John Hartley.

but Crew was galvanised into action.

Soper had persuaded Austin of the Pillar's importance and they decided on an early start to have a full day at it. They could not believe their ears as they approached the crag to hear the metallic woodpecker-type sounds as Crew hammered at a piton. Central Pillar (E2 5b) was the most audacious of the pirates' bag of routes in the Lakeland valleys. However base his motives Crew injected new attitudes into Cumbrian climbing and although he never climbed there again, there was nothing to equal that frenzied few days climbing during June 1962.

The same day as Central Pillar was produced, Soper rose from the ashes of his ambitions and in desperation scanned the rest of the crag. First he produced the appropriately-named Black Sunday (Hard Very Severe 5a), 'a justifiably popular climb' which follows a series of cracks and grooves, but it was Red Edge (E1 5a) which helped to ease the loss of their great plum. It merits three stars and is a superb and exposed climb in a thrilling position. When Ken Wilson's book 'Hard Rock' came out in 1975, it contained the best hard climbs in each mountain area of the British Isles, Eleven climbs were selected for the Lake District:

CENTRAL BUTTRESS	1914	HVS 5b	Siegfried Herford
THE CRACK	1928	VS 4c	A.B.Reynolds
ENGINEERS SLAB	1934	VS 4c	Fred Balcombe
KIPLING GROOVE	1948	HVS 5a	Arthur Dolphin
DEER BIELD BUTTRESS	1951	E1 5b	Arthur Dolphin
NORTH CRAG ELIMINATE	1952	E1 5b	Harold Drasdo
ICHABOD	1960	E2 5c	Geoff Oliver
EXTOL	1960	E2 5c	Don Whillans
GORMENGHAST	1960	HVS 5b	Les Brown
CENTRAL PILLAR	1962	E2 5b	Peter Crew
PRAYING MANTIS	1965	HVS 5b	Les Brown

Over the fifty-year span in which they were produced, five of these routes were compressed into the period from 1960 to 1965, and although a decade passed between Les Brown's Praying Mantis and 'Hard Rock' in 1975 no other routes came in to the list, which may reflect a shift of attention to other areas, especially Anglesey and The Peak. Two of the routes were from Arthur Dolphin and two from Les Brown. Oliver and Crew had their place, but others should have been included, particularly Birkett's Overhanging Bastion and Perhaps Not.

Similar to the situation before the Second World War predatory top Welsh climbers had left the land of Arfon to grab some of the untouched prizes on Cumbrian Rock. Both the Rock and Ice and the Alpha have left their significant climbs for future generations to see in the first ascent lists in the guide-books. A new phase was about to start and several circumstances combined to make the intruders leave Lakeland. The awesomely-serious crags of the sea-washed Gogarth on Anglesey were about to claim their full attention and Lakeland could breathe more easily again.

Opposite: Above left: Harold Drasdo.   Photo: R.F. Allen.
            Above right: Allan Austin.   Photo: R.F. Allen.
            Below left: Harold Drasdo on Overhanging Wall.   Photo: H. Drasdo.
            Below right: Geoff Oliver leading complete with hammer in back pocket!   Photo: Geoff Oliver.

Geoff Milburn after a Langdale weekend in 1961

Ken and Geoff Milburn shortly before Cumbrian Rock was completed

Trevor Jones on the way to Pillar in 1954

Trevor Jones, the Author, in 1987

Opposite: Top left: Pat Fearnehough
            Top right: Paul Nunn on the 2nd ascent of Samson.
            Bottom left: Paul Nunn on the 2nd ascent of Post Mortem, Eagle Crag.
            Bottom right: Paul Nunn.

Photo: Ian Roper.

Photos: Paul Nunn.
Photo: R.F. Allen.

Austin's superb route The Red Edge (1962) on Esk Buttress.

Photo: Bob Allen.

White Knight

In the middle-Sixties there was an explosion of new routes and one of the reasons was the development of much better protection devices. Crew and Jack Soper had relied extensively on drilled-out nuts, of differing sizes, strung on to nylon line slings, so that the assembly looked like a Polynesian necklace. Soper invented a revolutionary device, a cast aluminium wedge, swaged onto a sturdy wire sling, the wedge taking the place of the inserted chockstone, extensively used by the Rock and Ice, and the later development — the drilled-out nut. Soper unwittingly tested his prototype during a fall from the final crack of Joe Brown's test-piece, Vector (E2 5c) on the Tremadog cliffs in North Wales. Whilst dangling on the rope he decided on a major re-design. He then improved his casting methods so successfully that his invention was able to absorb the shock load of a long leader-fall. The modern method of protecting cracks of differing widths had been invented. The drilled-out nuts had a bad mechanical design: threading rope through them meant that the line was stressed over a narrow radius so increasing the possibility of failure during a fall. Soper's basic wedge design over the years has led to much smaller wired wedges and made the protection of narrow cracks much safer. It was a world-first and credit is due to him. Before his invention pitons were often hammered into the rock, but he started the decline in the use of pegs. Other climbers started to make wedges, and one of Les Brown's friends, 'Killer' Henderson, produced quite an array, all of which were made in a North-Eastern shipyard where he worked. On Fisher's Folly on Shepherds Crag, they lifted out as he climbed up then slid into a spiky bundle. Whillans happened to be passing underneath, and shouted up, "Don't think yer'll be able to get ITV wi' that aerial."

Paul Ross, always a controversial climber, had twelve traumatic months in a sanatorium, having contracted tuberculosis of the spine, which resulted in two collapsed vertebrae. While they slowly mended he became a horizontal hospital bookmaker and made so much money that when he was discharged he was able to convalesce on the French Riviera for six weeks. He was told that he would have to wear a plaster corset for months, possibly years; then promptly soloed Little Chamonix. While still under the plaster constraint he discovered Reecastle Crag in the Watendlath valley and recorded its first route — The Gibbet (E1 5b).

One man who helped to make 1962 an important year was Ray McHaffie who was just as colourful as Ross. He came from Carlisle and before he took up climbing he had been the leader of a gang of Teddy boys. During one fracas with a rival gang, he was struck in the face with an axe and lost the sight of an eye. He became interested in walking and became captivated by the Lakeland fells. One weekend in the Lakes he decided to take to the water, but getting out of a rubber dinghy cut his foot badly on a broken bottle, the wound requiring eight stitches. The following weekend he lagged far behind his fellow walkers because he had to wear a carpet slipper on the injured foot and a nailed boot on the other. Suddenly alone at the foot of Kern Knotts, he soloed Kern Knotts Crack (V.S.) in his bizarre footwear. Back in Keswick, he rejoined his walking friends and pointed out an Abrahams photograph of the Crack — his first climb. They didn't believe him so, stung into action, he soloed it again the next week in nailed boots in front of his amazed friends. Twenty-five years after his heyday,

McHaffie still climbs E2 5c in his sixth decade, and has amassed a total of nearly two hundred new routes — nearly all in Borrowdale.

Others of his generation who climbed just for glory gave up when they were overtaken by a younger generation, whereas Ray has carried on. Climbing in bizarre footwear has been one of his specialities. Wearing roller skates and boxing gloves, he has climbed Little Chamonix on Shepherds Crag three times. Thirty years ago he did it for a bet of twenty pounds, worth two hundred pounds today. Again he repeated the performance for the Daily Express and finally for B.B.C. television, the secret being that roller skates have plates which stick out and can be placed on holds just like a tricouni nail. The other part of the trick is that boxing gloves are not so thickly padded on their inners and it is possible to feel the rock through the fabric palm.

McHaffie eventually became one of the better Borrowdale climbers. He regularly gave a colourful account of each day's activities and his penetrating voice in pubs became ever louder as each evening wore on. Rumour has it that he even had time for girl friends and prudently kept a supply of engagement rings to keep his female flock tethered.

In 1962 he started to climb with Ado Liddell. Interloper (E1 5b) (aid used on first ascent) on Falcon Crag was their first new route. There was a prominent niche just to its left and McHaffie saw it as a superb possibility. He and Liddell produced The Niche (E2 5c) a classic climb. McHaffie described their ascent:

'We wondered why this line had not been climbed by Paul Ross. We spun a coin to see who was going to lead the first pitch. Adrian won the toss and set off up the steep wall. About fifteen feet below the Niche he had no runners on and decided to put a peg in, then climbed up a few feet and made the very difficult traverse into the Niche. He belayed on a piton. I set off to climb the pitch which I found to be very difficult. I left the piton in place. I came off on the traverse into the Niche. I set off on the second pitch and put two pitons under the roof.'

They had used aid to get up the route, but so had Joe Brown and Ross on some of their routes. A quarter of a century later McHaffie can get fourteen running belays on the first pitch which has made it much safer. The aid caused a lively controversy, but Rob Matheson, a future star, summed up the attitude of a later generation:

'Perhaps 'The Niche' controversy illustrates the attitude of the Northern approach. A few mates, a little imagination and several letters later the scene was set. A manufactured controversy. The Borrowdale team had made themselves a little more famous and a little richer from payment for letters and had had a good laugh; but let's face it, the most important thing of all was the route. The cynics of other areas could sense the atmosphere of steel and there can be no doubt as to their astuteness. Progress — competition — conflict: leading to an inevitable stretching of the traditional ethics and means. Progress is leading today to a 'purifying' process and this has been obvious in the case of Borrowdale. Difficulty undoubtedly increases as a result of aid reduction, and great difficulty breeds great doubt!'

During McHaffie's ascent he was unnerved by an alarming crash as a large block hit the ground. For part of its fall Les Brown had been reluctantly attached to it, whilst trying a new climb, an old piton plucked him away to dangling safety. The ledge from which the block had become airborne was immediately named Les's Ledge. The following weekend, another strong university/Alpha team attacked the route, Oliver Woolcock and new Borrowdale hard man Paul Nunn, and produced the appropri-

Opposite: Above: Ed Grindley, Ian Roper and Jack Soper.
            Below: Paul Ross, ?, and Brian Henderson below Goat Crag in 1965.   Photo: Ken Wilson.

ately-named Plagiarism (E2 5b). Nunn became one of the top gregarious Peak climbers and in the early Sixties made Keswick his mountain home at weekends and Borrowdale benefited as a result. There was also a plentiful supply of pleasant girls, in contrast to the Llanberis maidens who spurned the advances of English climbers. He was particularly tough, and on one occasion while near the top of the Alpine super-severe Philip-Flamm in the Dolomites, a rock plummeted, breaking his leg, as well as jamming his peg hammer into it. He pulled the hammer out, splinted the broken leg with slings and hopped upwards to finish the route.

Nunn enriched Keswick Saturday nights with probably the loudest laugh in the British Isles climbing community. Although he did not raise the top Lakeland standards set by Ross in his early career, Nunn contributed to the relentless drive for new routes in which his contemporaries were involved. On the unfinished route which housed Les's ledge, he too came upon a loose block, and prudently hammered in a piton to produce Plagiarism (E2 5b); a climb demanding strength, with which the Alpha climbers were obsessed. Powerful lines through overhanging rock were among their specialities.

In 1963 whilst Ross lay between clean white sheets in the sanatorium, his arch-rival Allan Austin was hard at work in Langdale. On the high reaches of Gimmer Crag, just left of Kipling Groove, a line had attracted great climbers such as Joe Brown and Robin Smith. Both had done a pitch and the whole line had all been climbed in sections. Austin gathered them together with Gimmer String (E1 5b) which dispensed with the piton which Robin Smith had been forced to use. The 1980 guide-book says:

> 'The climb is attractively laid out with its major difficulties in fine open positions on the arete, and gives one of the more enjoyable climbs on Gimmer.'

Austin also helped to restore Lakeland pride by doing the third ascent of Dovedale Grooves and even added another pitch:

> 'Off again, full of hope. And sure enough after a bit of effort, I found myself above the overhang in a sort of slabby groove, except that it was not really slabby, only in comparison with the overhanging walls on either side. The holds were sloping too. A few feet more and I decided it looked too gripping ahead and too desperate below. Once again I wished I was somewhere else. "My trouble is that I am just a coward", I called to Jack as I selected a piton. "I'm not built for bold leading", I said, hammering it home into a fat crack on the wall. Suddenly there was a shudder and a jerk and part of the wall slid down. I was frightened. "It's a judgement", I thought, staring at the flake hanging above my head and willing it to stay there. "What shall I do?" I wailed. "Get out", said Jack, so off I rushed up the previously impossible groove, a peg in my teeth and the hammer dragging along between my feet. At last the top and a place to put the peg. I hammered it in, gently at first and then with increasing confidence as it rang higher and higher. Time to relax now and take stock of my position. Damn! There was a jug just over the top! I thought of the peg I had just put in. I could take it out or I could leave it for Jack. I left it, and rushed over the top.'

1964 dawned with a resurgence in West Cumbrian climbing, particularly on Pillar Rock, a favourite with Victorian climbers, since it was first climbed in the Eighteen-Twenties. After Kelly's series of excellent climbs just after the First World War it had gradually gone out of favour. There were occasional raids by leaders from particular periods, then the Old Stone slumbered again. Geoff Cram who changed its status quo

Opposite: Peter Crew and Jancis Allinson on an early ascent of The Praying Mantis (1965), Goat Crag.   Photo: Ken Wilson.
      Inset: Les Brown.   Photo: Trevor Jones.

lived in Whitehaven, started climbing when he was fifteen and often cycled fifteen miles from his home to Pillar Rock, where he cut his teeth on its traditional Victorian climbing gems. When he was eighteen, in 1963, he did his first new route Scylla, a useful V.S. By the time he went to Imperial College, London, he was one of the leading Lakeland climbers. On the college fresher's meet, he astonished the senior under-graduates by leading Cenotaph Corner, Joe Brown's outstanding Llanberis climb. In the summer of 1964 on the return journey from a long Alpine season he stopped the car at the foot of Castle Rock of Triermain to try a line to the right of Ross's Rigor Mortis. He produced The Ghost, which is both steep and strenuous and which had a dangerous loose block, which menaced the crux moves. It was his first E2 5b and it immediately made him one of the hard Cumbrian climbers. Some years later Chris Bonington abseiled down and removed the loose block and made the climb much harder and nowadays the easier 'loop' variation is used.

Across the valley from Castle Rock is Raven Crag, Thirlmere, which is an entirely different proposition altogether as it is a dark cliff, topped by firs and pines. It is often wet, and had only been lightly explored at that time. A huge cave at its centre made the only possibilities for the Sixties climbers on its flanks. Martin Boysen was one of the most brilliant rock gymnasts, trained on the sandstone teeth of Harrison's Rocks. He impressed the old fox Joe Brown on a joint new route in Wales, with a languid solution to hard moves which had pressed Joe. Boysen became intrigued by the gloomy Raven Crag, Thirlmere and saw a faint chance in a hanging groove on the left side, which was guarded at its foot by a slender tree. He tried it in winter but the rock was cold and deadened his fingers, and he retreated. He returned with a product of public school, Sandhurst and Cranwell, an ex-army officer, who is now our best-known mountain-eer, Chris Bonington. Bonington suggested that he should make the first attempt on the smooth-looking initial wall. Boysen, the better climber, secretly thought he would fail. Craftily Bonington slid in a hand-inserted piton to protect his moves into the unknown, but pulled it out as soon as he moved beyond it. He reached the foot of a tempting corner, which soared up above his head then announced: "I think I'll go to the top."

Boysen suspecting lese-majeste said firmly, "No you don't. It's my bloody route." He took over after asserting his right and surged into the second pitch. In the very steep corner he was forced to stand in a sling round a spike which unfortunately snapped off leaving him suspended by his hands, but he recovered to finish the climb. They named it The Medlar (E2 5b) (now E3 6a in its free state) although the tree at the foot is in fact a different species being a Sorbus, of the rose or whitebeam family.

About this time Boysen attempted Ross's Thirlmere Eliminate on Castle Rock, where he found progress both slow and tiring. While he was contemplating the crux Ross appeared and told him that he was on Rigor Mortis. Unperturbed, Boysen carried on to make its first free ascent, and just to prove his excellent form did both Triermain and North Crag Eliminates as well the same day. Even in his forties, he still climbs 6b, adjusts his glasses on hard moves, then glides elegantly up. Not long after The Medlar, Bonington returned with Mike Thompson to force a way up the right-hand flank of Raven Crag with Totalitarian (E2 5c) (after Ed Grindley freed the top pitch and made this forbidding cliff more popular. Bonington's clipped public school accent and obsession with remoter parts of the world might give the impression that he is a latter-day Victorian explorer. In fact, he still leads E3 with the same dedication to rock-climbing as twenty-five years ago. His commanding presence can occasionally help in difficult circumstances. Once he and Trevor Jones went into a stockbroker-belt

Opposite: Left: Paul Nunn on Plastic Happiness, Upper Falcon Crag.   Photo: Bonington collection.
            Top right: Paul Nunn on Eagle Crag.   Photo: Paul Nunn.
            Bottom right: Oliver Woolcock on 2nd ascent of Samson, High Crag.   Photo: Paul Nunn.

pub still dressed in tattered climbing gear. Inside the landlord at the bar was stroking an exotic-looking dog. When they appeared a disgusted look came over his face, but before he could speak, Bonington bellowed, "What a splendid animal! I've not seen one since I met the Lion of Judaea on the Blue Nile Expedition." The landlord's face distorted into incredulity as he realised Chris's true identity and he treated them to free whiskies for the rest of the evening.

In 1965 Bonington turned his attention to the hard man's crag, the East Buttress of Scafell, with Mike Thompson. They reasoned that the 1938 Girdle Traverse was incomplete, and so they started off from the left-hand end. Bonington made a succession of committing moves until he got stuck. Fortunately three young soldiers were passing underneath, and in his best parade-ground voice Bonington ordered them to produce a top-rope. However, with a great deal of push he managed to climb the mauvais pas, and consequently produced The Holy Ghost (E2 5c). The name caused some protest, as some thought that he was referring to himself, whereas others felt that it was blasphemy,

Borrowdale came into the news again, principally because of the insatiable curiosity of Ray McHaffie who discovered Goat Crag. Certainly it did not offer much promise. Hanging gardens of creepers, moss and bushes gave it a miserable appearance. Some climbers even doubted that there was a crag. McHaffie tried a promising crack but was stopped by vegetation. Later, with Les Brown, he went to try a fierce crack on Great Gable. They failed, not surprisingly as it was to be the first E3 in Cumbria. That day McHaffie told Brown about the possibilities of Goat Crag. Brown went to have a look but he too was defeated by vegetation after climbing two pitches of McHaffie's line. Brown abseiled down the route the following weekend and thoroughly cleaned it, and seven days later in May 1965 completed Praying Mantis. Graded Extreme it was thought at first to be one of the hardest routes in the valley. Later after further ascents it became a classic Hard Very Severe 5b. Les Brown not only produced hard new routes, he also developed new crags and buttresses such as the central part of Heron Crag, so that any of his activities were subject to close scrutiny by the opposition. Paul Nunn wrote of the interest before Brown did Praying Mantis:

'One spring Saturday evening he sat in the corner pen listening to the amber-reflecting glasses chinking, hedged in by the intensity of his companions' stares and shrinking ever deeper into his shell before salvoes of their questions. His words became fewer and fewer. The more acute the probes, the more vehement the interrogation, the less was the response. At last his assailants spluttered into silence. The beer won in a few moments; a new topic was broached and the main issue was forgotten. Later he disappeared into the night without any hint on the prize topic. His interrogators reconsidered it all while driving down the valley. 'He must be imagining it. Where in the Lakes is there so high a piece of unclimbed stone? Getting on for 300 feet? It's absurd...' There were hints that it had taken all winter. The following day a wife was sent on a hunch to spy and she was sitting at the foot when the big team arrived. Obliged to finish by an unwanted female observer the Silent One ate the final pitches. By evening it was all over. Somewhere amid the dark vegetated walls had emerged a great climb.'

Later Pete Whillance summed up its effect:

'...a magnificent route which was destined to become one of the best and most popular in the Lakes. Brown's route triggered off such a spate of activity from the valley's regular climbers,

Opposite: Pete Livesey on the 1st ascent of Lunatic, E2 5c, on Chapel Head Scar.   Photo: John Sheard.

that it resembled a modern gold rush! None of the routes that followed managed to match the quality of Praying Mantis but several excellent routes materialised from beneath the carpets of grass. In less than two years Goat Crag was transformed from an obscure vegetated hillside into a major crag that boasted twenty-eight new climbs.'

Later that summer Boysen became intrigued with an unclimbed possibility between Hiraeth and Extol on Dove, but was defeated by loose overhangs. He went back, but this time the second man became marooned in the middle of the face. The ropes then jammed and not surprisingly Boysen lost interest in the line. Geoff Cram eventually repeated it and called it Mordor (E3 5c) meaning the bad land — as a dig against the Welsh marauders. There is a top corner which could provide a top pitch and still awaits an ascent. Although the route can be claimed to be the first real E3 in the Lakes, its looseness has made it unpopular.

It was inevitable that the Borrowdale team would rear its head again in 1965 and Paul Nunn did Daedalus (E2 5c) on Eagle Crag supported by Paul Ross. The climb was a milestone as Ross's days of new routes (in England) were nearly over. It was the Alpha Club which now played the major role in Borrowdale and elsewhere. Amongst the Alpha there was a feeling that Les Brown and Nunn dominated Lakeland climbing, Crew Ingle and Boysen were the leading forces in Wales, whilst in the Peak they all combined to dominate its development.

A major problem in Borrowdale was the lack of an up-to-date guide-book, and as McHaffie and Ross were not members of the Fell and Rock information regarding new routes was lacking. McHaffie produced his own guide-book which was then expanded and developed by Ross and Mike Thompson, as the Fell and Rock equivalent still seemed to be some way off. The 1966 'pirate' guide to Borrowdale included several aid routes and was regarded with some horror by the Establishment. The Fell and Rock had realised the danger and decided to look for a literate iconoclast who was also a good climber. Jack Soper had gravitated to Allan Austin's Langdale team so Soper asked the bustling Nunn to join the Fell and Rock and take over the vital Borrowdale guide-book. Nunn was then involved in ten more hard new routes, many with Ross, who then departed for the U.S.A. Nunn and Woolcock eventually produced their long-awaited guide-book in 1968.

Jack Soper was climbing regularly with Allan Austin in 1965 and together with a young apprentice Ian (Sherpa) Roper, they all went to Eagle Crag in Buttermere in one of Austin's rare excursions to the higher Lakeland crags. Carnival (E1 5b) was the result with the youthful Roper leading the crucial pitches. However Austin's thoughts were in Langdale and he made a determined effort with Man of Straw (E1 5b) on White Ghyll and Rainmaker (E1 5b) on Pavey Ark. He had to use a piton on both routes and perhaps it is worth quoting his own thoughts on the use of pegs in new routes:

'Climbers seem to be choosing a line and using just enough aid to get up them without really considering whether the climb is possible without... In general there is too much of a rush to do a route and get it into print.'

With the dawn of 1966 it was sensed in Keswick climbing circles that the time was ripe for another Les Brown onslaught, this time on the main face of Scafell. He was cross-questioned and blandly replied that he intended to go to Far East Buzzard Crag so while the Inquisition scanned its guide-books for this mythical crag, Brown produced The Nazgul (E2 5c) (some aid). It was another Les Brown masterpiece and

Opposite: Bill Birkett moving off the end of the ramp on Shere Khan (Cleasby and Matheson 1977), on Scafell East Buttress. Rick Graham is the
second.   Photo: Al Phizacklea.

his last major contribution to Lakeland climbing before he departed for Scotland.

Evergreen Austin that same year produced Chimney Variant (E1 5b) in White Ghyll. Drasdo in his prime had tried it and failed; and it eventually proved to be one of Austin's more spectacular pitches, with a sidle along an undercut gangway to a hanging groove at its end, whose only footholds seemed to be at shoulder height.

Not long afterwards Allan Austin produced the first guide-book to Great Langdale for seventeen years. It aroused a storm of protest even before it was published. When he presented his manuscript to the Fell and Rock Guide-book Committee, Kelly was still editor, despite being in his eighties. Austin wanted to include Dolphin's Babylon, the first new Extreme in which a woman (Marie Ball) was involved. It was on East Raven Crag in Langdale, which Kelly dismissed as a scruffy irrelevance. When Austin entered the meeting-room, Kelly threw the manuscript at Austin, who only grabbed a few sheets before they fluttered to the floor. A long silence ensued, followed by a bitter discussion about ethics and finally Kelly resigned.

The change in Fell and Rock guide-book management resulted in three guide-books in 1967, Austin's Great Langdale, a revised Eastern Crags and a much-needed Scafell Guide from Geoff Oliver and Joe Griffin.

A lot of Austin's verbal barbs were directed at Paul Ross, who had done aid routes in Langdale just to annoy him. Austin was involved in over a hundred new routes in the Lakes and only put in half a dozen pegs; this was certainly the lowest total number of any leading innovator of that time and helped to buttress his purist approach. It should be remembered that Joe Brown had set a limit of two points of aid per pitch and this was an ethic which the British climbing community generally accepted. Perhaps it is worth quoting Austin:

> 'I am not proud of my pegs, I am weak like the rest, but having said that I can stand back and look at them and realise that they are blunders, but I don't try to back my blunders up!'

Even Peter Crew was not above suspicion. Ray McHaffie saw him hammering chockstones into Triermain Eliminate, then using them for aid. McHaffie politely told Crew that it was a free climb.

About that time Ken Wilson was collecting material for his classic book, Hard Rock. It was mandatory to approach Austin on two counts: for his stature in the climbing world and also as respect for his lucid climbing articles. Wilson offered him a copy at wholesale price in return for an article. Austin retorted that he could get one at that price in his own climbing shop and demanded a free copy plus £20. Wilson reluctantly agreed, but ten years later Austin was rummaging through ancient office records, when a dusty £20 cheque fell to the floor. Wilson had won in the end.

Far away from controversy Geoff Cram was still hard at work on Pillar Rock. Early in 1965 he had put up Sheol (E2 5b) a 300-foot climb right of Grooved Wall on the North Face. He then moved a compass point to the West Face of High Man which had a bulging arete on the left of Kelly's Gomorrah. This produced Gondor (E2 5c), meaning the 'good land' which was quite appropriate after the bitter controversies of the Sixties.

Latterly Ross had kept the Lamplighter Cafe to cater for the needs of climbers returning from Borrowdale, then in the evening he used to entertain them with folksongs.

By the end of 1968 however he had emigrated. Of the others Les Brown had moved to Scotland, and Crew had fallen under the spell of Joe Brown and no longer went

e exposed position on Minotaur (1968), Scafell East Buttress.

Photo: Ian Roper.

North. Austin was one of the only active innovators left from the early Sixties and still had several fruitful Langdale years ahead of him up to his E2 ceiling. Austin was undoubtedly spurred on by the increasing number of hard men coming onto the scene and became intrigued with a small steep crag just below the summit of The Band in Langdale. Some would contend that Neckband Crag is mossy, faces North-East, and is often damp; but Austin had noticed a wealth of tempting unclimbed narrow cracks, ideal for a gritstone expert. It took nearly an hour to get there. Unfortunately Austin greatly disliked walking because he had broken several leg bones as a result of gritstone falls. One foot eventually became a different size from the other. On several occasions after bone-breaking falls on Yorkshire grit, he hopped to crags on a pair of crutches, but was still more able than his friends on the hardest problems.

Austin first went to Neckband Crag for guide-book investigations, to check a route called Virgo, a serious Hard Very Severe, which was wet. The first pitch looked like a vertical skating rink. After clipping into an ancient peg, Austin tried a mantelshelf move, then realised to his horror that he couldn't reverse it. He fell and during his fifty-foot plummet the second man rushed down the hillside to lessen the shock on the piton which had to take the strain of the fall. Austin survived his flight and returned with Ken Wood for a consolation prize, Razor Crack, Hard Very Severe 5a, a superb crack splitting a steep wall. Whilst doing the climb they noticed another intriguing possibility which led onto a narrow slab followed by a steep groove. Wood was not bothered about new routes and his name does not often appear in the first ascent lists, but experts often pushed Wood into the lead if conditions were damp. It was almost two years before he returned with Austin to produce Gillette (E2 5c) one of the hardest climbs in the valley at the time.

1969 was a momentous year. Bill Lounds who lived near Lancaster, became a fast, fluent mover on rock, then started producing quite a number of steep hard routes on limestone cliffs near Lancaster. Together with Chris Eilbeck who worked in the new university Lounds added a top pitch to Gillette, then produced his own free version of Black Widow (E2 5b) on Pillar.

However, the obsession of 1969 was in a valley not previously associated with climbing, Kentmere at the gateway to the Lakes. A crag was discovered called Rainsborrow. Good climbers became obsessed with it, even comparing it with the East Buttress of Scafell, despite the fact that the main features of Rainsborrow were its vegetation and a lack of rock. There were rumours flying about which caused a sort of Goat Crag gold rush, and even Joe Brown visited for a route. His route The Groan (E2 5c) was done at the age of 39, after he had been at the top for twenty years. The crux of The Groan was a vicious crack, the type that Brown and Whillans had excelled at for two decades. Brown still feels that the techniques he and Don developed for hard crack climbs have not been exceeded. Intensive training and obsession with climbing walls have made young climbers exceptional on overhanging walls, while a route such as Whillans's ultimate crack test-piece on Burbage Edge — Goliath E4 6a — is studiously avoided by the young gritstone elite.

The most surprising event of 1969 was the solution of the big unclimbed crack on Great Gable which had defeated Les Brown, and from which Eric 'Matie' Metcalf had fallen and broken his leg. The surprising victor was Richard McHardy, a capable Welsh climber who was not considered to be in the front rank in Wales. He came to the Lake District one momentous 1969 weekend with Paul (Tut) Braithwaite. They did Leverage, Ichabod and Hell's Groove, then tired of using the rope soloed Mickledore Grooves, Trinity, Chartreuse and Overhanging Wall. They were obviously in excellent

Opposite: Top left: Mike Mortimer.   Photo: Ian Roper.
           Top right: Ray McHaffie.   Photo: Ian Roper.
           Bottom left: John Wilkinson.   Photo: Ian Roper.
           Bottom right: David Miller.   Photo: R.F. Allen.

condition and McHardy snatched one of the plum routes on Great Gable, The Viking, which was the first popular E3 5c in the Lake District.

During the closing stages of Les Brown's Lakeland climbing career, he lived in the North-East and frequently gave a lift to two teenagers who embraced his climbing philosophy. They were Colin Read and Johnny Adams, who in a twelve-month period spanning 1968/1969 put up hard routes on five separate crags: the East Buttress of Scafell, Scafell Shamrock, Deer Bield Crag, Goat Crag and Great End Crag in Borrowdale. They generally climbed at E2 standard, but some of their productions were destined to be either E3s or had a 6a pitch and required aid.

The East Buttress of Scafell gave them their great 1969 prize, the three-star Lord of The Rings (E2 5b) which is over 1100 feet long and is described by the 1984 guide-book as: 'A long arduous and magnificent expedition which takes in some of the best pitches and situations on the cliff.'

Chris Bonington had made an attempt on the line with Holy Ghost. On the second 5c pitch he had been forced to veer away, and had left a decaying runner as a symbol of his traumas. Read and Adams approached the unsolved problem with precise exploration. They took a sequence of panoramic photographs and studied them during winter evenings. One day when spring arrived, they studied the cliff with binoculars; the weather was awful, but hypnotised by the possibilities they bivouacked at the foot of the crag. Unfortunately despite their enthusiasm they were forced to retreat because of thick mist and driving rain. As soon as the weather improved they went back, with little time to spare, as Johnny had arranged to go on an overland expedition to India. Again they bivouacked. Later Read described the second crucial pitch:

'Now came the moment of truth, as the descent, on virgin rock, of the wall below began. Down a few feet, then working back a little left to the top of a shallow indefinite groove, down this, not too bad at first, but progressively growing thinner and thinner. A few feet below a poor ledge led rightwards to a possible stance, the next few moves towards it were indescribably thin. Holding my breath as a foot roamed in search of the elusive ledge, gingerly down, then balancing across until being able to see right down into Hell's Groove, banging in a Yankee angle (a broad piton) and sorting things out I began seeping in the warm glow of satisfaction. For John the pitch was utterly serious. As he rounded the edge on Holy Ghost, the situation became alarming — the rope fell away sweeping down across the wall, towards the only two meagre runners on the pitch. He juggled with the 5c moves, for a moment hesitating. I gripped the rope tightly, watching intently, a fall from there would result in a tremendous pendulum with messy consequences. This must have been spinning through his mind, as he dithered, then braced himself moving very steadily. Things relaxed as the first runner was approached, descending the wall with protection made that part acceptable......'

They climbed for eleven hours before returning to their rocky bed at the foot of the crag. Next day after eight further hours, they wearily climbed the last pitch of Mickledore Grooves and were rewarded with one of the longest hard climbs in the Lake District.

Athanor on Goat Crag was another of their remarkable achievements. Only twenty feet right of Praying Mantis was an awesomely steep line which Read and Adams climbed at 6a using aid to overcome it. Nowadays hard men step upwards from the highest rung gained by their predecessors.

Mortimer on The Viking (1969), Great Gable.

Phto: Bob Allen.

Dave Miller and Terry Parker on Tarkus (1972) Dow Crag.

Photo: Ian R

Adams and Read had a clear-cut ethic, if they used aid they recorded it. If either was second and did the route with less aid, they recorded the greater amount. If they repeated the route the following week and reduced the aid, the original recorded amount was left to stand. It would have been easy to say that they had not advanced standards, but they showed remarkable energy, with routes over the high and low crags. Perhaps it is best to label them 'the change-over team' as they spanned the old and new climbing ideologies.

Unfortunately a bad accident while at work, sliced off Read's thumb, and damaged the rest of his hand so severely that he was unable to climb hard again. Johnny Adams is still as keen as ever. When he climbed with Colin Read their top standard was E2/3 but with the increase in methods of protection he can now lead E4. Some time ago he decided that he was not living in the right place for maximum climbing productivity and worked out the optimum place to live. From an atlas he worked out that Kendal gave maximum access to all climbing areas, with minimum travel costs.

At the same time as Adams and Read started to make an impact, another man appeared on the scene. Rob Matheson started climbing with his father at the age of seven, did his first Severe at the age of ten, then followed this with a classical education in Very Difficults until he was able to lead his father up Gimmer Crack when he was fifteen.

Matheson soon showed a natural new route ability and put up the impressive Paladin on White Ghyll in 1970. He used a considerable amount of aid, but led it clean six months later to give a sustained E3 5c. However it was in Austin country and the manner of its ascent annoyed Austin, which resulted in a barrage of verbal grapeshot fired at Matheson. But in his 1973 Great Langdale guide-book, Austin ignored Matheson's free ascent and wrote in the 'Mountain' magazine: 'I do not see crags as impressive backcloths where ruthless men can construct their climbs'. Matheson's reply was swift:

> 'All I wanted when I did this route was a good end-product, and it took me an inspection and two ascents to attain this. As in the case of all routes ascended in this manner, the critics will say: "Why didn't you leave it to someone else?" The only answer is that we are all human, and few of us are strong-willed enough, or care enough, to throw the limited numbers of lines on to the open market. So the end-product of Paladin was a hard, free route, which was reported honestly for anyone who wished to follow. It started out as a partially-aided route and was converted into a free route. The Fell and Rock guide-writers thought it unethical for a first ascensionist to free climb his own route. They therefore reduced what had become a very fine and ferocious free line to its original aided status, pari passu their own ascent.'

Austin left fifty routes out of the guide-book, and reasoned that just because climbers operated at the Extreme level it did not mean their excessively-aided routes should be included. (Nobody however took him to task for omitting some Difficult and Severe climbs.) The disputes rumbled on for years and one suspects that Austin enjoyed being in the thick of it. Rob Matheson, poked fun at Austin and his Langdale Inquisition in an article which was written under a pseudonym — Henry Ford, which was an amusingly sly dig at Allan's surname:

> 'The Wise Owl'd Judge of the English Lake District wryly smiles at the evidence in hand. The jury of wide-eyed spies, hangers-on, apprentices and informers await eagerly, full of conjecture about the inevitable judgement to come. "He's a bastard, a liar and a cheat!"

Catacomb (1972) on Dow Crag.

ff Lamb on Phobos (1972), Dove Crag.

proclaims the beaming judge. (Stupendous applause) "He was seen to top-rope the bloody thing at fifteen hundred hours." A stifling silence ensues. "Excommunication — send him to Wales — that's all!" The atmosphere was one of fear and respect. It was a demagogue's dream; the situation called for more. "We must maintain the Status Quo or fall into the pit of vice and modern perversion. These 'bastard practices' must be cut out. 'On sight' is the thing. Top-roping, abseiling down, pegging, skyhooking, lying and the like demonstrate this modern perversion and they must be challenged and erased from the record."

Austin commented caustically on the use of aid on hard routes:

'All the protests come from Jumped-up XS men who complain that their aid route had been left out. Just because they climb at that standard, they think that their particular brand of ethics should count.'

Perhaps to show that he could still climb Austin produced one of his hardest climbs on Pavey Ark, The Bracken-clock (E2 5c) but had to use a piton which was dispensed with the following year.

Disputes still rumbled on with Austin happily at the centre, but in the early Seventies a be-spectacled, climber Peter Livesey was to change British climbing for ever.

Opposite: Top left: Rod Valentine   Photo: Ian Roper.
            Top right: Ken Wood.   Photo: Ian Roper.
            Bottom left: Geoff Cram on Troutdale Pinnacle Direct.   Photo: R.F. Allen.
            Bottom right: Paul 'Tut' Braithwaite.   Photo: R.F. Allen.

Rock Athlete

Before Peter Livesey took up athletic rock-climbing in 1970 there was still a thread of the old gentlemanly tradition that competition was socially unacceptable. Livesey made sure that such attitudes were dumped overboard. He was the first of the ruthless, competitive rock athletes. His external appearance — glasses and a straggle of frizzy hair — masked an exceptional determination and a latent physical strength fuelled by rigorous, scientifically-planned training which made him a winner at whatever sport he took up.

From an early age he had a precious physical spark that made him Northern Counties Junior Steeplechase Champion, and it took him to a third place in the AAA Championships. He then had to cast around for some time, before he found his true outdoor metier. However just to prove he was not just a fitness freak, one year he became Electrical Engineering Apprentice of the Year. Canoeing gave him strong forearms; caving, then cave-diving, heightened his exploratory feelings — particularly after a year in Jamaica employed by a millionaire to explore virgin river caves.

About this time he decided to become the best climber in the country by incessant training on a climbing wall in Scunthorpe. Training, training, followed by yet more training put him in the running to become the leading climber in the country. Jim Perrin has analysed his climbing:

> 'Livesey's style is ordinariness brought to a fine art: fast, powerful, perfect and completely unremarkable except in its breathtaking efficiency.'

Nobody before Livesey had analysed the mental and physical demands required, not only to reach the top but to become good enough to produce galaxies of much harder new routes than had been known before. Livesey's analysis is as follows:

> 'The basic principle is that of overload, and overload means working the muscle near its maximum for as long as possible and training effect is only achieved when this is happening. When the muscle is cruising there is little or no training effect. Lots of overload in a short length of time is achieved by doing repetitions of the action with something like 70% of the maximun load possible for one action...A snow mountaineer, for example, may require 95% endurance and 5% speed/strength energy development, whereas a crag-rat may require 80% speed/strength energy and 20% medium duration energy...one should never deny that climbing is physical and that much of the inherent pleasure is distinctly physical. That pleasure is almost certainly heightened by a sense of physical well-being, or perhaps even athletic competence; fitness training of some kind is the way to heighten or ensure that experience.'

Livesey is a Yorkshireman, from a county which has enriched Cumbrian climbing. His first hard new Cumbrian climb was Sally Free and Easy (E2 5c) on the right wall of Stony Buttress on Pavey Ark. Subsequently Rodney Valentine and Austin claimed that their Ragman's Trumpet (E2 5c) covered the same ground. Livesey insisted that they

Opposite: Ed Cleasby on Footless Crow (1974), Goat Crag.   Photo: Ian Roper.
Inset: Pete Livesey on Gates of Delirium.

had repeated his pitch, then traversed fearfully away from his serious 5c second pitch. There followed a ferocious printed battle which Austin waged with zest:

'I believe that the first line on a new wall or buttress must be a natural one. Direct routes, 'eliminate' type routes, various hybrids and so on can come later. Essentially a great mountaineering line like this must follow the easiest way. One may wish that this fine corner was the only way, or that that line of jugs over there was somewhere else, but one can't ignore the fact of their existence. The correct solution to a rock problem must be the easy one. The finish produced by Pete Livesey is a very fine one, but it isn't even direct...'

A leader of the next generation, Ron Fawcett, felt impelled to come to Livesey's defence:

'On the Stony Buttress, Livesey's long and serious route, Sally Free and Easy, met with a considerable opposition from Fell and Rock pundits who claimed that their inferior Ragman's Trumpet was the real route up that piece of rock. Time and subsequent ascents have shown the way and Sally Free and Easy is now the established route.'

Sally Free and Easy was not in itself an epoch-making climb; even Livesey had to build up to a climax and it was to be another three years before he made his major impact on the Lakeland crags. During the early Seventies he popularised the advantages of climbing in perpetual summer sunshine in the Yosemite Valley in California, and on the thousand-foot limestone cliffs of the Verdon gorge in Provence, in contrast to previous summer practice of waiting in Chamonix for the Aiguilles to come into condition after frequent bad-weather periods. He summed up in a few words the main advantage that training gave him over the leading climbers before him:

'Having the strength not just to climb the route, but to hang around long enough to select and place your running belays and then have the strength to go on climbing.'

Livesey's activities on Pavey Ark should not obscure the fact that on the same day as Ragman's Trumpet, Austin went to White Ghyll and put up one of his best Lakeland pitches, a bulging 5c crack pitch, to complete Haste Not Direct.

Rob Matheson well remembers climbing with Allan Austin; a memorable experience when he became overawed and climbed badly.

Matheson became intrigued by the possibilities on Deer Bield. A slim groove on the left of the crag cried out for attention. Matheson claimed it as The Graduate (E3 6a), but he had pre-placed a long sling and piton by abseil which reduced its present technical grade. He then discovered that Les Brown had done the line some years before with a similar amount of aid but had not recorded it.

An interesting clash of fundamental principles was now taking place. There was the total-war-on-the-crags concept, initiated by Livesey, then the purist approach argued by Austin, whose career as a pioneer was nearing its end.

Rob Matheson and his close friend Ed Cleasby were really the last top climbers from the classical background of an apprenticeship on easier climbs progressing eventually to the top, without intensive or scientific training. The event of 1971 was Matheson's production of Holocaust on Dow Crag. He used two points of aid to force the first pitch but later freed it to claim it at its present grade (E4 6a). Some miles away on

Opposite: Bob Smith leading Edge of Eriador (Matheson and Cleasby 1977) on Scafell East Buttress.   Photo: Al Phizacklea.

Scafell Chris Bonington forced a direct line from the foot of Botterill's Slab, White Wizard (E3 5c). The name seems curiously appropriate, considering Bonington's obsession with the eternal snows. The climb proved to be popular, steep and interesting, but the general opinion was that Bonington had aided it into submission and that it was fortunate that he was out of range of the Langdale polemic artillery commanded by Austin.

Bonington's time was heavily taxed, with his continual membership of expeditions and media extravaganzas as described by Mike Thompson:

> 'He was already involved in early planning stages of a live Eiger broadcast. Despite the massive inroads that they made upon his time, he kept both options open and eventually was faced with an agonising dilemma. Since they were scheduled to take place at the same time, he could not go on both of them. Clearly, Everest was the more important, yet its outcome was less certain and what is more the Eiger broadcast, unlike Everest would go on with or without him. The prospect that, if he went to Everest, somebody else would cavort across the television screens of Europe was almost too much for him to bear, and it was only after he had tried, unsuccessfully, to have the Eiger programme re-scheduled that he was forced to accept, grudgingly, that even he could not manage to be in two places at once.'

1972 proved to be the year of pitons pre-placed from abseil ropes. Two routes were done using this method, both in Langdale, and this caused a storm of protest from Austin, who was in the final stages of his second guide-book to the area. Matheson started from the foot of Austin's Arcturus on Pavey Ark below Jack's Rake then surged up an undercut rib forming the right-hand edge of the upper wall. It was hard and beautifully set up and resulted in Cruel Sister (E3 5c). In addition to the pre-placed piton, he used a long sling and sky-hook for aid. This was against Austin's rigid principles and so the route was omitted from his guide book. The reason in Austin's own words was quite simply:

> '...because I did not believe it had been climbed. I cannot see how a party can claim to have been successful when, having failed on the crux, they have simply gone round to the top of the cliff, hung a sling down over it and then swarmed up from below. Surely rock-climbing is a challenge, and superb lines like this rib throw down their challenge to succeeding generations of climbers, until eventually along comes someone who can do the climb.'

On Raven Crag in Langdale, Livesey also pre-placed a peg and a sling for aid to produce Fine Time and another apoplectic explosion came from Austin. Both Livesey and Matheson had separately come to believe that the way ahead for hard new routes was the carving out of climbs by intensive preparation, e.g. the pre-placement of the minimum acceptable limit of protection. Fine Time with its nerve-racking pull over the initial overhang below the smooth upper wall, was not repeated for another four years.

Ed Grindley had already put up Risus on Pavey Ark. Austin had top-roped its subsequent second pitch and declared it impossible. Grindley's solution showed his future potential. He realised that there was still considerable potential on Pavey Ark and forced one of the last natural unclimbed lines, Fallen Angel (E4 6a, with two pegs for aid on the main pitch). When he got to the foot of the climb, he found that he had forgotten his PAs and had to borrow his partner's (Ian 'Sherpa' Roper) which were two sizes too big.

Opposite: Pulling through the Issel Roof (1977) Ed Cleasby's E2 6a route on Dow Crag.   Photo: Al Phizacklea.

'The most important thing of all was that my first ascents were reported honestly, no secrets being kept from other climbers.'

However new routes which had pitons made it a challenge for others to do it free.

'The Day of the Jackal was thus born; it being realized that fame and satisfaction could just as easily be found by making free second ascents...'

Grindley described some of the problems:

'...In fact, all seemed well until the overlarge PAs began to uncurl from their dimple holds and attempts to rest by leaning on the left wall of the groove were frustrated by a bunch of pegs clipped to my waist; stabbing me and the groove and making the whole business decidedly precarious. Fumble as I might, I couldn't get the bunch out of the way. If downward progress was to be avoided, what was called for was upward movement. Another difficult pull did nothing to solve the PA problem; the last runner below the poor peg was 25 ft. away and with grass blocking the crack ahead a gardening peg seemed the only possibility. Reason prevailed and in went the peg, in enough to lessen the panic and in enough to consolidate a rest for the removal of the grass. Sure as dammit a perfect nut spec (placement) came to light beneath the grass — if only Pete had gardened while he'd abseiled, he usually did! The groove was difficult with the overlarge PAs still showing reluctance to stick to the small holds but soon the right wall dropped back. Above, a short steep crack led up to Astra's stance; to the right another fainter groove split the upper wall. By now, further problems had arisen, principally tiredness, but also a thicker carpet of moss on the traverse to a tiny stance at the foot of the upper groove (most of the groove had needed clearing of some moss on the way up).'

Standards were inching ever higher and it became the time of the 'jackal' — someone who went around reducing or eliminating aid which had been used to force a first ascent. This happened to Fallen Angel when the powerful Jeff Lamb managed to free the climb to produce the first free E4 in the Lake District.

However Colin Read and Johnny Adams took pride of place in 1972 for routes of stature combined with quality, particularly on Dove Crag which frowns from its high perch down towards Brotherswater. They put up Phobos (E2 5c). The name means 'a servant of the god of war' and is described as 'a steep wall climb', taking the challenge that Hiraeth avoids. Crew must have noticed when he did Hiraeth, that the wall would add to the difficulty of his route. He decided to leave it; and Read and Adams solved its complexities. Adams had to overcome the danger of a loose block on the first pitch and was forced to use a point of aid. During a repeat ascent the block was pushed off and when the sulphurous smells caused by its plunge had dispersed a tiny ledge came to light to be used as a hold.

Bad weather did not deter Read and Adams. When most climbers retired to the pub or stayed at home, they still carried on doing Extreme climbs such as Gimmer String in pouring rain, using the well-tried dodge of pulling a pair of socks over their PAs.

In 1969 they had opened up Greatend Crag when they did the Pillar. During its ascent Read had noticed an intriguing line to the left, but its intricacies swallowed up the daylight hours and they had to retreat. Twelve months went by before he could persuade Adams to return for another attempt. Adams gave him a strict time limit as

ob Matheson on Rough (1973), Dow Crag,

Pete Livesey leading Silence (1973) on A Buttress, Dow Crag.

Photo: R.F. Aller

he felt it would take too much gardening, but Read triumphed with Nagasaki Grooves, one of the show pieces of the Borrowdale valley. It is now E4 6b as Read had to use aid to climb the 150-foot pitch. It was freed two years later by Livesey climbing solo with a back-rope, i.e. tied to a rope secured at ground level, with tied-off loops at intervals for clipping into running belays. When Adams repeated the climb years later, he found that when he got to the point where Read had used some aid, some delicate flakes had been smashed to provide holds. The culprit has never been identified.

Read and Adams had a strict ethic. If one of them gardened a pitch, supported by tension or a sling, and the other was able to climb the difficulties using less or no aid the exact amount of aid used by the leader was declared.

On another of their restless excursions they went to Eagle Crag, Buttermere to try Carnival but there was already a slow party of three on the route so they decided to try a line just to the right of it, but only managed two pitches before it got dark. As soon as possible they returned as it was late October and the cliffs were already getting chilly from the first frosts of winter. They finished the route in the dark, with snowflakes swirling about them and covering the fellside with a white mantle. Deimos (E3 5c) (some aid) was nearly five hundred feet long and the guide-book gives it three stars saying that it 'raised standards in the valley by a full grade'. Although it must be mentioned that Jeff Lamb did the first free ascent. Ed Grindley was drawn back to Pavey Ark in 1973 and paused at Stickle Tarn to look at a series of grooves on the left-hand side of the East Wall. Matheson had noticed it too and had abseiled down and placed a piton under the top overhang. He had already done two E2s with his father on Dow Crag in 1973, Pink Panther and Hesperus, and it would have been nice to complete the trilogy with the tempting grooves on Pavey's East Wall but the controversy over his methods put him off:

'The wall was so steep that I doubted if it would be possible to hang around without any biscuits in order to place protection. Shortly afterwards I got so cheesed off with the haggling and criticism I was experiencing that I virtually gave up climbing and left the line for someone else. Grindley was quickly on the scene. He removed the offending piton from a rope, but then replaced it during his ascent and used it for a rest, before completing the climb. The interesting fact about this route is that the horrific second pitch is not as difficult as the rather insignificant-looking first pitch, which involves a very long reach on tiny finger-holds. In fact, Jeff Lamb failed here shortly before making a free ascent of Fallen Angel!'

Grindley was so nervous that the route might be taken from him, that he sent his young climbing apprentice Pete Long at the crack of dawn to guard the foot of the intended climb till he joined him. Brain Damage (E3 6a) gets an approving star and although Grindley had to rest on a sling after placing the peg on the second pitch he did not have any wire slings and used just two small spikes for protectiom on the first pitch. It was a major event. Allan Austin tried to climb it shortly afterwards, failed, and had to pass over the lead to young Rodney Valentine who, as Austin charmingly puts it 'had grown past him'.

Valentine overcame the difficulties and when it came to Austin's turn he still had trouble and whispered for a tight rope. Valentine in his loudest Lancastrian tones shouted "Do you want a pull Allan?"

As autumn approached another pair of invaders came to the Lake District from the Peak's climbing crucible — Keith Myhill and Ken Jones. Myhill had noticed a tempting line on Raven Crag, Thirlmere. He became so paranoid at the thought of the route being poached from him, that he gave out invitations to a mythical party in Sheffield on the critical weekend to ensure that any likely competitors would be absent from the scene! The goal was a wall of light-coloured rock over two hundred feet high scored by the faintest sequence of inter-linked grooves. They called the route Empire (E3 6a), and two points of aid were used to reduce the difficulties, which would have been quite acceptable in the climate of that time. Myhill and Jones however exaggerated its difficulties and insultingly referred to the local climbing atmosphere as 'the insular Lakeland scene'. Fortunately a strong man appeared to restore local dignity; within weeks Jeff Lamb repeated the climb completely free. Lamb apart from becoming a leading figure on the new-route scene was also a super-jackal and freed many new routes where less strong leaders had been forced to use aid to overcome crux pitches.

Perhaps the most important man to appear on the scene in 1973 was Pete Whillance. Although he had some serious falls during his explorations, they only seemed to inspire him to greater efforts. During the following winter he put up his first major new route, Brutus (E3 5c) on Buckstone How. The rock was poor in parts, and when Lamb tried to repeat it he fell when a block came loose and he broke his leg.

Whillance and Livesey were to dominate Lakeland climbing for several years. Whillance wasn't as ruthless as Livesey and it took some years before he caught up. However whilst Livesey did fewer than twenty major Lakeland climbs, Whillance did many times that number. In 1974 Livesey gave up his job as a Scunthorpe teacher to give himself a year off to climb all the time.

Livesey reasoned that the way forward was by abseil inspection of a potential new route, removing detritus, and possibly practising the crux moves on a rope; and also pointed out that for standards to move upwards ethics had to change and he was the man to force them through:

> 'Climbing will only retain interest if standards continue to rise. Improved gear, etc., would only mean too many people climbing at a top standard, and consequent boredom — a state reached in French rock-climbing a few years ago, where, because of the style and use of equipment nearly everyone could climb every route. We need mental and physical advancement to ensure a receding horizon to head towards;'

Whillance fully realised the radical steps that Livesey had taken:

> 'He adopted a new approach, a fierce attitude to climbing that hadn't really been taken before. He also took what some people think of as a ruthless attitude towards the sport. He prepared his routes very carefully so that he knew exactly what he was doing before he started.'

There were several Peak District climbers who were technically as able as Livesey, but in positions high above the ground with no protection, he outstripped them all:

> 'There are, claims Livesey, hundreds of extremely good, skilful rock-climbers who have never done difficult routes. They can do anything you want on boulders, or on climbing walls, but when they try to climb something high up, their potential drops three or four grades because they haven't got this mental capability of concentrating on the task in hand, or displacing the fear of what's to come; their coping techniques are not sufficiently developed.'

To train himself for this he climbed many hard routes solo. It is quite clear that he knew he was taking dangerous risks but it was all part of his master plan and later he outlined his thoughts about new routes:

'Royal Robbins has something to say; "…concept of climbs as not just lines but as creations containing line and style…"' To this I would add my own more important concept of creative quality in a new route — that of the aesthetic enjoyment possibly from the physical movement involved in the climb — the exhilaration felt after ascending a series of continuously demanding moves. A climb must have this quality to be a worthy creation.'

In early 1974 Livesey had an eight-week period that shook the climbing world, and his two epoch-making climbs were to herald the new age. One was in the Llanberis Pass — Right Wall on Dinas Cromlech; and the other, Footless Crow, was on Goat Crag in Borrowdale. They were both E5s. Wales was at that time the hotbed of hard climbing, and as Right Wall immediately became the most serious climb in Wales it was generally assumed there that it must be the harder of the two routes. Livesey, however, wrote in the 37th issue of Mountain magazine:

'Right Wall doesn't really compare with the two recent Goat Crag routes, Footless Crow and Bitter Oasis. They are harder, bolder, more strenuous and infinitely finer and more grand than Right Wall and are on what I consider a more impressive lump of rock.'

Now the dust has settled, his comments have proved correct. Both Footless Crow and Right Wall are still E5, but Footless Crow has a gripping 6b pitch whilst Right Wall is 'only' 6a. Bitter Oasis has surprisingly settled down to a relatively modest E3 5c. Dinas Cromlech is set imposingly high on the hillside for all to see, whilst Goat Crag is relatively scattered, lacks continuity and has copious vegetation, but it took Livesey to realise the awesome free-climbing potential of the great wall to the right of Praying Mantis.

The main pitch of Footless Crow is at least 165 feet, and is still one of the longest Extreme pitches in the country. To succeed Livesey had to use all his techniques of abseil inspection, crux practice, and wire-brushing to remove moss and lichen. Most of his protective gear was brought back from the Yosemite Valley the previous year. He failed on his first attempt because of 'inability and fright'. None of his usual companions was available and as he was so desperate to get to grips with the route again, he found a non-climbing sailor named Witham to hold his ropes. Even with all Livesey's meticulous preparation he still had to overcome the innermost terrors of the unknown. At one crucial point he was so far above indifferent protection that a fall might have had fatal consequences. When he had run out his one hundred and fifty feet of rope he had to finish the last part solo and Witham had to let the ropes go. The seconds on later ascents invariably found themselves climbing at the same time as the leader in order to allow an extra twenty to thirty feet of rope.

Pete Whillance who had also started his Lakeland new route career and even then was amongst the front rank of existing hard men, summed up the effect that Livesey's Borrowdale routes had on him:

'I'd say the person I most admire would be Livesey. I think a lot of what Livesey's done. I'm not one that nowadays throws stones at him. There are a lot of climbers about today in Wales, the Lakes and the Peak who will try and ignore what he did in the mid-70s and try to knock him. Quite a few in the Lakes say that Livesey never instigated any new move in the

70s and there was no real increase in the grade and there were a lot of people climbing about the same standard. But I was there and I know differently. He's done so much and climbed in so many different areas... He brought a new approach. It might have been ruthless and professional, but he had that urge within himself that he was going to do things; he was going to push standards, go for the hard lines — and he stood on his own and went for them.'

Footless Crow was attempted by the Lakeland hard men but it was too hard for them. Apart from its difficulty, they were still bound by the principle that one climbed up from the ground and any pre-inspection was done in a very low-key manner in order to attract minimum controversy. Furthermore, they were accustomed to the blanket grading of Extremely Severe, although this had been sub-divided into three brackets — Hard Extreme, Extreme and Mild Extreme. Since Footless Crow required a grade of E5, it is not surprising that Lakeland hard men had difficulty coming to terms with it. Even now after his retirement from the vertical scene, Livesey feels that although today's intense young men are fitter they are less brave. During his climbing career he did not shine at that alone, he also took part in an outdoor television athletic competition, in which the other contenders included top athletes and rugby players. He competed in a variety of events and by virtue of his fierce drive he came first and won £500. As a result he was invited to take part in a similar international event organised by an American T.V. company in New Zealand and he came fourth and won £8000. His will to win whatever the activity made one of his close friends comment:

'...he is not a gentleman, but a competitor'.

The local Lakeland climbers strove even further to try to catch up with Livesey, but he still carried on with rich pickings available on every Cumbrian cliff. Only three weeks after Livesey's Goat Crag triumphs, attention switched to Esk Buttress. One of its great unclimbed features has been described:

'...awe-inspiring....sensationally positioned, left-slanting cleft, high on the front face.'

Rodney Valentine examined it, then tried it in the traditional manner without a Livesey-type inspection. He had to use two points of aid on the initial wall which guarded the approach to the slim cleft. He then placed a poor nut but was unable to get any more placements above and fell thirty feet, held only by the flimsy nut. Next day it was Paul (Tut) Braithwaite's turn. He placed a piton above the nut which had stopped Valentine, then finished the pitch to produce The Cumbrian (E4 6b) in its modern free state; a major new climb from the Oldham experts. Their delight was short-lived as their methods to overcome it provoked a furious reaction from Livesey:

'Braithwaite and Valentine pulled the lowest trick in years. It was Valentine and his FRCC cronies who had a lot to say about leaving routes with aid out of the guide-books. "Avoid the rush to get into print", they said. "If you can't do it without aid then leave it for someone better". The various factions operating in the Lakes couldn't help but agree with these strictures, so we all had a look at this Esk Buttress line and left it to someone better. The new guide was about to go into print and who rushed to get it in but Valentine and Tut.'

He summed up quite simply his owm ethics:

> 'I see the finished product, the route, as the important aspect of climbing new routes on British rock. It is perhaps better, therefore, to sacrifice some purity of approach in favour of leaving a clean, aid-free creation.'

There is some special pleading here, leading to a contradiction: Livesey favoured his own kind of 'cleanness' even at the expense of purity. When it came to Livesey's turn to repeat The Cumbrian, he had to use aid — although one point less than Braithwaite and Valentine.

It had only been five years since the first E3, The Viking, was put up, and already standards were in the E5 bracket. If we accept the present E grading system of numbers and translate it to Livesey's record of his dominance in the Lake District from 1974 to 1978, and tot up for each year the cumulative number of new E points, 1974 gave by far the greatest with a grand total of nineteen. The significant routes were: Footless Crow (E5 6b), Bitter Oasis (E3 5c), Eastern Hammer (E3 6a), Dry Grasp (E4 6a) and Nagasaki Grooves (E4 6b). Interestingly four were in Borrowdale and only one in Langdale.

When a clever able gadfly such as Livesey emerges, many people hope that his routes can be denigrated or found to be quite reasonable, but his hard routes repelled elite climbers for years. Fourteen years have passed; new younger men have taken over, written guide-books and assessed the worth of his routes. If the above routes are examined it will be seen that Footless Crow, Bitter Oasis, and Nagasaki Grooves are all given the rare three-star accolade whilst the other two are awarded two stars.

One June summer day in 1974 Livesey waited for some friends who didn't show up. Anxious not to waste the next day, he talked to the irrepressible Ray McHaffie. With tongue firmly in cheek, McHaffie casually pointed out a supposedly-unclimbed line. It was in fact Nagasaki Grooves on Greatend Crag which had been climbed with aid by Read and Adams. Livesey climbed it solo, with a tied-off back-rope, and tie-off loops for protection. As if to prove the system's viability he fell from the hard moves into the foot of the main groove but still triumphed. Earlier in the year he had done Bitter Oasis on Goat Crag, and his fellow Yorkshireman Ron Fawcett was impressed by it:

> 'A gritstone-like wall that doesn't relent for 80 feet, all without a rest and, as its name suggests, a real throat-wrencher. Protection is poor low down and only fair higher up; a real wall of horrors.'

It was in keeping with Livesey's character that one of his memorable raids in 1974 was on Gimmer Crag to free Ross's old aid route — If, situated on the front of the crag. The repeat ascents required the new technique known as the yo-yo: after becoming exhausted the leader lowered off from the highest runner. The pitch was still littered with old pitons which had been cheekily placed by Ross to upset the crusty Austin. The faint crack which gave the line of the route was ideal for small wire placements so Livesey was in no danger despite the difficulty. It was later alleged that he had abseiled down and knocked the old pegs out even after using them for protection, but Livesey stoutly maintained that during his abseil descent he only broke off by hand rusted bits of metal which were blocking the crack.

During the same season Rob Matheson was joined by Ed Cleasby who started climbing in 1973 and led his first Extreme within three months. He saw a picture of Matheson in a climbing magazine and resolved to be 'as good as that bastard'. Matheson had lost some of his drive, but the two combined well and Cleasby felt that he would not have started many hard pitches without the support of Matheson. Perhaps Martin Berzins' dry comment about Cleasby suffices: 'he's good at the necky stuff'. In the late Seventies and early Eighties, Cleasby and Matheson became one of the most productive Lakeland teams.

Cleasby's swarthy good looks and bandido moustache gave him the appearance of a hard man. This was soon confirmed on a very hard pitch on which he failed to put in any runners, which so alarmed his second that he named him Kamikaze Ed. He had a narrow escape on an early repeat of Lord of The Rings. Whilst he was belayed, his leader above dislodged some large blocks, which hit a prow just above him and split asunder with a shower of sparks and sulphurous smells. The razor-edged fragments shredded the rope, tore his pockets off, and ripped away his slings and karabiners, but miraculously he was completely unscathed.

The North Lakes team comprised Pete Whillance ably supported by Dave Armstrong, Jeff Lamb and Pete Botterill who became a technician of the highest ability, helped by his chunky Rock-and-Ice-type physique. Trained as a pharmacist he moved to Carlisle and started climbing with Jeff Lamb, an immensely strong joiner who trained Botterill in the finer points of Extreme climbing. Lamb was so powerfully built that he often had difficulty resting amongst overhangs; but Whillance, being smaller, could crouch quite happily in tiny alcoves in extremis. In the next few years fifty 6b Extreme climbs were produced in Cumbria and Botterill was involved in fifteen of them.

It was Whillance however who set the standard for Cumbrian climbers. He moved to Carlisle in 1973 and set out on a relentless training programme. With the local climbers he often went to a climbing wall in Whitehaven, and in the early spring evenings even though it was dark made trips to the jutting sandstone outcrops at Armathwaite, with the holds lit up by head torches. During the day Whillance squeezed two tennis balls for extra finger-strength and he even took a job as a scaffolder which helped to overcome exposure problems.

At weekends Lakeland weather was often poor, so the Carlisle team often went southwards in search of drier rock. They often ended up at the Leeds climbing wall to ensure that they did some climbing despite the adverse weather. Including the return back to their Carlisle base it gave a round trip of two hundred and fifty miles.

It might be useful to use Footless Crow as a yardstick in relation to the two groups of Lakeland climbers. Cleasby and Matheson did not lead it at that time, although Cleasby tried it on several occasions. It was 1982 before Dave Armstrong of the Carlisle team finally overcame it, although the standard of new routes of both groups eventually broke through the E5 barrier.

Borrowdale continued to be an attractive area for producing new routes, and the evergreen McHaffie carried on with his explorations and was joined by Colin Downer who emerged from a Nottinghamshire coal-mine to work at an Outdoor Pursuits Centre near Keswick. For the next few years Downer was the most prolific Borrowdale pioneer, buttressed by harder climbers from the Carlisle team, particularly Whillance and Pete Botterill. Downer started his campaign on Greatend Crag with a team of fellow enthusiasts. There was so much vegetation that they had to work as a team in an entirely novel manner. Four of them, suspended from separate ropes,

Opposite: Ron Fawcett on Pete Botterill's intimidating E5 route Creation (1976) on Raven Crag, Thirlmere.   Photo: Rob Matheson.

synchronised their leg-leverage to dislodge areas of connected vegetation which eventually unrolled like a vast green carpet and thudded to the ground, leaving hundreds of square feet of untouched rock. As a result Great End Corner and Earthstrip (both Hard Very Severe 5a) were produced in a three-day period in 1975 giving nearly eight hundred feet of new rock.

His friends too, were just as keen as Downer in the search for new routes. A contemporary photograph shows one of them climbing with a yard brush trailing from his peg-hammer holster. Ropes too were left in position to speed up the production of a route. Downer started to prusik up one line and after fifty feet realised that the rope was sliding downwards as it wasn't tied off at the top. Fortunately by grabbing the other rope he was able to stop. In the course of his adventures Downer has produced nearly a hundred climbs up to E3 over the last twelve years.

In 1976 chalk started to be generally used. It had been widely used in the Yosemite Valley where Livesey had seen its beneficial effects in improving the adhesion of sweaty fingers on warm, smooth rock. Its introduction sparked off a lively debate:

> '...Chalk is like E.B.s; it makes the actual physical act more elegant, and more dynamic and more self-fulfilling. Nuts get better every year and make climbing psychologically easier and safer, and therefore less of a challenge. All kinds of silly yobs can bumble their way up Welsh Extremes and Malham VSs now, with above-the-head wire protection.'

This gave Ed Cleasby an opportunity to reply and also take a swipe at Livesey's preparatory work on new routes:

> 'I believe there to be intelligent and unintelligent ways of using chalk, but anyone stating that it should be outlawed is being totally unrealistic. Incidentally, chalk has been used in the Lakes for some time now. Many of the area's leading climbers, such as Botterill, Whillance and Matheson use it. I realize that its use is now quite widespread in the Peak, but in our own far-flung corner of Britain ethical problems relating to its use have never really arisen. The bastard practices of certain marauding parties, such as top-roping and practising moves etc., raises far more of an outcry.'

During 1976 there was an explosion of routes which reflected a widespread exploration. Pete Botterill was the most active leader within the E4 grade which was being solidly reinforced; but there were no E5 routes to follow the epoch-making Footless Crow — despite the fact that two years had passed. By July three teams were to climb important routes within four days. Firstly Botterill and Clegg forced Shadowfax (E4 6a) up the wall left of Botterill's slab. The next day Cleasby and Matheson produced another good performance on Pavey Ark, on an E3 5c line where Cleasby found the only holds widely spaced and used up so much of his strength that he had to knock in a piton:

> 'Mother Courage gives food for thought. If Cleasby had placed the piton runner before his ascent, he might have been able to climb the route completely free. Another alternative would have been to adopt a tactic that many Yorkshire climbers seem to favour — the practice of using tension from a runner above the waist. Needless to say, a well-drilled second can help the leader quite effectively in this fashion, without it coming to the notice of any interested spectators. Everyone knows that this is aid, and of course everyone is free to use the method, but guilty parties should never claim free ascents, especially if they are doing first

Opposite: Below: Ed Cleasby on the First hard section of Imagination, Deer Bield Crag.
           Above: Ed Cleasby on the upper section of Warrior (1977) White Ghyll.   Photos: Rob Matheson

ascents or jackal ascents. The crux of the matter is honesty; report the truth, even if it doesn't match your ethics and theoretical desires. Cleasby's other alternatives on Mother Courage could have included continuous yo-yoing until a free ascent was achieved (wasn't Finger-licker climbed in this way?), or he could have fallen off until he had rested enough to complete the last few moves.'

Two days later on Scafell the scene was set for a major discovery, although the final grade was not as hard as might have been expected.

There are few climbs that can be described as magnificent, but the setting for Saxon (E2 5b) has few equals in the British Isles. On the right-hand side of the Great Flake of Central Buttress is a sheer wall and Saxon makes maximum use of its position and frowning beauty. It naturally gathered three stars during its four-hundred-foot length. At one point Eastham thought he would have to use aid, but Cleasby shouted, "Don't spoil it. For God's sake don't spoil it". Eastham resisted the temptation and they produced one of the best climbs in Lakeland.

Matheson and Cleasby soon struck again on Black Crag, Borrowdale. Their route Grand Alliance (E3 5b, 6a) developed a reputation for stopping leaders in their tracks, and huge chalk blotches on the rock indicated the point where falling leaders hit rock again. During the summer of 1976 Botterill and Clegg produced two further test pieces on Raven, Thirlmere, firstly a brilliant route, The Gates of Delirium (E4 6a, 6a) then Creation (E4 6a, 6a).

> 'Some dangerously-wide bridging up a short blank corner brings a doubtful block in the right wall to hand. Any sighs of relief are temporary for the calves start to pull and the hardest moves follow. By pushing hard on the toes you can be ready to vacate the groove, hands searching for a sloping hold on the left rib. I recall grasping the hold as my infamous feet shot off; a few moments of panic followed as they fruitlessly pedalled against blank rock. Then, after a vain attempt to mantelshelf and contemplation of a long fall, Jerry Peel's words came to mind; "Tried to mantelshelf a number of times myself — no chance, thought I was going to live up to my name, then I looked down to the left and, amazingly, there was a beautiful little foothold. Part with the left foot and stand easy."
>
> Up above, a short well-protected wall involves a long reach, then it's all over. However, whether you succeed or not you can't fail to be impressed.'

On Pavey Ark Pete Whillance made a hard push backed by Botterill and Steve Clegg another fine climber, forced Eclipse (E4 6a) but the big route of the autumn belonged to Livesey. Lost Horizons (E4 6b, 5c) was yet another brilliant line (with aid) on the East Buttress.

In the previous years of Lakeland climbing, too many routes had been put up by means of what is known as 'frigging' — resting on protection, practising moves by abseil, accompanied by convenient attacks of amnesia when the route was written up. When Livesey did Footless Crow he realised that the grading system at that time was unsatisfactory and made some useful suggestions to reform it. This included subdividing some of the better-known Extremes into a graded list of the hardest Lakeland climbs:

XS	Astra	Medlar (1 peg)	Praying Mantis Direct
	Dovedale Groove	Nagasaki Groove	Rigor Mortis
	Eliminot	The Niche	Risus
	The Ghost	Phoenix	Silence
	The Hobbit	Phobos	Ichabod
	Post Mortem	Holy Ghost	Pink Panther

HXS	Fallen Angel	Holocaust (1 peg, 1 nut)	The Viking
	Hydra	Cruel Sister (1 sling)	Paladin
	Gillette Direct	Peccadillo (2 pegs)	Brain Damage
	Ragman's Trumpet Sally	Empire	
	Free and Easy (1 nut)		

HARDER STILL

	Athanor	Fine Time (1 peg)	Footless Crow
	Dry Grasp	Cumbrian	
	Eastern Hammer	Bitter Oasis	

It was a start, and soon others thought about improving the system. Pete Botterill had the idea of a numerical progression in the Extreme grades: Extremely Severes should be graded as E1, E2, E3, and so on. These original thoughts were quickly taken up by others, particularly Ed Cleasby and soon a table was produced fitting together the new ideas allied to the hardest climbs:

E4 — Footless Crow, Gates of Delirium

E3 — White Wizard, Fallen Angel, Abraxas, Tumble, Nagasaki Grooves, Holocaust, Grand Alliance, Dry Grasp, Iago, Eastern Hammer, Verdict.

E2 — Cruel Sister, Mother Courage (1 resting peg), Eclipse, Brain Damage, Problem Child, Explosion, Nazgul, Zeus, Incubus (1 peg), The Viking, Shadowfax, Risus, Paladin, Pearls Before Swine, Peccadillo (1 peg), Bitter Oasis, Cumbrian (1 nut), Empire, Fine Time (1 peg), Deimos, Rat Race, Route 1 (Falcon), Niche, Balrog.

E1 — Astra, Extol, Equus, Saxon, Ichabod, Dyad, Holy Ghost, Poacher, Chimney Variant, Phobos, Philistine, Tumbleweed Connection, Dangler, Bludgeon, Man of Straw, White Ghyll Eliminate, Rigor Mortis, Medlar (1 peg), Pink Panther, Phoenix, Lord of the Rings, Hiraeth.

In 1976 a twenty-one-year-old Yorkshireman, Ron Fawcett, made the second ascent of Footless Crow and also of Right Wall in Wales. Even at fourteen years of age Fawcett not only had been moving up into the top echelon of climbers; and when Livesey gave up in 1980 Fawcett took over his pre-eminent position. His fitness even in the fanatical scene which had developed was legendary, and at one stage he nonchalantly managed two hundred press-ups then was surprised when others thought that this was exceptional. Much later he soloed one hundred gritstone Extremes in a day including E5s. However his influence in the Lake District was small compared with Livesey but he highlighted an increasing trend of hard men to concentrate their climbing in the Peak with occasional excursions to fashionable crags in Wales.

Opposite: Al Phizacklea on Incantations, Great Gable (Whillance and Armstrong).   Photo: Penny Melville.

By 1977 Livesey had not pioneered any more climbs in Lakeland which might compare with Footless Crow, but perhaps Fawcett's repetition of it spurred him into action. He teamed up with Peter Gomersall, who was one of his students at Bingley College and as they were able to snatch time off during the week they could investigate new lines. About this time Livesey broke his ankle. It had just mended when John Sheard decided to make an early repetition of Grand Alliance. He spent two hours trying to solve the crux traverse, then relinquished the lead to Livesey. To Sheard's chagrin, Livesey hopped across the difficulties at his first attempt. One of Livesey's main ambitions was to solo Botterill's Gates of Delirium on Raven, Thirlmere. He took on the challenge and even managed the first pitch but had to retreat from the second. However he did notice a line to the left of The Medlar. It had been partially cleaned by Cleasby and Matheson, who had decided that the lower overhangs were too much for them. Gomersall and Livesey abseiled down it and decided that it might be feasible. During the attempt Livesey became so exhausted placing a vital nut on the first pitch that he had to retreat. Gomersall took over, then promptly led the whole pitch. The 1979 guide-book states: 'The main pitch was split just below the crux'. However a stance was not taken according to Gomersall, and the true sequence of events is as described above. The name was a triumph too, Peels of Laughter (E5 6b), Botterill and Clegg had first cleaned the line, then couldn't do it. They in turn enlisted the help of Martin Berzins, who couldn't even do it on a top-rope. This turned out to be the reason why Livesey and Gomersall were surprised to find holds on the wall chalked up prior to their ascent.

They realised there was more potential on the crag, and in particular a free version of an aid route Blitz. Livesey proposed an abseil inspection using a hawthorn sapling as an anchor. When Gomersall jibbed at its frailty, Livesey announced loftily that he had carried out a thorough testing programme on their tensile strengths and that the future was quite safe. After cleaning the route they came back and produced Blitzkrieg (E4 6a), an audacious assault on the headwall of the big cave which is the main feature of the crag. They noticed another line next to Blitzkrieg, which was so overhanging that it was impossible to clean all the pitches. When they returned it took five attempts over three days to solve the first 6b pitch. Livesey kept falling from the desperately hard traverse and once managed to grab a spike and perch like a surprised bespectacled bird. The attempt failed however so Gomersall arranged to meet Livesey a week later, and arrived at the crag to find him hard at work practising the hard moves of the first pitch. The crux sequence involved an overhanging section followed by exquisite delicacy. Livesey managed it with only one fall then magnanimously offered Gomersall the second pitch. Not only was it the same standard, but it was also covered with lichen, and they had to go back again, and spend a whole afternoon removing the lichen before Gomersall could lead it. Das Kapital (E6 6b, 6b) was to be Livesey's last hard route in the Lake District. For four years he had led the way towards the present stage of the sport, in which specialised training, intensive preparation of routes, and a minute definition of grades put climbing in the hi-tech, highly competitive world of the Seventies and Eighties. His account of his own methods is characteristically candid:

> 'Abseiling down new lines to clean them has been a crucial cheating technique and I am perhaps more guilty, or better at it, than the rest. One develops a sequence memory of moves for the whole pitch which certainly cuts down the required climbing time; it's rather like the downhill skier memorising his line down the course. It is difficult to avoid this form of

'n S. Special (1977), Raven Crag, Langdale. John Eastham sharp ending.

Photo: Rob Matheson.

cheating unless one doesn't garden routes beforehand. I can't honestly say that I recommend trying on-sight leads of hard new routes, i.e. with no gardening beforehand. Our rock is usually just not good enough for climbing at this standard to be done without cleaning. I would, however, decry the practice on subsequent ascents. It may well make the second and third ascents harder undertakings than the first, but it does make sure the climb is clean and stands without a long history of first ascent aid to live down.'

Opposite: Top left: Pete Whillance.   Photo: Rob Matheson.
           Top right: Rob Matheson on Vertigo, Black Crag.
           Bottom left: Rob Matheson on Prana (1977), Black Crag.
           Bottom right: Pete Gomersall.

Small is Beautiful

With the imminent departure of Livesey from the front rank of Lakeland climbers, rivalry intensified between the North and South Cumbrian teams. Both made raids into each other's territory, causing mutual irritation which often flared up into public controversy.

Cleasby and Matheson had already embraced Livesey's method of top-rope inspection and were audacious enough to use it on an unclimbed arete which Whillance had cleaned on Deer Bield Crag. This gave Cleasby, Imagination (E4 6a) but four days later Whillance returned, repeated the route and was enraged when he found out the method of the first ascent. He mutilated Cleasby's written description in the new-route book and renamed it Life In the Fast Lane. The two sides met in the bar of the Golden Rule pub in Ambleside, angry words were exchanged and Botterill said bitterly "It's like a bloody war" a remark which was distorted in the climbing magazines to "From now on this is war", to suggest even greater animosity.

After the Golden Rule row Cleasby, with tongue in cheek named a route in White Ghyll, Ethics of War. An uneasy feeling was developing that, once a climb was claimed, it might mean that either illicit aid or methods had been used. When the second ascensionist came to repeat it, not knowing the circumstances of the first ascent, he would face even more problems than the originators.

The following year, 1978, brought another innovation in climbing protective gear, designed with the aid of a computer. An American aerospace engineer and Yosemite climber Ray Jardine conceived the idea of four spring-loaded aluminium serrated cams with curved edges, that locked even tighter into a crack when a leader's shock-load came onto them. Straight-sided cracks often refused to accept the aluminium-wedged wire sling. The new cam-devices, called Friends, helped to overcome this, and even made it possible to protect the dreaded flared cracks which were such a feature of hard American climbing. Adjustability was not the main advantage; it was the speed with which they could be placed in a menacing crux situation by a harassed leader which turned out to be the main benefit. Whillance needed these devices less than most hard men and deserved the nickname 'Mr Cool' as Pete Botterill dubbed him. On rock which was less than vertical where Whillance was in finger-tip control he at that time had few, if any, equals. Such daring carried risks and he had several horrific falls. Fortunately none of them caused him serious damage and usually he dusted himself down and carried on despite his injuries.

Although better gear had reduced the potential hideous burns which could result from a leader fall, the hands of seconds made of vulnerable flesh might still have to absorb increasing shock loads. Consequently the sticht plate was invented. It was a simple, thick, circular aluminium disc with two slots cut into it so that the rope could be pushed through and locked inside a screw-gate karabiner attached to a harness. If the leader fell the whole system was designed to tighten up very quickly, absorb some shockload and lock off the leader's rope. Long leader-falls such as those experienced by Whillance came to be much safer, and he commented on his thought processes in extremis:

'Your brain will not allow you to get that close to your actual level of ability, where you might overstretch yourself. The ability to climb at the very edge of your limit and remain cool is something else entirely. It needs a lot of mental control to prevent the brain starting to wander. Nervousness makes you lose energy and everything goes to pieces. Once that happens you are going to fall off.'

Perhaps stung into action on Deer Bield Crag in 1978 by Cleasby's feat of Imagination (E4 6a) the previous year, Whillance did a new girdle traverse that gave him a good view of the whole crag. He became attracted to the impressive serious front face of the cliff, and to his surprise discovered that someone had already chipped some of the holds. He decided that it was time for action along with Dave Armstrong and commented on his subsequent ascent:

'Take it to the Limit (E5,6b,5b,5b) proved to be a major undertaking with probably the most serious 6b pitch in the Lakes to date. Perhaps I should mention that the peg runner, which has already appeared in a description in the Lake District South guide-book, is just a joke. I'll be surprised if the wind hasn't blown it off by now. As Dave and I were completing the first ascent, Ron Fawcett and Steve Foster were preparing to make the second. Ron's lead was particularly impressive as he did not have the advantage of a prior abseil inspection, and he had already done Stiletto and Peccadillo that day.

Surprisingly Fawcett had a hard time repeating the route under the watchful eyes of Whillance and Armstrong, despite the fact that he had done the second ascent of Footless Crow which had defeated all the Lakeland teams. Fawcett was also to put up the hardest climb in the Lake District, Hell's Wall in Borrowdale, the following year. His nervous ascent of Take it to the Limit only reinforces the realisation of Whillance's bravery in dangerous situations.

When Livesey heard about it he commented sourly in one of the magazines that it was 'pathetically easy' and although still at the height of his powers, he made no effort to repeat it. Take it to the Limit can be described as Whillance's breakthrough into the elite league of hard climbers. The route has still not been repeated as a large protruding block from Deer Bield Chimney which provided an essential hold was knocked off during a recent big rock fall from the detached buttress between Deer Bield Crack and Deer Bield Chimney and damaged the lower rib of Imagination, huge chunks, some almost as big as small houses, now perched precariously on the scree slopes at its foot; they have an alien look, their clean- cut, menacing faces are bare of any lichen or moss to mask their sharp steel-grey finish.

Another of Whillance's routes on Deer Bield Crag he named Desperado (E5 6a). The name summing him up — 'an adventurer...driven to extremity' which perhaps summed up his restless wanderings. He did not confine himself to the Lake District and like Livesey, made major contributions in Wales. He also went much farther afield and helped to propagate the new E5 standard in Scotland and in winter the Carlisle caravan visited the vertical limestone cliffs of South Pembroke and put up many new routes on St Govan's Head.

Dave Armstrong kept files on each climbing area and when new routes were published in climbing magazines they were photostated and kept in an appropriate file for reference when they visited the area. They and the South Lakes team were mainly responsible for the enduring hard classic climbs put up in the late Seventies and early

Eighties, when the top British standard was being propagated on routes all over the Lake District, even though the available lines were becoming hard to see.

Whillance gave up work during the summer to spend the maximum amount of time on the crags and his admiring rival Ed Cleasby wrote of him:

'Indeed, many of the names Whillance has bestowed upon his routes illustrate only too well their appalling seriousness: Edge of Extinction, The Risk Business, The Long Run, Stayin' Alive, Take it to the Limit. All are at the top of the real E grades and few have been repeated; there may be hundreds of climbers operating at 6a and above, but few have the mental stability and conviction to do so without regular protection...

Whillance was establishing himself as one of the Lakes leading climbers, with a growing tally of routes to his credit, his forte being just off-vertical walls with minimal holds and protection. In search of new lines he would spend hours reading and re-reading guides, books, reports and studying photographs for sight or mention of unclimbed rock — particularly large blank walls.'

The Carlisle team did not just rest on Whillance's achievements. Pete Botterill and Jeff Lamb also added their share for the common good. Lamb was awesomely strong as a result of his job as a joiner and could nonchalantly cling in overwhelming situations working out the proper fitting of protection, which to him seemed like metallic solutions to similar problems he had tackled during his working day. It was inevitable that Scafell would again have to be reckoned with. It had drawn explorers ever since Coleridge, one hundred and seventy-five years before. Ron Fawcett neatly summed up the problems associated with climbing on its mist-shrouded buttresses:

'If you can face the slog up Brown Tongue and the perpetual cold and damp that stiffens the limbs and deadens the fingers, or the wet crux that throws you off, making you disbelieve Newton's theory as the water droplets drip away from the crag (or is it really that steep?), if you can face all that then the routes you will find hereabouts are superb.'

Cleasby and Matheson were drawn to it as well, and Shere Khan (E5 6a) (one point of aid) was one of their best efforts being a modern classic. In 1978 Botterill and Lamb excelled with five routes; one of the hardest of the quartet was Carahadras (E5 6b,6b), Lamb led the first 6b pitch, then Botterill had to use two points of aid to follow the muscleman, but on the next 6b pitch with its thin crack Lamb failed and Botterill took over and led it. His apprenticeship days were over. However his career on Scafell was nearly terminated one day on Overhanging Grooves Direct when his companion above him dislodged a chockstone which splintered in its fall. Several pieces sliced into Botterill's back. At Whitehaven hospital, although the doctor had not been told of the circumstances of his injuries he asked Pete on which climb the injuries had happened. Botterill and Lamb produced many top grade routes over the next few years and not only helped to raise Lakeland standards but also beneficially influenced local climbers.

Perhaps it was inevitable that there would be another Cumbrian invasion by Yorkshire climbers. This time it was an exceptionally tall trio, the Berzins brothers, Martin and Bob, together with Ron Fawcett. Fawcett and Livesey climbed together often and helped each other to solve some of the country's hardest problems. Fawcett had more natural talent, but Livesey offset this by being more intensely driven with a better eye for a new route on improbable-looking rock. Like Livesey, Fawcett's quota of Lakeland routes was relatively small. Fawcett had been attracted to the roadside

Bowderstone Crag in Borrowdale. The cliff was only just over a hundred feet high but it housed a large open corner with an awe-inspiringly smooth left wall containing an old Sixties aid route. Fawcett had climbed Hell's Wall the previous year but the holds were so small and the difficulties so unrelenting that he had been forced to use two points of aid. During the winter he became determined to free it and its eventual grading of E6 6c made it the hardest climb in the Lake District right up to the present day. Fawcett had to resort to siege tactics over several days before its thin, tendon-tearing cracks were forced into submission.

The Berzins brothers were shrewd enough to notice a good line on the unattractively-named Flat Crags on Bowfell, and soon tackled a prominent groove in an overhanging wall which did not yield easily:

> '...it was so overhanging we virtually had to aid-climb down to stay anywhere near the rock. Next morning bright and early, we slogged back up the hill, and set about the route. I had first go. The start was an easy-looking jam crack through a roof that we hadn't bothered to clean. After ten minutes of thrutching I finally grovelled my way up it, with some impressively mangled hands to my credit. I then set off up the thin crack above, slotting in lots of lovely runners, until I ground to a halt where the crack ran out. The moves above looked desperate — from poor pinchgrips on a fin of rock you had to launch into a lay-back position with feet frictioning on an overhanging wall. All this on top of fifty feet of strenuous climbing was too much for me — I flopped onto the top runner and was lowered down to the ground exhausted.
>
> Martin tied on and quickly climbed up to the high point. He swung into a layback and hand sliding, he didn't stay there very long! Then straight back onto the rock and this time he made no mistake and pulled his way up the last twenty feet of overhanging rock, and crawled up the slabs above to the top.
>
> Looking for a name we settled on Ataxia — a medical term meaning total loss of bodily control which seemed quite appropriate really.'

Ataxia provided another 6b pitch for the Lakeland repertoire of hard climbs, but it was just a dress rehearsal for yet another product of difficulty in Borrowdale. Ataxia had been a respectable one hundred and sixty feet long. The Berzins breach in Borrowdale proved to be yet another E6 pitch, Exclamation, for one of Lakeland's most beautiful valleys. However it was only sixty feet long, which may have seemed to be just a large boulder problem, ludicrously overhanging, and although it was 6b in technical difficulty, it was the general acceptance of its shortness which was most significant.

Shortness was not a feature of the Berzins brothers; towering over most of their contemporaries made them comment that if someone of their height could find a particular move 5c, someone only five-foot-nine might probably find the problems increased to 6a, and a tiny five-footer might find the same problems 6b or even impossible.

Even with their height the Berzins had to pre-place protection in neighbouring Shepherd's Chimney, before they were able to overcome its overwhelming problems.

During 1979 the rich Borrowdale seam produced two E6's, two E4's, four E2's backed up by six E1's. This made it into one of the most rapidly expanding climbing areas with routes to appeal to all young hard climbers. Climbers from different areas had different attitudes. Those who frequented Wales knew about the hard Welsh climbs — where they could rest, the amount of protection available and so on — but

Opposite: Rob Matheson having started up The Medlar is starting the traverse on Decline and Fall, Raven Thirlmere.

Photo: R. Matheson collection.

they usually knew little about even the hardest Cumbrian climbs, although the best Cumbrians knew the Welsh secrets. On the Lakes crags there was more mystery and protection was more subtle.

The Berzins brothers had become fascinated by Scafell and were involved in its development for over a decade. With Chris Sowden they were responsible for ten of the hard good routes on its buttresses. Their first encounter gave the brothers Ringwraith (E4 6a). It repelled efforts to repeat it even by Ed Cleasby and much later Al Phizacklea and George Smith made the second ascent with difficulty:

'After a rest on the ledge I gained my high point, overcoming the awkward section by pinching the right rib of the groove and throwing myself into a wide, high bridge. Gasping for breath I lurched for a finger jug on the tip of the roof with my right hand, then slotted my left next to it. It didn't take long to realise that was a bad mistake — my legs were rattling, and with the fingers slowly creaking open I let out one desperate cry before catapulting through the air. I was furious, kicking the rock and swearing loudly, a far cry from Fred Botterill's gentlemanly conduct on that legendary first ascent of his slab: there would be no raised hat today. Ten minutes later I was back up there, struggling to keep in contact with the rock. George was encouraging me, verbally pushing my weakening resolve for one last move, then another, onto a terrific resting place where I slumped, totally exhausted...'
"Y'know lad," I mused, "It's a bloody shame we put in all that effort for nowt but a second ascent. By hell, it's worth it though!"

It could be said that 1979 was Borrowdale's year, for all the hard men involved in Lakeland development made a contribution there, each in his own distinctive style. Inevitably Whillance was one of them. Reecastle Crag, in the tiny Watendlath valley branching off from the road down Borrowdale, was another small very steep cliff that struggled to exceed a hundred feet. Jeff Lamb had noticed a bulging thin crack which gave him White Noise (E3 5c). Then Whillance climbed a bulging wall which gave him The Executioner (E4 6a). It had little protection, and a fall from its sustained difficulties could have had fatal consequences. It had the typical Whillance trade marks of hard technical climbing combined with a high degree of danger. Later he summed up his thoughts on these contrasting factors:

'Climbers desire to see their sport, their vocation, their obsession as above competitiveness. And this, perhaps, stems from its root as a sport for gentlemen, who prefer to lose honourably rather than to win dishonourably. 'I look at the sport of rock climbing as any other sport, whether it's football, cricket, golf or whatever one is doing. You are trying to improve your skill and ability — but with climbing you back that skill against your life; if you are not up to it you may well hurt yourself. It's just another sort of challenge added to the main theme of testing your ability. Even if I kill myself, I can look at it quite clearly and say that, subjectively, it will be my fault and I will have made an error of judgement.'

1980 provided high interest, but not in the spheres normally associated with the stop press. There were three aspects that interested people. An entirely new crag was developed — Hodge Close Quarry — which added a new dimension to lakeland climbing. A new guide-book was also produced to Great Langdale, inevitably by another Yorkshireman, Mike Mortimer, who had shown a 'cosmopolitan' attitude to his climbing by being the only person single-handed to have done a guide-book to both a Lakes and a Welsh area (Tremadog). To the uninitiated it might have seemed that, as Austin had retired, the new guide-book would have had a smooth entry into the climbing community.

Copies had hardly reached the shelves of climbing shops before the first shots were fired and Livesey's review of it was cutting:

> 'Fine Time is debased with the comment "Yet another preplaced peg and sling for aid", inferring that "It is no solution at all to fail, and then go round to the top and abseil down and place a fixed piton and hanging sling which can be reached from below, in order to bypass a particularly troublesome spot". Both insults are totally untrue, ill-conceived and unnecessary; Fine Time was climbed on sight and the route's aid point was already in place, complete with an old sling (it was of course an old aid route). There was no "pre-preparation" as there is on most modern (i.e. since 1970) first ascents. The Ragman's Trumpet/Sally Free and Easy confusion is still not sorted out, the dates again being wrongly recorded. Sally Free and Easy was climbed in two attempts, the first pitch being the major pitch (indeed the only real pitch) of Ragman's Trumpet, but climbed nine days before that route, neither is the upper pitch loose as described — it is eminently sound and holdless...
>
> Why doesn't the historical comment mention the much more serious trends evidenced by recent routes; the preplaced nut on Warrior, the profusion of manufactured holds on Desperado, Peccadillo and Take it to the Limit, or the almost universal practising of crucial moves on a top-rope prior to the first ascent? Such practices, particularly the last one, should be mentioned; they have a profound effect on the seriousness of a subsequent ascent, particularly on unprotected routes. The style of ascent of older routes such as Cruel Sister and Peccadillo criticised in the text is considerably "whiter" by comparison.'

A counterblast from fellow Yorkshireman Martin Berzins was equally scathing about Livesey:

> 'John Hartley saw Livesey practise the overhang on Fine Time. Furthermore, in Mountain 39 Livesey himself states that Fine Time was omitted from the last guide because it had aid placed from above and that this was a brave but correct decision on the part of the guide writers. As for the now famous sling — it was very conveniently positioned for Livesey who probably couldn't have done the route without it at the time. Sally Free and Easy is a fine line but only a mind lobotomised by some of the more tottering attractions of Langcliffe and Gordale would describe it as "eminently sound and holdless".

The climbing world stood back with some delight at the Yorkshiremen sniping away at each other.

It seems surprising that the major cliff discovery of 1980 by the North Lakes team of Whillance, Armstrong and Botterill was in a hole in the ground — Hodge Close Quarry, two miles north of Coniston. The first climb there was Stiff Little Fingers (E3 6a), a fine sustained finger crack and during a frenzied period in March they produced five routes there, one E4, two E3s an E1 and a Very Severe characteristically called Behind The Lines just to rub their discovery in to Cleasby and Matheson. As soon as April dawned the South Lakes team jumped into action with their own inventions. The quarry was an unattractive place, with plenty of loose rock, and a gloomy pool to enhance its serious nature. Amazingly enough the pioneers hoped that it might be the Lakeland equivalent to the sunny seaside Tremadog cliffs in North Wales. Some people felt that climbing in a quarry was not proper climbing and that one had to be either brave or stupid or both to climb there, also that it was a scruffy place and that it was better to fall or fail on a proper crag not in a hole in the ground.

These feelings were accentuated by the lack of protection and when it was suggested that bolts should be used to protect leaders there was an immediate veto from the North Lakes team. Cleasby and Matheson set to work in their own right in April, but the use of the cliff as a popular climbing ground continued to be controversial. Although the North and South teams continued with its development until Whillance topped everyone else with Life in the Fast Lane (E5 6a), which neatly summed up a loose wet cliff below ground level with minimal protection, the latter climb was justly summed up in the guide-book as requiring 'a controlled and courageous approach...' Perhaps this route embodied all that Whillance looked for in a new climb:

> '...go round a corner and look at something else, perhaps find the dream route, the imaginary ultimate route. You never do but you tend to find things that are worthwhile on the way. For me that's a lot of it now — just to get away from the traditional climbing haunts and have a look.'

To be impartial it was a little before its time, as quarries and limestone cliffs in other areas were developed intensively a few years later, (e.g. the slate quarries at Dinorwig, Llanberis) and bolts for protection became normal, but as Hodge Close Quarry was so close to the other mountain crags there was a resistance to them anywhere inside the Lakeland frontiers for some years. Reaction from other climbers was apprehensive when details of all the climbs were published in the 1984 Scafell, Dow Crag & Eskdale guide-book. Comments were published in climbing magazines:

> 'Stiff Little Fingers is a great route, but the gradually-widening crack line raises doubts as to how long it will continue in its present form...' '..there have been several lucky escapes...'

Another salvo was launched against the guide-book — 'the new guide grossly underrates the serious nature of the climbing.' Perhaps climbers felt reluctantly drawn there as a lot of new climbs were less than a hundred feet in length and Hodge Close was a hundred and fifty feet high. Things had hardly simmered down in 1980 when news came of a huge fall on an almost unknown small bulging crag called Raven Crag, Threshwaite Cove which branches steeply up from the tiny hamlet of Hartsop near Brotherswater, a collection of ancient houses some with galleries.

Rick Graham and Ian (Squawk) Dunn went up to it to try an unclimbed shield of rock which they had partially cleaned by abseil, when Whillance arrived looking displeased at an encroachment on his preserve. Graham set off but couldn't climb a groove which had not been cleaned. With the aid of a Friend he removed the detritus. Dunn took over, climbed twenty feet above the Friend but gave up, ever conscious of the restless Whillance at the foot of the crag. The ropes were passed to him, but by this time it was raining and eventually he came to a slab covered with oozing green slime, from which he fell a total of a hundred and twenty feet and hit the ground with his face on the extension of the rope. He had snapped the top nut runner, torn open two karabiners, pulled out several other pieces of protection and was finally stopped by the Friend put in by Graham despite the fact that it had a broken trigger. His face was badly lacerated. In almost complete darkness the whole party went to hospital, but when he was told his wounds would need many stitches, he discharged himself and went home for his tea. He returned to finish the route which became Top Gear (E4 6a).

It would be wrong to pass over 1980 without mentioning some strenuous efforts on Dove Crag's overhanging North Buttress which had lured several generations to tackle its two hundred-foot leering rock plate. Many had faltered, littering the face with ironmongery in their vain attempts to advance or retreat. Bill Birkett and Rick Graham used some aid on an initial route on it during which Birkett found himself in a parlous position:

> '...the rising traverse left got lonelier and lonelier culminating in technical and precarious climbing on pumped arms to an in-situ nut, below a pod, nestling beneath the greatest overhangs. The nut we had fixed by abseil (stopper 5), and I knew it to be poor and on a very short sling.
>
> Breathing quickly, slight body movement saw the nut rotating, fulcrumed too high on its wedge for comfortable stability. I clipped it. Unable to free-climb past this point, I knew there was a very thin crack high on the right of the pod, and after much heart-searching I decided to insert a knife-blade peg. Heart-searching soon changed to heart-fluttering as I strained at full stretch to insert the piton. Absolutely at the limit and beyond, the peg was part pushed, part tapped in. No way would it take a fall, but would it take dead weight? If it popped, so would I, and the fall would be long and damaging.'

Fortunately he did not fail, and they both finished the route Broken Arrow (E5 6a). Even with two points of aid it was a powerful addition. However they were back again the following month of June with Rick Graham in charge.He started from the same point as Broken Arrow and produced Fear and Fascination (E5 6a), one of the finest three-starred routes on the crag. It was twenty-one years since Bill's father, Jim Birkett, had done his last hard climb, Harlot Face. Birkett was certainly carrying on the splendid family tradition.

1981 was another great boom year, and Whillance and the Carlisle team were soon in action. Their output was prodigious and Whillance was inevitably in the forefront, particularly in Borrowdale, with sixteen new climbs including five E5s all with 6b pitches. One exception was at the start on Reecastle Crag when after many exhausting joint efforts, Dave Armstrong came up with Penal Servitude (E5 6b), and it might have been thought that the mighty Whillance would have forced it, but he had suffered his hideous fall not long before and it was left to Armstrong to be in the rare position of the pusher who finally got over the problems.

There were others who felt the desperate urge for untouched rock, whatever the methods used to get up. There was a growing realisation that the 6b technical standard was about the limit that nearly all elite climbers could cling to without prior knowledge by abseil inspection and continual practising of the moves as initiated by Livesey or climbing deliberately into a falling-off situation where modern protection ensured that a modern leader in most cases would be quite safe. For a hundred years it had been a sacred doctrine that a leader should never fall, since it would almost always have resulted in death. By the early Nineteen-Eighties protection had advanced so much that the leader's fear of death or injury had been largely removed, particularly on any pitch which contained anything up to a fist-sized crack which could then be protected. The way was open for the strong and less brave to force lines into submission. One of these was produced on Pavey Ark in 1981, Sixpence (E4 6b/c), by A. Atkinson. Its technical standard was at the critical point of adhesion without pre-inspection and the manner of its ascent was roundly condemned in Lakes New Climbs 1981/1982 by

Armstrong and Whillance:

> 'Above the mentioned resting sling, a series of short falls was taken whilst progressing up the hanging groove. The leader did not lower back down between these falls and some intermittent hanging on rope and runners took place. The exact amount, extent, and indeed interpretation of this 'hanging around' is now disputed between the first ascensionists and eye-witness reports. The writers' best assessment of the events, for future aspirants is "several rest points".

It was a couple of years before Chris Hamper and Bill Birkett climbed it in an acceptable manner. They re-named it Equinox and upped its grade to E5 but kept its technical grade at 6b. This climb highlighted another growing trend, that just because a line had been ascended in a ruthless manner unacceptable to popular local ethics it was quite in order to repeat it by acceptable means and then rename the climb. Perhaps Sixpence highlighted a growing division amongst the climbing community. There were the rank and file who adhered to the historical traditions, and there was a separate elite which created its own ethics or (lack of them) in an attitude towards a new climb by any cheating method possible, fuelled by aggressive competition and a complete lack of traditional enjoyment which had previously been one of the pleasures of climbing in high remote places. Soloing and boldness were looked on as dangerous but commendable. There was another angry explosion in Langdale caused by a route, The Beatles, on Middle Scout Crag. One wonders what Allan Austin thought of all the aided controversy, bearing in mind his rigid free-climbing rules for many years. The Beatles was, like Sixpence, climbed with several rest points by Tom Walkington and the subsequent ascent by Nick Dixon caused even more heavy flak in the climbing magazines which stung Dixon into a quick reply:

> 'On The Beatles I pre-placed two very poor R.P. nuts, then after a top-rope inspection, I led the route. The style of ascent of Elvis was similar with 1 in-situ Rock 1. Would as much fuss have been created if I had placed pegs? I think not, so why this odd prejudice against situ nuts? Could it be that Bill Birkett's criticism stems from the insular and retarded attitudes in the Lake District climbing scene, and perhaps even an inability to do the routes? Elvis had several repeats last year and its quality was confirmed; I believe The Beatles is at least as good. The routes are approximately the same length as 'Cock Block' in the Llanberis Pass; I do not remember much criticism regarding the length of that route.'

Far above the controversies, on Dove Crag Bill Birkett had a novel idea. Other sports had sponsorship and money provided for top athletes so it seemed reasonable for him to do the same for climbing. He approached several equipment makers to see if they would like their products immortalised in a name of a new route. He then did a new route on Dove Crag and called it Asolo (E3 6a), the name of a popular range of Italian boots. His bank balance did not have a great influx of lira, and although there was some predictable sniping at his thoughts and actions, others repeated the route and decided that it was an excellent E3. However favourable the comments on its quality, commercial naming of new routes did not catch on. Dove Crag is one of the finest high crags in the Eastern Fells. Bill Birkett and Rick Graham solved its intricacies.

It was inevitable that the Botterill/Lamb team would make significant contributions in 1981. On the East Buttress of Scafell there was a thin, fierce-looking overhanging crack and although it was only sixty feet long it gave Pete Botterill one of his hardest but most satisfying struggles. The Almighty (E5 6b) was seconded by muscleman Lamb in his trainers. It was the last of their great joint contributions to Scafell and almost the last climb that Lamb did in the Lake District. The following week he top-roped the ferocious boulder-problem climb, Parting Shot (6b), and then emigrated to Australia. Even though August had not finished Lamb had been involved in twenty-five new routes in the early crowded months of 1981. Some time after his arrival in Australia he was found dead in his car after succumbing to severe head injuries sustained whilst climbing alone. (It is thought that he had been hit on the head by people throwing rocks from the top of the cliff.) His strength and ability had done much for his partnerships in the Carlisle team, particularly with Botterill, and he had made a considerable mark on Lakeland climbing, not only because of his new routes but as one of the original 'jackals', who free-climbed routes which had been put up with aid.

Whillance was not bound to other people's views and one of his best discoveries was an untouched buttress on Iron Crag in the Thirlmere area. The 1979 guide-book had been particularly scathing about it:

'...one of the loosest cliffs in the Lake District, having an abundance of detached blocks and friable holds. There is plenty of unclimbed rock; it deserves to remain so.'

This was true about the main buttress but there were two others, one being high on the left. Whillance found sound steep rock and there, partnered by Dave Armstrong, was rewarded with half a dozen routes, the best of which was Black Gold (E4 6a), led by Armstrong.

Rick Graham had become one of the new leading lights of a rejuvenated South Lakes team based in his Ambleside home; and one of his finds was on Goat Crag, after a careful examination of the Footless Crow wall. Mirage (E5 6b) was certainly comparable to its famous neighbour. He climbed the 6b first pitch and linked it with a 6a pitch which Pete Botterill had espied in 1977.

1981 saw a broadening of the E5 grade, and other E grades leading up to it, all over the Lakeland cliffs; more routes in Hodge Close, additions of climbs under a hundred feet, and a vast increase in the number of climbers.

Rock gymnastics became the norm and those who embraced this philosophy polarised to the White and Dark Peak with occasional trips to Wales. The Lakes was still being served by a devoted few, and remained a beautiful place of outdoor pilgrimage for the walker and traditional climbers, but for the teenage extremist it seemed to have little to offer.

One of these hypertrained muscled teenagers, Jerry Moffatt, had been fired in the Peak furnace. In 1982 he visited Borrowdale and started off with some hard climb/boulder problems on The Bowderstone, then felt bolder still when he was attracted to the steep face from which Fawcett had plucked Hell's Wall. He climbed a tempting flying arete to produce De Quincey (E5 6b), which the guide-book credits with 'mind-blowing situations', then he top-roped a smooth plate of rock on Shepherds Crag and called it Father Ape. Finally he recleaned and climbed Footless Crow and brought it into such a spruce condition that many others soon followed in his footsteps.

1982 proved to be a sad farewell to Pete Botterill, who had been involved in nearly fifty new Extreme climbs with the ever-active Carlisle team. He chose Goat Crag for his last bow, with Wild Times (E5 6b), which took him three grim days of yo-yo tactics

Opposite   Top right: Dougie Hall on Heaven's Gate, Bowderstone Crag.
           Top left: A taste of Hodge Close Quarry!
           Bottom left: Bill Birkett, Ian 'Squawk' Dunn and Rick Graham.   Photo: Rob Matheson.
           Bottom right: Nick Dixon.

before it reluctantly succumbed. As one of his last philanthropic climbing duties, together with Whillance, Jeff Lamb, Dave Armstrong and the Berzins brothers, he had spent considerable time compiling an overall assessment of the fifty hardest Lakeland climbs, and of these they selected eight as requiring the ultimate in people who attempted them:

THE LAKES TECHNICAL TOP ROUTES

ROUTE NAME	CRAG	FIRST ASCENT OR FIRST YEAR FREE ASCENT TEAM	
Hell's Wall	Bowderstone	Fawcett	(1979)
Exclamation	Shepherds	B. Berzins/M. Berzins	(1979)
Penal Servitude	Reecastle	Armstrong/Whillance	(1981)
High Performance	Raven (Threshthwaite)	Botterill/Lamb	(1981)
Rough Boys	Shepherds	Wilford/Lindehorne	(1981)
Wild West Show	Buckbarrow (Wasdale)	Armstrong/Whillance	(1981)
Coroner's Crack	Eagle (Borrowdale)	Whillance/Armstrong	(1981)
Ataxia	Flat Crags	M. Berzins/B. Berzins	(1979)

Even after three years Hell's Wall by Ron Fawcett, was still judged the hardest free climb in the Lakes, despite the multiplicity of hard climbs from the native Cumbrian climbers.

The Berzins brothers also had a good 1982, particularly on the East Buttress of Scafell. Martin free-climbed Incubus and made it another E5 6b, but did not have such good fortune on Livesey's Lost Horizons and faltered on the second pitch:

'...the first corner is good, honest bridging and laybacking. The sloping ledge above is guarded by a manky peg, so pathetic that it can only have been used for cleaning. Above, the corner leans and narrows. Fifteen feet higher is another ledge, and in between is the second peg. A fierce pull enables it to be reached — smashed in to the hilt right by the crux, it's obviously not just for decoration. A bit of cunning enables you to free-climb until the peg is at waist level but the ledge is still tantalisingly out of reach.

The next move, the crux, involves easing up from a precarious bridging position to reach the ledge. There was some dispute about whether Livesey free-climbed the next move on the first ascent. What is certain is that I, for one, grabbed the peg, and that the move was unquestionably free-climbed by both Bob Berzins and Alan Murray some five years after the first ascent.'

It was good to see the old firm of Cleasby and Matheson still in action. Matheson had started in the new-route business when Allan Austin ruled his Langdale fiefdom with a rod of iron. By 1982 his rigid views seemed light years away. It was eleven years since Matheson had done his first new route on Dow Crag. Now, in the evening of their partnership, he and Ed Cleasby did their last two new routes on Dow Crag on the same day in the high summer. They too, like their rival Pete Botterill, had contributed dozens of routes all over the Cumbrian crags.

On Dow they triumphed on Security Risk (E3 6a), and then on a long-standing, handsome, untouched groove behind Woodhouse's Pinnacle which gave them Close to Critical (E4 6b), as hard as they could ever do, and deserving its guide-book two stars. Their last high hard route was on the East Buttress of Scafell, Shikasta (E4 6a),

Opposite: George Smith on the 1st ascent of The Route of All Evil, Chapel Head Scar.   Photo: Al Phizacklea.
    Inset: Paul Cornforth goes for his bolt gun. A serious threat or the way forward?   Photo: Paul Cornforth collection.

its final pitch forcing a prominent prow above the White Slab by two top men out of the classical mould, who did their climbs with bravery and ability. Scafell is a wet place not climbable for weeks, sometimes months, at a time. Other areas such as Wales have good cliffs, in the rain shadow of the mountains. The seaside cliffs of Tremadog and Gogarth are good examples. Unfortunately there are no unclimbed cliffs rising out of the Solway Firth and although the massive sandstone cliffs at St Bee's had a brief period of popularity interest in them soon waned.

Only a dozen miles away from Dow Crag was a limestone cliff, Chapel Head Scar. There were those of the old guard who said that it was not part of the Lake District. The details of its climbs were already in the Lancashire guide-book. Tradition was certainly against its inclusion in the patchwork of Lakeland climbing. However its proximity to the sea and the lack of rainfall has made it a place of Extremely Severe pilgrimage for the young hard men of Cumbria who see it as the greatest concentration of very hard Extremes — a doctrine not acceptable to those who have reached the advanced age of twenty-five or above. In North Wales the seaside limestone cliffs attached to the Little and Great Ormes have been accepted as part of alternatives available when the high crags are wet. It seems that acceptance of Cumbrian limestone as Lakeland cliffs is still a little way off. The cliff also has the advantage of receiving any sunlight and the white rock of Chapel Head Scar rises a hundred and twenty feet thus making it the equivalent of many of its Derbyshire and Yorkshire competitors.

In the early days would-be pioneers were faced with an irascible armed gamekeeper, whose shotgun caused instant compliance with his orders. The cliff had a slow rise to fame until Ron Fawcett produced Moonchild (E3 5c), followed shortly afterwards by Pete Livesey with Lunatic (E3 5c). The actions of the Yorkshiremen spurred the Kamikaze Kid — Ed Cleasby — into action. He decided to top their efforts on the highest unclimbed part of the cliff — Great Buttress. He climbed it with the aid of a tree which was so flimsy that he tied it to the cliff with a length of frail tent guy-line and then had to tie his leg to the tree so that he could place the cliff's first bolt. He was surprised at the relatively small amount of flak for placing the bolt and was rewarded with a good climb consisting of a single hundred-and-fifty- foot pitch — Android (E3 5c).

1983 was a quiet time for very hard new routes in high Lakeland and Chapel Head Scar was again a focus of interest. Everyone knew the crag had great potential but its smooth nature meant that protection was sparse and it needed bolt protection.

In the summer of 1983, another Yorkshireman Martin (Basher) Atkinson, one of Northern Limestone's most powerful and muscular climbers, powered up the smooth wall to the right of Great Gully with True Path (E5 6b).

In 1984 a small climbing wall in Ambleside came to the rescue of the local climbers; its influence was profound. With three midweek nights' training local climbers raised their standards in a few months from E4 to E6.

Another limestone cliff, Humphrey Head, was developed right next to Morecambe Bay, but unfortunately it was crowned with sixty feet of vertical grass and loose rock which made belaying at the top impossible. Ace climber-photographer Al Phizacklea decided on drastic action and armed himself with a hired electric generator and bolt-placing equipment and placed thirteen in one day. They were four inches long and half an inch thick, with stainless steel hangers to offset the battery effect of sea water. Most of them were strategically placed to be used as belays at the top and this helped the Lake District to have a seaside cliff like Wales. Phizacklea waited tensely for the reaction. Bill Birkett's column in Climber and Rambler had a headline scream 'Bolt placed in Lakeland Rock' despite the fact that the cliff was in the Lancashire guide-

book.

Phizacklea with Ambleside-climbing-wall-trained fingers forced War Games (E5 6b), the first route to breach the overhanging start of the Great Buttress. The first person to repeat it was dashing Dougie Hall, one of the best on-sight climbers, who for some years worked in West Cumbria during the week.

If the weather was fine he arranged for a friend to pick him up from the factory gates and was able to get to Borrowdale in forty-five minutes. They could even get to the East buttress of Scafell if they ran up Brown Tongue. In this manner he repeated Botterill's The Almighty (E5 6b) one evening plus two other routes. Sunny-smiled Dougie lived too far away for climbing-wall training and because of his young family he only spent two weekends in the Lake District in four years. During one of them he went to the third buttress of Iron Crag, the lower one, and produced, a hundred-and-thirty-foot long climb, which overhangs thirty feet. He was in a hurry to finish it as he had to be at a wedding in Oldham by 5 p.m. He placed more protection pitons than he needed as he didn't have long enough to clean it, then fell off, dusted himself down, then produced Western Union (E6 6c), the hardest climb in the whole of the Eastern Fells, and still reached the wedding with ease by 5 p.m. At the end of 1986, he had dashed up a thousand routes during the year, many of a high E grade. During a good summer weekend he could clock up twenty Extreme climbs.

Whillance and Armstrong worked on a juicy thin crack next to a previous pace-setter, The Viking, on Great Gable. On a warm August evening they abseiled down and brushed away the delicate lichen which held the key to success. Whillance placed a piton by abseil in a critical crux sequence that only the longer reach of Armstrong could clip with a karabiner, to produce Incantations (E5 6b), which was filmed by Border Television.

Important but sad, as it was one of Whillance's last great routes in the Lake District as he soon left the area. Whillance had trained relentlessly, but he had been brave too, not afraid of forcing a new climb in potential death situations. He had a standard of fearless Extreme climbing that very few were able to emulate.

There was a useful development in Langdale on the Crinkle Gill walls spearheaded by Bill Birkett. The climbs were under a hundred feet high, but were very hard, and provided one of the highest concentrations of hard climbs in the valley. 1984 saw the development of a new crag Bleak How by ace earth-mover Colin Downer. It was set high on the hillside at the entrance to the valley through which the Langstrath Beck tumbles down from Angle Tarn, hard under Esk Pike. Every one of the dozen or so routes put up in its first couple of years was single-pitch, but each could stand up to comparison with most single pitches anywhere in the Lakes, particularly Downer's Brush Off (Hard Very Severe 4c), with worrying moves just a few feet up, when it seemed as if the protection might lift out, and a foot might slip. Downer took time off from his excavations to produce Inquisition (E3 6a) on Reecastle Crag in the Watendlath valley. Lakeland climbing was fortunate that Downer was so productive with copious numbers of lower E grade routes as there are still thousands of climbers eager for such routes. Although the E6s have the final glamour, only a small percentage of climbers actually get up them and certainly very few in good style.

1984 should not be left without commenting on the crowning of the steep, remote and attractive Raven Crag, Threshwaite Cove, where Phil Rigby and Al Murray came up with Liquid Engineering (E5 6b) which embraced all that a climb should have in its steep magnificence.

In 1985, on Chapel Head Scar, Paul Cornforth audaciously produced Super-

Dupont (E5 6c) the first of that technical standard on the cliff, but more important, at last there was a Cumbrian climber able to technically match the Yorkshire predators. He was helped by Al Phizacklea who worked at Vickers in Barrow-in-Furness and was able to get huge bolts normally used to tether atomic reactors in nuclear submarines. He placed the huge bolts in critical positions marked by a cross by Paul Cornforth from an abseil rope. The long bolts were needed as often the rock had a tough outer skin and was much softer underneath, and a long bolt penetrated the two layers.

Paul Ingham went to live in the Lakes in 1985 and although he was thirty-five years of age his fanatical devotion to training and climbing soon put him amongst the leaders, and he too became one of the pioneers of Chapel Head Scar. Now that the locals were so fit their ethics changed too, so they too practised the hard bits of new routes until they memorised the critical sequences. Initially they just bouldered the moves until they fell off into space protected by bolts. They produced a nucleus of hard men and when Ingham was accepted into their midst he unconsciously embraced their high norms.

Multitudes of new climbs appeared in Borrowdale in the guide-book published in 1986, which listed nearly eight hundred routes. A large percentage of the recent ones came from the nimble feet of Colin Downer and Ray McHaffie. Paul Ingham came into prominence when he climbed Jerry Moffatt's top-rope test-piece, Father Ape. He renamed it Geronimo (E6 6c). Unfortunately it is felt that it should be E7 and represents a continuation of Lakeland undergrading which deters off-comers, who would lose face if they failed on such a route. It might have been better if the grading had been left open for some leading climber from elsewhere to give an unbiased decision without any fear of loss of face on his part.

However it is resented by Lakeland hard men that their climbs are undergraded. They point out that the E grading system was invented by the Carlisle climbers and that it is other areas such as North Wales which are out of phase. Dave Armstrong says that he and Whillance found Welsh climbs half a grade easier than their Lakeland equivalents. When they did eight routes on Eagle Crag in the early Eighties, they graded the hardest E4, to ensure they did not over-grade them; three of them have now been upgraded to E5.

Another of Ingham's conquests was a much-tried groove on Deer Bield Crag which on his second day of attempts gave him Pretty in Pink (another E6 6c). The name was derived from his colourful attire not to any personal beauty.

Away beyond the very head of Borrowdale's tributary valleys on the bulging East Buttress of Scafell, Martin Berzins was well rewarded for his persistence in the summer of 1986 when he produced the high route of the year with Borderline (E6 6c). Martin and Chris Sowden had abseiled down to brush away lichen and moss from its tiny holds. The pitch was so overhanging that they had to tie themselves into protection to clean it. They then left the gear in place, including two expensive Friends, which were gone when they returned. Martin had to threaten the removal men before they would give them back. On the final successful push, he ran out of strength on the first 6c pitch but placed several runners before his strength oozed away, enabling Chris Sowden to take over. It was still twelve weary hours before one of the 'last unclimbed lines' succumbed.

Martin Berzins is an example of the mature, hyper-trained rock athlete with an intense training programme which includes aerobics, circuit training, weight training, and running, as well as training on both climbing-walls near his home in Leeds. Whenever his experienced team goes to the climbing-wall the undergraduate climbers

Opposite: Top left: Dougie Hall on Centre Fold.
            Top right: Dougie Hall on Exclamation.
            Bottom left: Al Phizacklea on Rudolf Nureyev, Side Pike, 1983.
            Bottom right: Dougie Hall on Hiddenite on the intimidating Iron Crag.   Photos: D. Hall collection.

move elsewhere.

Down in the southern lowlands on Chapel Head Scar the five-month ban on climbing caused a lull, and the Lakeland jeunesse dispersed to sunny French limestone. As soon as the ban was lifted the leading teams were ready with cordless drills and handfuls of bolts. Paul Cornforth produced Super-Duper Dupont (E6 6c), whilst the other Paul, Ingham, did the first 7a pitch on Zantom Phone (E6).

There was a ludicrously overhanging challenge to the left of Great Gully, which obsessed Cornforth. During one attempt at the end of a big roof a hold broke off and he fell into space. He found the missing hold, abseiled down and glued it back in place. Then Pat Mcvay on the same line broke another hold off, and again Cornforth glued it back. On one unsuccessful attempt Paul even jumped to get a critical finger-jam but failed. Eventually he was successful with Maboulisme Merveilleux (E7 6c), the first of that standard produced by a local climber in the whole of Lakeland.

As 1986 drew to a close, the mountain cliffs had their hardest routes as follows:

Hell's Wall	E6 6c	R.Fawcett
Borderline	E6 6c	M.Berzins & C. Sowden
Pretty in Pink	E6 6c	P.Ingham
Western Union	E6 6c	D.Hall
Geronimo	E6 6c	P.Ingham
Centrefold	E6 6b/c	T.W.Birkett

Activity at the highest level in 1987 focussed on small vicious unclimbed problems, which were still available on Reecastle Crag in the Watendlath valley. Four E6s were produced during the awful 1987 summer by Paul Ingham, ably buttressed by Paul Cornforth. Ingham's hardest was Short Sharp Shock (E6 6c) followed by Cornforth with The Torture Board of a similar standard and grading.

There were those who thought that such short routes were not part of mountain life, yet a century ago, Haskett Smith had conquered Napes Needle which was also a modest height, and had climbed it solo. One would like to think that he would have approved of modern Lakeland trends in rock-climbing which he had started.

Nowadays most young climbers want to climb routes with high E numbers for the kudos that goes with them as opposed to pure enjoyment. But to climb at E6 and above requires incessant training, which is not compatible with a professional career, so that the dedicated unemployed still dominate the top echelons.

The hordes of brightly-clad teenagers of the Nineteen Eighties are a far cry from Haskett Smith tying his handkerchief to the top of the Napes Needle a century ago. There are however isolated crags in peaceful valleys waiting for the climber who wishes to escape and even traditional crags such as Pillar Rock are often away from the mainstream climbing scene. For those who do not mind a long approach walk there is still much untouched rock in the Lake District — even on Scafell — but some of the hardest lines that remain are lacking in protection and will need a bold approach from someone who is prepared to take the risk. Then, when the clouds roll away from the great cliffs the next chapters will unfold. High above Cumbria's many jewelled lakes the crags hidden among the rocky fells await the next generation of rock-climbers.

256

INDEX OF CLIMBERS

Opposite: Pete Whillance on Grand Prix, Raven Crag, Threshthwaite Cove. Photo Pete Botterill.
Over: Paul Cornforth on the 1st ascent of Maboulisme Merveilleux, on Chapel Head Scar, the first E7 in the Lake District area.
Photo: Al Phizacklea.

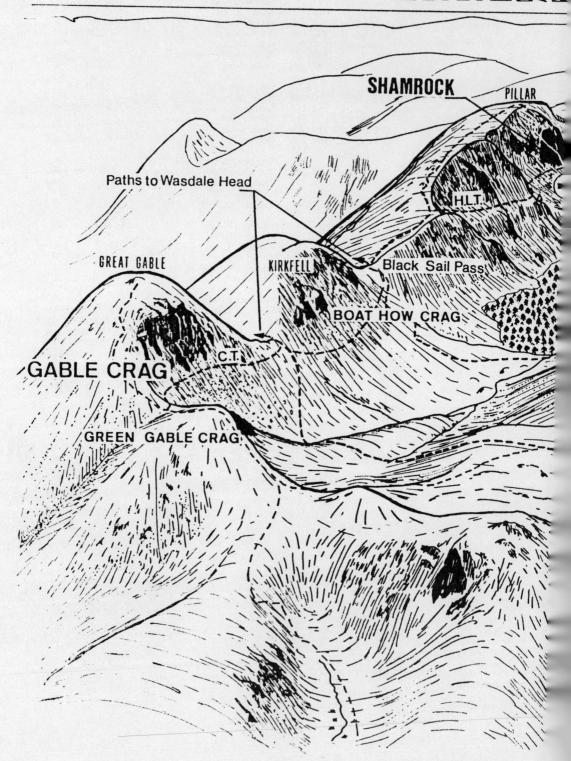

SHAMROCK

PILLAR

Paths to Wasdale Head

GREAT GABLE

KIRKFELL

H.L.T.

Black Sail Pass

BOAT HOW CRAG

GABLE CRAG

C.T.

GREEN GABLE CRAG